ENDEAVOR FOR
RENEWAL

THE BROKEN JUG SERIES – 12

ENDEAVOR FOR RENEWAL

Droplets of Wisdom from the Heart

M. Fethullah Gülen

NEW JERSEY • LONDON • FRANKFURT • CAIRO • JAKARTA

TUGHRA
BOOKS
New Jersey

Contents

Preface

The beginning of all good deed or beneficial work is important because it is the first step on a path that, hopefully, leads to a good conclusion. Yet it is only a beginning; a beginning alone is not sufficient for the continuity of goodness. There are so many good beginnings that do not reach the spring and are buried in history, leaving broken dreams behind. Every journey or action that blooms to existence and smiles at life needs further positive dynamics to realize its own identity and become a tree that yields fruit and maintains its liveliness. The most important of these dynamics is the will and struggle for self-renewal. Everything is kept alive by renewal; when renewal stops, decay and decomposition begin, and a once promising endeavor becomes like a corpse whose soul has been taken.

The most important thing is understanding renewal correctly. Self-renewal should definitely not be confused with a fancy for renewal. True renewal is realized by retaining the purity of the seed and the root, and by synthesizing an entire inheritance of values with new thoughts and wisdom appropriate to the age. Thus, one can reach clearer horizons of reflection. Self-renewal is a purely metaphysical phenomenon, a spiritual revival; one must stay true to the sacred values. In other words, a thorough revival can only be realized with the efforts of the spirit, intellect, feelings, and willpower working in concert. Utilizing the spirit's power to the fullest, making flawless use of the knowledge inherited from the past, being constantly open to spiritual breezes of inspiration, not being trapped by blind imitation, and always following a sound methodology are some dynamics of an ideal renewal.

A person leads an impulsive and energetic life in their youth. When the age of maturity comes, everything finds its right place and the person begins to lead a life shaped by sound judgment and reason. But there sometimes comes a phase when feelings and thoughts lose their color and become dull. This does not signify maturation of character; on the contrary, this state expresses losing the spirit of things that once meant a great deal to you.

Actually, such transformations experienced by individuals also hold true for collectives and communities. In their heyday, strong communities flow like rivers. They beam with smiles at their periods of youth and maturity, but then begin to dull with the fall of their seasons. By utilizing their inner dynamics well, some survive for a long time and some for a shorter period, but they all move toward their destined ends.

In this respect, both in individual and social life, one's eyes must be directed to peaks, one's wings must be open wide to reach higher levels, and one must pursue noble ideals. Without such determination, these ideals will never come true. Without such resolve, stagnancy and disintegration become inevitable. In the person of the Prophet's blessed Companions, the Qur'an calls believers to such a revival: *"Has not the time yet come for those who believe that their hearts should soften with humility and submit (to God to strive in His cause) in the face of God's Remembrance (the Qur'an) and what has come down of the truth (the Divine teachings)?"* (al-Hadid 57:16).

Believers who respond positively to this call must maintain enthusiasm for progress, so that they will be protected by Divine providence, will stay fresh as long as possible, and will not topple over. They must do this so that they are not blown adrift by every new wave of change and transformation.

It is possible to speak up with a new voice and offer the world a new righteous understanding of civilization. But it should never be forgotten that the realization of this ideal depends on the human factor. It depends on individuals who think, judge, draw on sound reasoning, and experiment; who have a say in every field, from sciences to arts, technology to metaphysics; who seek ways of deepening their knowledge of every issue that concerns them; who use a constructive spirit to realize self-renewal without losing respect for the Divine Essence, and who oppose all kinds of narrow-mindedness. These vigorous souls with steel willpower must keep running on the path of serving humanity with an insatiable love for research, an ever-evolving passion for knowledge of God, and an otherworldly profundity beyond comprehension. This book conveys the feelings and thoughts of a person who has dedicated his life for the coming of such a generation and who suffers, in heart and mind, for this ideal.

Religiousness and Religious Sensitivity

Question: *Could you explain the meanings conveyed by the terms "religiousness" and "religious sensitivity"?*

Answer: Religiousness has different degrees, from being reverent toward religious principles in theory, to practicing religious commandments and making religion the pervading spirit in one's life. For example, some people know and believe in the essentials of faith and observe daily worship accordingly. On the other hand, some take faith in a rather immense sense; they follow what it commands and keep away from what it forbids with this approach. They go so far that, in addition to refraining from sin and fulfilling the obligatory commandments, they even take a stance against doubtful things, concerned about the possibility of committing something forbidden. They try to lead their lives as God-fearing believers. As for those who practice religion with a deeper consciousness, they always observe worship with a feeling of offering it to Divine inspection, and live with a full consciousness of God and His omnipresence. In this respect, there are various degrees of religiousness, stretching from the ground level to the stars in the sky. Incidentally, let me add that even with its primary level, religiousness bears a crucial value for people, and it should never be dismissed whatsoever.

As for religious sensitivity, it refers to very meticulous observation of religious principles in one's personal life first, and then being exceedingly sensitive about the religious practices of one's family members, close environment, and other people willing to benefit from his or her spiritual guidance. In other words, religious sensitivity means living with the fervor and enthusiasm as expressed by a saintly figure: "If only all people in the world loved the One I love; if only all of our words would be a narrative of the Beloved One" (Yahya of Taşlıca).

I Wish I Could Kindle Love of God in Hearts

A believer with religious sensitivity has the following feeling and thought about others: "How I wish I could tell these brothers and sisters about God and kindle love for Him in their hearts! How I wish I could evoke a passion of togetherness with God in them! How I wish, they could feel so close to God as to supplicate every time they raise their hands, as if saying: 'My God, I am asking from You forgiveness, goodness, Your good pleasure, Your care, Divine zephyrs, company, closeness, the ability to love You as becomes Your glory, togetherness, protection, victories with Your help, and for You to be my guardian.'"

According to his or her degree, a believer who has such sensitivity will calculate how to help others attain such horizons, not only for people in their close sphere for but all of humanity. They will figure out how to evoke such enthusiasm in everyone. His cause will be to make others love the noble Spirit of the Master of Humankind, peace and blessings be upon him, to the degree of feeling a spasm deep in their spine when his majestic name is mentioned. On the other hand, such a believer feels agonized by witnessing people stagger, fall, or lapse, and exerts himself by finding out what else he can do to keep people away from the slippery grounds that cause people to fall into misguidance. In conclusion, he leads a very sensitive life with respect to guiding society, preventing falls, and putting a stop to detachment from religion.

Sensitivity of Bringing Others to Life

As we have described, a true believer is not content with the Prophet's blessed name ringing out from the minarets in his own country, but takes the *hadith* stating that his name will reach everywhere the sun rises and sets[1] as an ideal; thus, he tries to lead his life accordingly. While pursuing his ideals, he never worries about his own pettiness and does not say, "What can a man like me do?" Knowing that God makes little things realize great works,[2] he always keeps walking with determination and dynamism, and always acts with a spirit of responsibility. He holds the understanding: "If there is a bosom full of faith somewhere, he can find a way and let all the hearts feel the inspirations of his spirit." It needs to be known that if the horizons of one's ideals cover an entire nation, God lets that person achieve great tasks, which would normally take an entire nation. As it happened with Prophet Abraham and the Pride of Humanity, God Almighty grants the honor of accomplishing such a lofty duty to that person as well.

All of these indicate being very sensitive in religious life, far beyond being merely religious. In other words, you can name this as a sensitivity of reviving or giving life to others. In this respect, it can be said that being religious and having religious sensitivity are different. However, these two have certain parallels. The furthest limit of religiousness can be summarized as refraining from doubtful things,[3] seeing oneself like a murderer for having missed a Prayer, and carrying out the necessity of Divine commandments in a flawless fashion with the utmost sensitivity. This also includes feeling glad with a consciousness of having received a Divine blessing after having fulfilled God's commandments (instead of laying claim on that blessing and taking personal pride), and then having concerns as "I hope I did not adulterate this deed with sanctimonious considerations." These points, which are considered as the furthest levels of religiousness, mark the beginning

---

[1]   *Sahih Muslim*, Fitan, 19; *Sunan at-Tirmidhi*, Fitan, 14; *Sunan Abu Dawud*, Fitan, 1 (All footnotes were written by the editors.)

[2]   Bediüzzaman Said Nursi, *Lem'alar*, p. 350, 398–399; *Şualar*, p. 646

[3]   *Sunan at-Tirmidhi*, Qiyamah, 19; *Sunan ibn Majah*, Zuhd, 24

of religious sensitivity. As a consequence of that sensitivity, a believer who has a sensitivity of such immensity and depth wants to let others also experience what he feels and let them enjoy the blessings he enjoys.

Let Us Destroy the Monuments We Build to Ourselves First

People of these horizons are sufferers for their cause. They continuously think about their noble ideals and suffer mental anguish. They even continue their actions while—excuse me—answering a call of nature. They generate new thoughts and note down these new thoughts coming as soon as possible, and when they cannot note them down, they then save them in the neurons of their brains to consider later. Sometimes, the concern for their cause seizes those suffering souls to make them err at their Prayer. Even though there is no such established concept in terminology, we ascribe the errors of the *muqarrabin* (those closest to God) to such a lofty consideration. For example, concerning the Pride of Humanity's few minor mistakes in his Prayers,[4] we think, "God knows how the noble Spirit of the Master of Humankind, millions of peace and blessings be upon him, who is open to highest spiritual horizons, pursued such lofty goals that the Prayer remained, in a sense, secondary." He was not even dizzied by the Ascension (*Miraj*), and after he attained unattainable levels, he returned back as a necessity of his mission.[5] As a matter of fact, Abdul Quddus makes the following comment about this truth: "By God, Prophet Muhammad, peace and blessings be upon him, attained the unattainable and saw things impossible to see. He reached such levels that a man will never consent to return from there. By God, if I reached there, I would not return!" Another saintly figure who comments on this consideration says, "Here is the difference between a saint

---

[4]   *Sahih al- Bukhari*, Salah, 88; Adhan, 69; Sahw, 1; *Sahih Muslim*, Masajid, 97–99; *Sunan an-Nasa'i*, Sahw, 21

[5]   Al-Isra, 17:1; *Sahih al- Bukhari*, Badu'l-Khalq, 6; Manakıbu'l-Ansar, 42; *Sahih Muslim*, Iman, 264

and a Prophet." That is, a saint continues his spiritual journeys, ascending from one stage to the next; a Prophet does not only make personal progress but, after having reached the highest peaks, he returns back to guide people and direct them to the same horizons.

We can ascribe to the same consideration Umar ibn al-Khattab's mistake during a Prayer. After finishing the Prayer he led, the congregation told him that it was mistaken. He replied that he was transferring soldiers to the Iraqi region in his imagination.[6] As it is seen, the duty of glorifying the Name of God occupied his mind even during the gaps of Prayer. This is an indication of an amazingly sensitive concern for religion. It is not possible for a person of such religious sensitivity to be inclined toward temptations or to leave any cracks in observing the obligatory commandments.

In conclusion, a community whose members carry out worship in a casual manner with a consideration to get rid of it cannot possibly build up the statue of their souls and become heroes of revival. If we are to build a real monument to our spirit, a spectacular one that gives relief to and enchants those who see it, then we need to take an axe and destroy the monuments we built to ourselves. Then we need to build up a new monument that consists of religious commandments and whose cement is God's good pleasure, so that it does not ever come down. Therefore, a selfish understanding as "Observe your own Prayers and fasting; do not care about the rest," can never be acceptable, and such an understanding can never fulfill the responsibility of glorifying the Name of God.

---

[6]   *Sahih al-Bukhari*, Amal fi's-Salah, 18; Ibn Abi Shayba, *Al-Musannaf*, 2/186

Those Who Migrate for Noble Ideals and the Chivalrous Souls That Welcome Them

Q ue.stion: *After Prophet Lot, the Prophets were sent from among strong families.[7] Relatively speaking, can we consider the spiritual person of the Hizmet Movement as such a strong support (rukn al-shadid) for the volunteers in our time?*

Answer: Prophet Lot, who was Prophet Abraham's nephew,[8] was sent to the people who lived around the Dead Sea region, which included the cities of Sodom and Gomorrah. A certain immoral sexual act had become commonplace. The Qur'an refers to this issue in the context of different verses.[9] Before they were destroyed, God sent angels in human form to Prophet Lot as a miracle. They appeared as beautiful young men, as a final factor of Divine testing. When the people of Lot saw them, they became fixed on the newcomers as the target of their immoral behavior and it was the end of spoken address; they totally lost the test and were buried into the ground. God Almighty pun-

---

[7]   *Sunan at-Tirmidhi*, Tafsir as-Surah (12), 1; Ahmad ibn Hanbal, *Al-Musnad*, 2/533

[8]   As-Sa'labi, *Al-Kashf wa'l-Bayan*, 6/283; Al-Baghawi, *Ma'alimu't-Tanzil*, 3/251; Al-Qurtubi, *Al-Jami li Ahkami'l-Qur'an*, 13/339

[9]   Al-Hijr 15:51–77; ash-Shuara 26:160–175; an-Naml 27:53–58; al-Qamar 54:33–39

ished them with a shower of meteors.[10] So when those morally corrupted ones saw the angels near Prophet Lot and ran there drooling
with their indecent intent, Prophet Lot said: *"Would that I had power
to resist you, or that I could lean upon some strong support!"* (Hud 11:80).
Any decent person who was in that great Prophet's position would say
the same thing, but nobody would express it so neatly like a Prophet
did. For this reason, the Messenger of God stated that the helplessness
of Prophet Lot was accepted as a prayer: "And after him, God Almighty
sent every Prophet from among a large community in their people."[11]
That is, by sending every Prophet to come in later periods as a member
of a certain tribe, God Almighty did not let possible attackers reach
him right away, as the tribe served as a protective circle.

Divine Providence through the Veil of Causality

The Pride of Humanity was from the Banu Hashim tribe, which was a
very strong tribe in Mecca. His grandfather Abdul Muttalib was a distinguished figure in Mecca. After Abdul Muttalib passed, he was succeeded by his son Abu Talib, who was the Prophet's guardian during
his childhood and youth. So even the question of beating the noble
Prophet with a flick of one's little finger would be sufficient to cause
the Banu Hashim tribe to mobilize. For this reason, the pagans of
Mecca would not dare attacking the blessed Prophet. In the realm of
causes, God Almighty screened His Divine protection for His beloved
servant behind such apparent factors.

We can consider the event narrated in the second page of the chapter of Ya-Sin. Accordingly, God sent two messengers to a city, Antakya
according to most books of Qur'anic exegesis,[12] but the people of the
city refused to believe them. He reveals *"We reinforced them with a
third"* (Ya-Sin 36:13) that they have his support behind them and
they are not alone. A third one being added to the first two indicates
that a fourth may come if need be. This provides them with an oppor-

---

[10]   Hud 11:69–83

[11]   *Sunan at-Tirmidhi*, Tafsir as-Surah (12), 1; Al-Bukhari, *Al-Adabu'l-Mufrad*, p. 212

[12]   Az-Zamahshari, *Al-Kashshaf*, 4/10; Ar-Razi, *Mafatihu'l-Ghayb*, 26/45

tunity to carry out their duty further. When the history of the Prophets is considered, we can mention other cases to exemplify our point. I would like to leave that issue to the experts of the field and answer the second part of the question.

The devoted souls in our time travel to the four corners of the world with the love of humanity in their hearts. In some instances, only a few people, or even just a single person, go to a certain country. In the places they go, they face children of very different cultures who come from different backgrounds. They speak a different language, follow a different religion, and put emphasis on different values. For this reason, the volunteers who go to those countries might face various difficulties. As it is underlined in the question, the spiritual person of the movement can serve as a sound point of reliance and a safe haven. People of Anatolia supported this movement, and there were even some statesmen, who had political authority, who helped the volunteers wherever they went. In the same way, the support given by businessmen who went to those countries as investors sufficed to make the volunteers feel they were not alone. With such high morale, they made a very good impression on the people they encountered.

Language Olympiads, Relief for Hearts

When seen from this perspective, the language Olympiads that are annually held in Turkey can also be regarded as strong support for the volunteers serving in four corners of the world. Students from very different countries do not merely speak Turkish; with the language they speak, they present a view missed and expected by humanity, a view in the name of love, peace, and tolerance. The people of Turkey—from ordinary people to statesmen—sincerely appreciate these students and those who provide them with educational services. These activities are held in a growing circle. Though they used to be held only in the cities of Istanbul and Ankara, many other cities have joined the list. In the coming years, God knows how many more cities will open their arms to these activities, and students from four corners of the world will continue to relieve hearts with their hope inspiring poems, ballads, and songs. The fact that an entire nation, including people in administrative positions, applauds this issue will raise the volunteers' spirits and become a source of morale and strength for them.

I would like to express a different point about the issue. From the words of Prophet Lot *"Would that I had power to resist you, or that I could lean upon some strong support..."* we can infer that anybody who serves on the path of God needs to lean on a strong support. It is very important to have a source of power, a dynamo to boost their morale and help their trustworthiness be recognized by the people they address. For example, administrators in Turkey visited and gave sincere support to the educational institutions in the country. They stated they would continue their support and attended many institutional activities. All of these constitute a very important support for this movement, which has become a global event. Undoubtedly, God's power, help, and protection are the greatest support for a believer. However, it should not be forgotten that we live in a realm of causes and are responsible for fulfilling the requirements of causes. Therefore, we cannot ignore the causes before us.

Let me also point out that no matter what happens, while sharing our feelings, thoughts, and inspirations of our souls with others, we must absolutely refrain from arrogant considerations along with wishes or inclinations to impose our feelings on them. We must even keep away from attitudes and behaviors that might be perceived as pushing. We need to express our thoughts and feelings with a very soft manner that will be welcomed by the people we address. We should even not forget that besides the good and beneficial things others will learn from us, the same is true vice versa. In the globalized world of our time, very important things may have flourished in different regions of the world. Different ideas and considerations we will receive from others can take us to new combinations in our world of feeling and thoughts. Then what befalls on us is to take any beauties that can be good for serving humanity and try to benefit from them.

Markets Where Roses Are Bought and Sold

When it comes to making our beauties felt in others' hearts, we try to express any beautiful value we have through our system of education, and through our cultural centers and existing media organs. We try to make the issue virtually into a marketplace where everybody can reveal what they possess. Thus, the values that find their buyers reach people on demand. Pushing an entire heritage of values on others and presenting matters in a manner of looking down on them is the wrong approach. It must never be forgotten that even if your values are something others desperately need, a mistake of style will make people react against every outer element of goodness. In order not to cause such a reaction, it is necessary to approach the issue as an exchange of values where we learn good and beneficial things from them and present the beauties in our hands in an acceptable form.

Actually, our globalizing world badly needs such an interaction, because we can prevent disagreements and irreconcilable differences only through mutual contact and cultural exchange; thus we can build an atmosphere of peace to cover the whole of humanity. If such bridges of dialogue are not formed between different cultures and civilizations, differences and conflicts might drift humanity toward irrevocable fights and wars. Such a clash in our time will not resemble any of the two world wars. It will undoubtedly be much more deadly and destructive. There can be no winner in a war made with nuclear weapons. Such a war means the end of humanity. In order to protect humanity against such a danger, it is necessary to build bridges of peace between different understandings and cultures, receiving certain things from them while also conveying certain things to them, and thus showing that different societies and cultures are not alien and hostile. If this can be done, diverse cultures will recognize that there are no enormous, irreconcilable differences that should lead to conflict. At a period when understanding and reconciliation are seriously needed, such dialogue is a crucial service, done for the sake of humanity.

Measures against Polluted Minds

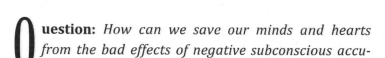

Question: *How can we save our minds and hearts from the bad effects of negative subconscious accumulation?*

Answer: Such a background that pollutes our mind, spirit, world of emotions, reasoning, and judgment, appears before us like an obstacle to block our mechanisms of reasoning and judgment, and can yield disturbing results. It is an unpleasant realization. It paralyzes a person's religious feelings and pollutes their spiritual subtle faculties. For this reason, one must try to give the willpower its due and try to get rid of such influences as much as possible. Such ugly and harmful accumulations may have emerged as a consequence of situations out of our own will. But it should not be forgotten that such negative factors become elements of the world testing us. Therefore, we need to see them as agents that trigger wrongdoing and sinning, and thus take due precautions. For example, the eye encounters a negative scene somewhere and the memory takes a picture of it. That picture, stored in the subconscious, can surface later on. This situation might drift the person toward obscene thoughts, ugly memories, and slippery grounds. To reiterate, it is necessary to give the willpower its due and keep it under control as much as possible. Indeed, when one feels ugly memories awakening, the verses of the Holy Qur'an recommend moving away from that atmosphere immediately.[13]

---

[13] Al-A'raf 7:200–201; Fussilat 41:36

Deadly Viruses and Preventive Medicine

To give an example, a mental picture left by an encounter with an obscene sight or an ugly expression might tempt a person at any moment. Therefore, one needs to rid oneself from that situation immediately, without giving it the slightest chance to survive. Because, as time passes, they make their presence felt and pressure the person in certain ways. They resemble viruses. Just as germs begin to prevail over the body during a physical weakness, subconscious viruses come to the stage in times of spiritual weakness and the absence of sublime feelings. They launch an attack and try to take the individual under control. For this reason, some spiritual figures planned their lives in a way that will not allow committing anything evil, even if one intends to do so. In other words, those great guides took such a stance with the precautions they took from the very beginning and thus blocked the ways of even minor heedlessness. Some even preferred to live as hermits in order to keep away from sins. They saw isolation as a barrier against evils that could tempt them. However, for those who are supposed to not only practice faith but also teach it to others, particularly for the inheritors of the Prophetic heritage, the truthful path to be taken is being with the Real, though in public. This is called *jalwat* (company of people) in Sufism. Togetherness with the Deity within the society is a Prophetic attitude. It is the essential duty of a believer to give one's hue to one's environment. As a believer wishes to keep pure at heart, it is necessary to endeavor to make the atmosphere he or she lives in into a pure place and to completely eliminate factors of evil from there.

Holes Filled in as a Precaution against Sinister Enemies

There is a parable about the beloved Prophet and noble Abu Bakr during their emigration from Mecca. When they reached the Cave of Thawr, Abu Bakr, may God be pleased with him, entered the cave first to check for any harmful animals and to clean the interior. Then he filled the holes he saw by tearing bits from his robe in order to prevent any vermin from harming the noble Prophet. Then the Messenger of God, peace and blessings be upon him, came in to have some rest. However, the pieces of cloth did not suffice for a final hole, which Abu Bakr eventually closed with his foot. Right at that moment, a snake came and bit his heel. Although this parable is not narrated in reliable sources, the gist of the story conveys certain truths for us. One of them is how loyal Abu Bakr was to the beloved Prophet. If there had been the danger of a snake attacking the blessed Prophet, noble Abu Bakr would have done anything to prevent it against all odds, even at the expense of pushing his heel into the mouth of a snake. The second lesson to be drawn from the story is that Believers must fill in all cracks and holes in their environment against every kind of danger that might harm their relationship with God and their spiritual life—including the holes that bear the possibility of turning dangerous. A true believer must fill that hole with one's own being if necessary and implore God thus: "My God, I might lose everything at this point in terms of my worldly life, but please protect me from any dangerous factor that can harm my relation with You, and consciousness of obedience to You; so let the monument of my spirit always stand upright and if it will ever bow down, let it bow down before nobody but You."

As I stated before, it is always possible to question the authenticity of this event but with respect to the meanings to be derived from its message, it not only conveys an example of loyalty but also an important lesson of heedfulness and taking precautions. In this second sense, the moral of the story is that "A believer gives his hue to his environment and builds a secure atmosphere where he can live in accordance with his own feelings and thoughts."

The Bad Friend and the Snake

Getting back to our main subject, we can list things we can do for the sake of ridding ourselves of ugly thoughts and images:

1. The noble Prophet counseled a pattern of action against a possible a corruptive feeling or thought as rage, which can drift one to perdition: "Rage is from Satan; Satan was created from fire, and fire is extin-

guished with water. Then when one of you is enraged, let him make ablutions."[14] Here, God's Messenger, peace and blessings be upon him, refers to a change of state and attitude. When the issue is analyzed from a perspective of human psychology, it will be seen that this advice is an effective course of action for controlling rage. Basing this on a saying of the noble Prophet, we can say that one must definitely have a change of state and environment for the sake of ridding oneself from the atmosphere of sinning. Thus, he will first be freed from the pressure of corruptive memories and images, and then by subscribing to a different atmosphere and different kinds of feelings and thoughts, he will be able to rid his mind and heart of the influence of those negativities.

2. A believer must always have righteous friends and be together with them. As I reiterated in many talks, the first thing they would teach a new student to learn religious discipline was a couplet meaning: "A bad friend is worse than a snake. If you come under his influence, he drifts you to Hell. As for a good friend, he takes you to Paradise."

It is of crucial importance to have good friends, because a person cannot keep standing by oneself all the time. If we compare a person to a tent, one cannot be both the main pole and the pegs of that entity at the same time. As a man bears the tent of being on his shoulders, like a main pole, he needs a few friends to serve as pegs holding its cloth in place. Only then can that structure remain standing. When stones forming a dome lean on one another, they do not fall. For this reason, the noble Prophet stated: "One traveler is a devil. Two travelers are two devils (who run the risk of agreeing on something evil). But three travelers are a group."[15] As the Messenger of God advised us to keep such company, a believer must adjust his or her atmosphere accordingly. Then what befalls on believers to always keep company with righteous and true friends. Thus, when we are inclined to a certain mistake, those friends will immediately warn us and try to bring us to our senses in the face of a possible wrong. Who knows, maybe

---

[14] *Sunan Abu Dawud*, Adab, 4
[15] *Sunan Abu Dawud*, Jihad, 86; *Sunan at-Tirmidhi*, Jihad, 4

most of the time, we will feel shame near those righteous ones and keep away from evil feelings and considerations.

At this point I would like to express one fact about my inner world. When my righteous friends warned me about certain mistakes of mine, I may have felt ashamed and embarrassed a bit. It may have been hard on me. But if looking at the issue in terms of the result it yielded, I always gratefully praised God for it, and felt sincerely thankful toward those friends. As a matter of fact, Bediüzzaman makes a wise warning by saying "If someone were to tell me that there is a scorpion on my neck or in my armpit, I would be grateful to him, not offended."[16] If a righteous believer warns a fellow believer as "You are not careful enough with what hits your eyes and ears!" then that person will probably be shaken like a car brought to a sudden halt while going downslope. However, when he or she looks at the issue with respect to the eternal life, then it will be clear that it is nothing at all to worry about. Such a warning will help coming to one's senses and being saved from falling into a vicious cycle. This is the reward of togetherness with righteous friends.

3. For a lifetime, a believer must be full of feelings and thoughts about the values he or she believes, must continuously read and think, and be fed by the essential sources without leaving a gap in one's personal life. In addition, with serious effort and heartfelt prayer in this respect, it is necessary to pray for protection, help, and guardianship from God with the confession, "O God, please save us from sinning and rebellion. Be our protector! Hold our hand, we cannot do without You!" In fact, the Messenger of God teaches us a course of action by praying as "O the All-Living and Self-Subsistent One! I seek assistance through the means of Your Mercy, correct for me all my affairs and do not entrust me to my soul for the moment of a blink of an eye."[17]

Let me make one final point, that as those who turned to God sincerely in a heartfelt manner did not remain on the road, those who adopt righteous company, and with the help of God, never became lost.

---

[16] Nursi, *Mektubat*, p. 66

[17] An-Nasa'i, *As-Sunanu'l-Kubra*, 6/147; Al-Bazzar, *Al-Musnad*, 13/49

A Common Disease and
Possible Cures

Question: *Individuals' being easily offended and harboring bitter feelings toward one another for a long time has almost become a widespread "disease" in our time. How do you think it is possible to cure this disease, which gives way to personal, familial, and social problems?*

Answer: In a situation as described in the question, individuals feel broken-hearted toward someone and consequently distance oneself from that person. They take a negative stance against that person, and refuse to continue friendly relations with him. It mostly entails other negative behaviors as well. For example, one who harbors resentment against a friend does not only stop there, but in time he or she begins to think negatively about that friend. This mood might even give way to backbiting or slandering that person. When a misfortune happens to the latter, the one harboring resentment feels glad about it. What is worse, as a resentful person lets oneself deeper into these negativities, he or she does not realize the greatness of their mistake and sin, owing to inclinations of seeing oneself as innocent. However, all of these are condemnable acts in the sight of God, which might cause one to fall into eternal ruin. The noble Prophet's warnings and advice on this issue are of crucial importance. In one instance he stated that it is not lawful for a Muslim to break relations with his brother (or her sister in religion) for more than three days.[18] That no matter what happens, a Muslim can continue such a state of bitterness for no more than three days. Incidentally, let me add that if the case of being offended is not based on reasonable grounds, or a sound reference (*manat*) as termed in Islamic Law, even a period of three days will not be allowed. If the causes that led to breaking relations are real and acceptable—only then—can they break off relations for three days, which is the uppermost limit. This period lets anger abate and bitter feelings disappear. It allows broken feelings to weaken, and it will be possible to reconsider the rights of the other person in a calmer mood. As a consequence, the feeling and thoughts of brotherhood or sisterhood will revive once more in the believer's spirit; they will fill the distance you put in between, and you will become close friends again. So by giving certain measures, the *hadith* teaches a way for freeing ourselves from resentment.

Bitter Feelings in the Real and Metaphorical Sense

Although there is no accustomed distinction as the real and metaphorical sense of the issue, we can make such a classification according to the intention and purpose of the people involved. Accordingly, harboring bitter feelings in the real sense is a condemnable condition, whereas its metaphorical version is a strategy that can be employed when necessary. A father can tell his own children "I was not expecting something like that from you!" and adopt an aloof manner toward them. The incident of *ila*[19]—when the beloved Prophet distanced himself from his wives for a temporary period—is an example of this. At this point, I would like to mention a memory of mine I had mentioned at some other talks. One day, my primary school teacher took hold of me and said, "and you also?" I guess if she had beaten me with fifty sticks instead, it would not make that much impact. Her words conveyed appreciation, reminding me of a good relation, and they were a warning, cautioning me to not destroy that relationship. That atti-

---

[18] *Sahih al-Bukhari*, Adab, 62; *Sahih Muslim*, Birr, 25
[19] At-Tahrim 66:1–5; *Sahih al-Bukhari*, Nikah, 83; *Sahih Muslim*, Talaq, 30

tude of the teacher was an appropriate one to bring me to my senses. This is what I mean by referring to turning aloof in the metaphorical sense; that is, using a negative stance as a method to effect a desired result on the person to be warned.

The Rights of Parents and Metaphorical Resentment

Parents should be exempted from the above mentioned situation. Concerning one's parents, God Almighty commands: *"Your Lord has decreed that you worship none but Him alone, and treat parents with the best of kindness. Should one of them, or both, attain old age in your lifetime, do not say "Ugh!" to them (as an indication of complaint or impatience), nor push them away, and always address them in gracious words"* (al-Isra 17:23). Every time I recite this verse during Prayer, I feel as if I get stabbed; for who knows, some of our attitudes might have broken their hearts unawares. My mother, father, grandfather, grandmother, sister, and aunts might have felt offended by my ill manners. When I take these into consideration, I feel as if a spear pierced through my chest. For this reason, when I remember the elderly people in my family, I pray as *"O our Lord! Forgive me, and my parents..."* (Ibrahim 14:41) and with the hope of fulfilling the due of their rights upon me, within the means God provided me with, I sometimes send people to pilgrimage on their behalf. Therefore, it must be out of the question to harbor any bitter feelings toward one's parents or the family elders, even in the metaphorical sense. Even if there are serious factors to cause one to feel offended, one should not be offended toward them. Even if one feels much offended, he or she must absolutely not offend them. On the contrary, one must try to keep them well-pleased. Otherwise, a day comes and one realizes his or her mistakes but it can be too late; it can be a point where it is impossible to compensate for the past. In this respect, it is necessary to plan our life in such a way that we do not express regret for the zigzags we have made and say, "I wish I had not acted that way but this way..." The Pride of Humanity stated that it is wrong to say "I wish..."[20] for it might imply a criticism of Divine Destiny. For this reason, one should agree with a friend to

---

[20]   *Sahih Muslim*, Qadr, 34; *Sunan ibn Majah*, Muqaddima, 10

act as his or her coach, who will warn and guide that person about wrongs that might cause one to express regret with "I wish..." It is said that many great rulers of the past kept certain people near them. As those people used to be chosen from among less cultivated groups, they would bluntly talk to the sultan. As the sultan gave them permission, he would not feel disturbed by their words. On the contrary, the sultan would take a lesson from their words and straighten up again and return to his right frequency. In the same way, it is possible, in our time, for individuals to have a mentor to constantly give them sound advice, guide them to truth, and avert them from committing wrongs that could make them say "I wish..." in regret; because, even if such wrongs make themselves felt as a pang of the conscience, this feeling does not suffice to compensate for them.

Getting back to our essential subject, it may be proper behavior to take a soft negative attitude as a form of metaphorical bitterness. It is possible to compare this situation to the "blows dealt by Divine compassion" as Bediüzzaman puts it. As a mother may slightly smack her children on the hips in response to a certain wrong and express her disapproval, she still tries to let them know that this warning and advice is out of her compassion and for their own good. On the other hand, it needs to be known that using such ways and means wisely takes a certain deal of mastering. Unfortunately, we witness serious mistakes of parenting on such issues, since couples who are to be married do not receive good and sufficient training. People are ignorant about the rights of their spouse, children, and parents according to Islam. As these are not known, they make very serious mistakes. For this reason, I hold the opinion that couples need to undergo good training to be certified as eligible for marriage, so that they can have a successful marriage.

The Deed that Brings Rewards Equivalent to Those Given for Worship

Let us briefly consider the real sense of taking offense. Sometimes, the people around us might really behave in a way that causes us offense. Even in such situations, we should strive not to take offense, as a requirement of our belief in God and the Hereafter, in spite of ourselves and our own feelings. Let us not forget that deciding not to take offense where one normally would bring otherworldly rewards as if that person offered worship. Because, it is a state of battling against one's carnal soul and rising up against one's inner tendencies of transgression, where one gives his or her willpower its due. As it is known, Bediüzzaman mentions three main types of patience and one of them is patience against troubles and misfortunes.[21] So it can easily be said that showing patience as we have described will bring the person otherworldly rewards to be gained by worship. We can sometimes face so many reasons to take offense. However, we need to see them as mere misfortunes and show due patience toward them. Even if somebody breaks relations with us, we should not. Even if they hurt us, we should not hurt another one. If others hurt us but we do not respond in the same way, act with certain flexibility, and find a way to give them a hug, then we will have made a very important sacrifice for the sake of faith and humanity; we will have enacted a very important virtue.

As for the social aspect of the issue, there are serious instances of taking offense, particularly between people who hold different worldviews and reflections of this situation in political life. Expectations of worldly gains as a high status add fuel to the flames. So much so that some people utter words they should not and make statements in conflict with the truth, and this leads to taking offense and harboring bitter feelings. If people do not act upon motives of seeking worldly status, it will be seen that there is a path and field for everybody to serve their people and humanity, and that there is a lane for everyone to run. As the members of a society, everybody can be on separate lanes but work for the common good, be hand in hand, and run toward the same target. This running does not include, nor should it include, a feeling of rivalry or considerations of "Let us leave them behind." May be it should be a form of competing at good acts to make us say, "Let me not remain behind at doing goodness, let me present a perfor-

---

[21] Nursi, *The Letters*, p. 300

mance no worse than those who run ahead of me." Therefore, when the road is so wide, there will not be cases of touching, hurting, and offending one another. The same principle is true about sharing the beauties of faith and the Qur'an with others. God Almighty states: *"Those (on the other hand) who strive hard for Our sake, We will most certainly guide them to Our ways (that We have established to lead them to salvation). Most assuredly, God is with those devoted to doing good, aware that God is seeing them"* (al-Ankabut 29:69). That is, God will guide them to Himself through not one but many ways.

Bediüzzaman underlines the fact that "The roads leading to God are as many as His creatures' breaths."[22] Given that this is the case, one can reach God through one way or another. If we give an example from Sufism, the ways of Naqshbandi, Qadiri, Shadhili, Rufai, Badawi, Khalidi and other orders all lead to Him. For this reason, differences should not be made into causes of harboring bitter feelings. It is necessary to avoid jealousy and rivalry on such issues and refrain from considerations as "They trespassed on our property."

As believers, we need to be as soft and mild as can be toward our brothers and sisters; we need to cherish feelings and thoughts that can smoothly be swallowed without hurting the throat at all. We should be able to present these feelings and thoughts in the same mildness.

Even though breaking relations with a certain person owing to taking offense is very ugly behavior, it might sometimes happen between the altruistic souls who have dedicated themselves to truthful knowledge and humanity. For this reason, I envision great benefit in forming teams for the sake of eliminating ill feelings between people from different sections of the society and different walks of life. As Bediüzzaman puts it, agreement and unity constitute an important means for inviting Divine help.[23] A relevant verse confirms this fact: "... *God's 'Hand'*[24] *is over their hands"* (al-Fath 48:10). That is, protection, help, and the graces of God are upon them. Concerning this verse, the noble

---

22 Nursi, *Al-Mathnawi Al-Nuri,* p. 369; Ibn Arabi, *Al-Futuhatu'l-Makkiyya,* 3/549; Al-Alusi, *Ruhu'l-Ma'ani,* 1/396, 6/165, 14/160

23 Nursi, *The Gleams,* p. 226

24 "Hand" or any other similar term is metaphorical when used about God Almighty.

Prophet stated "God's hand is with the community."[25] At another instance, the Messenger of God, peace and blessings be upon him a millions times, stated: "Whoever wants to be right in the middle of Paradise, let him (or her) not dissociate from the community."[26] That is, let that person not fall into factionalism. One who breaks off with the community owing to taking offense, harboring bitter feelings, resentment, intolerance or a similar feeling, will distance oneself from God's help as well.

There Is Nothing as "Little"

Taking all of these into consideration, we can understand how great a disaster people's breaking off relations with one another is, and what a virtuous act reconciliation is. Not dismissing any act of goodness as unimportant is essential in Islam. Sometimes, God Almighty may take people to the center of Paradise and let them enjoy the beauty of the Divine and experience feelings beyond imagination on the account of little acts of goodness they did. A *hadith* related to this fact states: "Be God-fearing and do not belittle anything from acts of goodness."[27] When we view things from this perspective, we understand that there is actually nothing that qualifies as little.

In another *hadith* where the Pride of Humanity refers to the same subject, behaviors such as smiling at another,[28] saying a good word to that person,[29] feeding a morsel to the mouth of one's wife,[30] and removing an obstacle that might inconvenience people passing[31] are all considered among good acts (*sadaqa*) to bring otherworldly rewards. Accordingly, placing a stone to a hole on the road in order to save passing cars' wheels from falling in or removing a thorn that might hurt people's feet

---

[25] *Sunan al-Tirmidhi*, Fitan, 7
[26] Ibid.
[27] Ahmad ibn Hanbal, *Al-Musnad*, 5:63
[28] *Sahih Muslim*, Birr, 144; *Sunan at-Tirmidhi*, Birr, 45; Ahmad ibn Hanbal, *Al-Musnad*, 3/360
[29] *Sahih al-Bukhari*, Jihad, 128; Adab, 34; *Sahih Muslim*, Zakah, 56
[30] *Sahih al-Bukhari*, Iman, 41, Janaiz, 37; Wasaya, 2; Manaqibu'l-Ansar, 47; *Sahih Muslim*, Wasiyya, 5
[31] *Sahih al-Bukhari*, Jihad, 128, Adab, 34; *Sahih Muslim*, Zakah, 56

from a walkway are considered among acts of worship. It is not certain which of such seemingly little deeds will be a means for settling right in the middle of Paradise. Let me relate a true story about this issue. Caliph Harun Rashid's wife, Zubaydah, was a great woman who carried out important services. At a certain period, pilgrims going to Arafat and Muzdalifa for their worship had to carry on their backs the water they needed. In the conditions of those days, she had waterways and fountains built from Mecca to Mina, Muzdalifa, and up until Arafat, thus committing a great act of goodness.[32] By God's grace, she provided millions of people with water to drink and make ablutions. God Almighty does not leave such a service unrewarded, of course. When I went to Hajj in 1968, I saw the fountains built thanks to that great woman. By making restorations, the Ottomans preserved that waterway for a long period. Those who saw that woman of such great service in dreams asked her how God treated her. Although she had done various good works, she told the deed that became the means of her deliverance thus: "One day the call to Prayer began to rise from the minarets. I told the people around me to be silent and listen. When I passed to the next world, they said 'God forgave you because of this.'"[33]

We never know how God values deeds that seem very little and simple to us in this world. We do not know which deed will become a means of gaining His good pleasure and a means of enjoying eternal bliss in Paradise. For this reason, we should try to carry out everything God commands, without discriminating between them as great or little.

Committees of Peace

I have told all of these stories for the sake of drawing attention to the significance of reconciling people who have broken off relations. Let me reiterate that as the issue is of great importance, it should not be left in a narrow sphere but it is necessary to form teams for this sake. Committees must be formed from experienced ones who have sound insight into human psychology to enable them to recognize their

---

[32]   Ibnu'l-Jawzi, *Al-Muntazam*, 10/277; Ibn Khallikan, *Wafayatu'l-A'yan*, 2/314

[33]   Ibn Ash-Shahin, *Al-Isharat*, p. 871

addressees' characters correctly, and who have competent powers of reasoning, judgment, and speech. This way, they can help people seized by bitter feelings and broken off relations.

Considering the people of Anatolia, they have respect for the sacred in spite of their ignorance in religious matters. For this reason, the universal principles and dynamics of Islam, which addresses everyone, can be a means for reconciliation, eliminating bitter feelings between people, and making them embrace one another again.

As this mission of reconciliation can be local, it is possible to implement it on a larger scale. That is, as you can carry out this beautiful act in a certain neighborhood, village, or city, you can practice it throughout a country. It is even possible to take it further and utilize it in terms of international relations. God's Messenger gave glad tidings for those who contribute to this issue: "Should I tell you about what is more virtuous than fasting, the Prayer, and alms?" They said yes. He said: "Reconciliation between people. Breaking of relations between people is a cut-off (of religion)."[34]

Actually, the dialogues the people of Anatolia are trying to realize worldwide can be considered within this category. Going to the four corners of the world in the name of dialogue, restoring broken relations between countries, constantly generating such plans, and developing effective projects is very important in terms of preventing possible conflicts, wars, and disorders. The most important means of struggling against conflict and discord is education. That is, you will bring up perfect individuals in terms of virtues and universal values, values such as peace, tolerance, and dialogue. Not only will they know a few languages, but they will have expertise in different sciences. At the same time, they will be cultivated with human values and virtues, full of the ideal of making others live. They will pursue PhD and postdoctoral studies everywhere they are for the sake of serving humanity. These exemplary personalities will serve as barriers against discord and transgression, and they will fulfill an important duty in this respect. In a way, it is a matter of reconciliation on global scale. Therefore, this matter, implemented at the micro or local plan, needs to be

---

[34] *Sunan Abu Dawud*, Adab, 58; *Sunan at-Tirmidhi*, Qiyamah, 57

implemented at the international level as well. Statesmen can come together with the goal of an alliance between civilizations. They can come to agreement on certain issues, and act cooperatively so that differences do not become a means of fighting. Surely, such an act is very important in the name of humanity; it is a laudable activity that deserves to be applauded. However, if such an understanding has not been internalized by the grassroots of the society, this kind of struggle will be doomed to fail. Therefore, it is necessary to seek ways to get people involved in this issue. You can see it as a way of facilitating the process initiated by statesmen through getting ordinary people involved in it; this is the key factor for permanence of the issue. During the cold war period, the communist and capitalist worlds kept fighting for a long time. Some of the smaller countries in between chose to join this or that pact. Each one of those countries experienced different troubles and difficulties as a consequence of such differentiation and polarization. I wonder whether any intellectuals, philosophers or thinkers spoke out loud that it could be handled without a fight as well, whether such an initiative for reconciliation came up or not. I guess not. On the contrary, there were different cases of provocation to make states confront one another. As some provoked their own men, others similarly provoked theirs, and a competition of armament began. Each pact occupied some land, exerted its influence there, and caused people to experience fear and terror that lasted for years. At a time when opportunities of communication and travel have developed and deadly weapons have become more powerful, I think it is an important act of worship to seek ways of reconciliation between nations by taking the issue to an international platform.

Passing to the Next World with a Pure Heart

Restoring relations between people signifies adopting Divine morality as well.[35] Some sayings of the noble Prophet refer to God Almighty's dealings that can be compared to reconciliation. For example, let us imagine that a certain man passes to the next world after having violated some rights of another, but this man has a certain degree of

---

[35] Al-Kalabazi, *At-Taarruf*, 1/5; Al-Ghazali, *Ihya Ulumiddin*, 4/306

worth in the sight of God. Let us assume that in the afterlife, God Almighty says to the rightful claimer, "You have lawful claims from this servant of Mine; if You consent to give up your claim, I will give you such and such reward..."[36] So we can apply such an approach to our individual, familial, and social life, and follow this Divine morality. If this is the way God Almighty treats people on the Day of Judgment, it is a very important reference for us at the same time. In my opinion, we need to take this Divine morality as guideline and strive for reconciliation between people who broke off relations. I do not remember having personally broken off relations with anyone by taking offense. There are people who have been writing against me for some forty or fifty years. They write against me alike when I smile and when I cry. Even if I stand somewhere in between, they definitely come up with something to oppose me. I did not, and will not, take offense; on the contrary, I feel pity for their condition. Then I think, they have difficulty in finding some other subject to write about. It goes against my nature to wish them to end up in Hell. At a certain time, when a person who had been in certain proximity to me made vicious statements, the idea of his being punished by God passed my mind; it is worse to see such hostility from a person who once had been near you. But still, I went to my room and said to myself "How dare I..." and God is my witness to how I sobbed. It is not easy to condemn a person to Hell. The evil he did to you does not mean condemning you to Hell. Even if it were, it is not fair to condemn a person to Hell who did the same to you. For this reason, I see no point in taking offense and harboring grudge against some people. We must go to God's presence with a pure heart and without harboring any resentment toward anyone. According to the relevant Arabic idiom, we must not have *ghil*—anything negative—toward anyone. As a lover runs to the beloved, we must respond to God's waiting for us by going to His presence with a pure heart. If we are invited as "You have always led a pure life, come now!" we need to respond by going there in a pure state. May God enable us to have such horizons and understanding while passing to the realms beyond, amin!

---

[36] Ibn Abi'd-Dunya, *Husn az-zan*, p. 109; Al-Ghazali, *Ihya Ulumiddin*, 4/523

A Major Sin: *Ghulul* (Defrauding)

It is not conceivable that a Prophet defrauds; and whoever defrauds (by stealing from public property or war-gains) will come with what he gained by his fraud on the Day of Resurrection. Then, every soul shall be repaid in full what it has earned (while in the world), and they will not be wronged. (Al Imran 3:161).

Question: *The verse mentions ghulul[37] (defrauding, misappropriation), which is considered among the major sins. Could you explain what ghulul is? Will you tell about the general frame of ghulul and what is the message to be drawn from the verse by contemporary believers?*

Answer: In its general meaning, *ghulul* means taking something unlawful for a person, benefiting from it, and breaching the trust. In a more specific context, it refers to stealing something from war-gains before they are distributed, and to take secretly from what belongs to the public and abusing what belongs to the state.

The Matchless Hero of Purity

The indefinite article before the word "Prophet" in the verse shows that all Prophets are included in the meaning. This fact conveys two important points:

---

[37] *Sahih al-Bukhari*, Jihad, 189; Khums, 8; *Sahih Muslim*, Iman, 182; Jihad, 32

Firstly, ethical purity is not peculiar to the Final Prophet but all of the Prophets, peace be upon them; Prophets Adam, Noah, Hud, Salih, Moses, Jesus or any other Prophet did not take anything to their person from what belongs to the people. They only took from what they believed to be one hundred per cent lawful given to them.

Secondly, as none of the Prophets committed such an act, it is obviously impossible for Prophet Muhammad, peace and blessings be upon him, who is the most illustrious fruit of this blessed tree, to do such a thing. If we compare the line of the Prophets to a set of Prayer beads, then the Pride of Humanity is the prime one among them. The set of beads became a string of prayer beads in the real sense and the circle became complete with him. With respect to the Divine purpose of creation, he is the seed and most perfected fruit of the universe.[38] Frames of concepts became clear with him. Meanings of phenomena that exist and take place around us found their explanation thanks to him. They were interpreted correctly, and by benefiting from them in terms of knowledge of God, truthful meanings were drawn from them. As the Pride of Humanity is the Paragon of Virtue who represents every good character in its peak, he also takes the lead in innocence and uprightness.

There are different reports about the reason for the revelation of the verse. One of these reports relates the verse to the Battle of Uhud. Accordingly, a group of immature people, most of whom were the Hypocrites of Medina, made baseless claims about the noble Prophet—may God forbid such an idea—that he would allocate some of the war-gains for himself.[39] The verse clearly reveals that defrauding is out of the question for that great figure who led a perfectly upright life from the beginning. Even one case suffices to show his staggering innocence: When the noble Prophet gave his last breath, his shield was held by a Jewish pawnbroker.[40] As he led his personal life in immense

[38] As-Suyuti, *Al-Hawi*, 1/325; Al-Halabi, *As-Siratu'l-Halabiyya*, 1/240

[39] As-Sa'labi, *Al-Kashf wa'l-Bayan*, 3/196; Al-Baghawi, *Ma'alimu't-Tanzil*, 1/366; Az-Zamahshari, *Al-Kashshaf*, 1/461

[40] *Sahih al-Bukhari*, Jihad, 89; *Sunan at-Tirmidhi*, Buyu, 7; *Sunan ibn Majah*, Ruhun, 1

and profound heedfulness, he also showed perfect sensitivity against anything that could raise the smallest doubt about his upright life.

Lawful Seeming Guises to Unlawful Gains

The verse continues as "...*whoever defrauds will come with what he gained by his fraud on the Day of Resurrection.*" As *ghulul* means taking secretly from war-gains, anything a person takes without a lawful right falls into the category of *ghulul*. For example, imagine that a man comes to certain position and makes personal gain by some speculations, misappropriates funds, and tries to justify his acts with claims as "I am exerting myself here. This much money could not be collected if it weren't for me!" All such things fall within the category of *ghulul*. We can even say that a person who steps forth for governing the people without being eligible for it violates the people's rights. According to this verse, which makes a specific address but conveys a general message, the followers of the Prophets should not commit it also. Regarding this issue, they should always be resolved to keep on the righteous path. Otherwise, they will be brought before God with what they took. Therefore, we can say that the verse warns all followers of the noble Prophet in the person of the Prophets. In fact, God's Messenger told his Companions one day about *ghulul* —this *hadith* could be considered as an interpretation of the relevant verse—and expressed what a great sin *ghulul* was and said: "I do not want any one of you to come on the Day of Resurrection with a groaning camel on his neck, saying,' O Muhammad!' and I will say: 'I cannot do anything for you, I conveyed the message.'" Then the noble Prophet voiced the same fact about other animals of this kind and different types of gains.[41]

The verse ends as follows: "*Then, every soul shall be repaid in full what it has earned (this can be goodness or evil depending on the deeds of the person), and they will not be wronged.*" May God save all of us from going to the next world with such ugliness as *ghulul* and laying our hands on anything we do not lawfully deserve. If we consider cases of embezzlement from state banks, wasting people's money, and push-

[41] *Sahih al-Bukhari*, Jihad, 189; *Sahih Muslim*, Imara, 24

ing people to poverty by burdening the state with loans, it will be better understood how grave a sin *ghulul* is.

Constant Self-Criticism In Order to Avoid *Ghulul*

Actually, the devoted souls should show more sensitivity in keeping away from *ghulul*. For example, if they gather together for the sake of servitude to God or worship, we need to have the thought within about whether it is our lawful right to step on the carpet under our feet. If we do not do that, then it means we have lost our sensitivity on this issue. I am not saying that it is not your right. Those who built these establishments bought the carpets for your use; this is a different issue. The point I am trying to make is that, we need to be so sensitive as to question ourselves about whether we deserve to use these carpets by prostrating ourselves on them and causing them to wear out a bit. We are eating from the food they serve us here, but are we really deserving of it? Having concerns, hesitations, and sensitivity about this issue is very important. Caring about where the morsel in one's mouth comes from, to whom it belonged, questioning is it really lawful or not, and showing great sensitivity in this respect is a very important duty that falls on a believer. You may be included in different units of serving faith and people, but let me give an example from the aid organization Kimse Yok Mu. As it is known and seen, Kimse Yok Mu fulfills a very important service of making humanitarian aid. In whichever part of the world a fracture appears, they go running to mend it and to lend a helping hand. However, it should not be forgotten that it is the people's donations that support this organization and goes to others' aid. Televisions advertise for it, phone calls pave the way for donations, and people join this goodness, even if it is only with a few liras. Eventually, the donations amount to a certain total. A person who works at such an organization should do this service for the sake of God, without asking any financial demand, if possible. But if he or she does not have any other income for a livelihood, it is possible to give that person a certain salary. However, it should definitely be a fixed amount clearly stated. Otherwise, those who handle the organization might think, "We have the financial means in our hands anyway. Then let us give our employees no less than a high-level journalist. After all, we go to so many different countries of the world and take serious pains. For this reason, a high salary is our right!" This thought is just another form of *ghulul*.

As for what needs to be done here, within the rules determined by the team that governs the organization, they should say to employees, "You can take this much as your monthly payment, and this is for the travel expenses." Nothing extra to that amount will be lawful for them. Otherwise, one might lose while seemingly being on the righteous path. While walking to God and having the means to gain His good pleasure, they might fall for Satan's trickery and—may God forbid!—become a fallen one.

The Ethical Conduct and Discipline of Making an Explanation to the People

Other people governing establishments of volunteers such as supplementary schools, cultural centers and the like must show the same sensitivity. The people who support this service trust the volunteers to the degree of comfortably saying, "You can take my soul" if a soul were needed somewhere. If there is a *ghulul* somewhere, even if it is as little as one-seventh of a grain of barley in worth, God will bring us to account for it. As a matter of fact, the Qur'an declares: "*Whoever does an atom's weight of good will see it; and whoever does an atom's weight of evil will see it*" (az-Zalzalah 99:8). Accordingly, we will be held liable for even smaller sins. The Arabic word *dharra* refers to the smallest particle of matter; it used to be called molecule, then atom, and then a subatomic particle... You can even call it luminiferous aether . So according to the verse, God Almighty will call us to account for evils we cannot even see with a microscope or x-rays.

Bediüzzaman also spent his life with the utmost sensitivity of this kind. In order not to shake the trust of society, he accounted for his very modest belongings: "This coat I wear, I bought it seven years ago as a second hand item. For five years I have been getting on four and a half liras for clothing, underwear, shoes, and socks." He did not leave any place for the slightest doubts to be raised about him. Then he explained that he possessed a chicken, which laid an egg every day in spite of the winter, and that its chick grew up and started to lay eggs no sooner than its mother was unable to lay eggs.[42] All of these are not simple stories. By doing that, he accounted for his belongings before the people.

Once I listened to Hacı Münir Effendi, who was a respected figure in our village. When soldiers, on the order of the new government, arrested Bediüzzaman during his retreat to Mount Erek, they stopped over in our village on the way. He was hosted at the inn of my grandfather. Münir Effendi described Bediüzzaman with the following words: "When I saw his condition, my eyes were filled with tears. As his shoes were torn, his feet and socks were soaked. I took his simple rubber shoes and brought him a new pair. God knows how difficult it was to convince him to accept it. At dusk, I brought him some soup and compote to break his fast. He took a few spoons from the soup and then said, let me not be wasteful, it is possible to eat the compote for the *sahur*.[43]" That great teacher could not even afford a pair of new rubber shoes. This was his degree of sensitivity. He did his best in order not to shake the people's trust in him and presented an example for us in this respect. People of such status, representing certain values, need to lead their lives with such sensitivity. As believers, our greatest credit is the people's trust. They keep asking "How do you find finance to support the schools?" We have the people's support. People give their support, for they have the belief; "There is no shadow of doubt and speculative purposes in these people's lives." Therefore, if you commit some form of *ghulul* by laying your hands on something that is not your lawful right, you will have, first of all, broken this trust. On the other hand, imagine that the people put their trust in you, but you betrayed them; God will bring one to account for that betrayal. But it is doubtful whether we can say anything meaningful during

---

[42] Nursi, *Mektubat*, p. 70

[43] Pre-dawn meal before fasting.

such questioning or not. The situation on Judgment Day will surely make the Pride of Humanity sad.

There are such essential values and disciplines in Islamic teaching that it is an entire case to be studied separately. God Almighty bestowed great blessings on Muslims, such as the Holy Qur'an, the Authenticated Sunnah, the Islamic teachings, and made this into the spirit of our lives. If Muslims still fail to erect the monument of their soul after so many blessings pouring down on them, then it means they are spending their lives in vain. Therefore, if we do not embarrass the noble Prophet in the Hereafter, and if we wish God's graces to keep coming in terms of good works in this world, then we have to show the utmost sensitivity on this issue. For the same reason I told certain people who have been my friends for 40 to 45 years, "You had better not own an apartment or car of your own." I am not such a sensitive person, but let me tell you one thing I did. So many times I opened my hands to God and prayed: "My God, please, here I am imploring You, do not grant worldly means to my own brothers." Because, if others see them enjoying some wealth, they can say, "Then he is taking something from somewhere." Praise be to my God, every one of them is employed somewhere as workers and I—the whole world is a witness to it—am not disturbed by this at all. Let them keep living—may God grant them long life—as laborers. I will not feel sad at all. I would be sad if they died as sinful people or if other people gossiped about their dishonesty; for it would mean discrediting a noble ideal the people gave heartfelt support to.

Thieves of Success

Let me express as a final point that *ghulul* can happen with not only material but also spiritual matters. For example Bediüzzaman mentions that the victory of an entire battalion cannot be ascribed to their commander only.[44] All the rewards and honor do not belong to the commander but the entire army. For this reason, laying claims on the accomplishment of an entire movement means associating partners

---

44   Nursi, *The Gleams*, p. 185

with God, on the one hand, and *ghulul* on the other. It is a great danger if a person lays claim to certain achievements by disregarding the efforts of millions and asserting his role by saying, "my plans and projects, my insight and thoughts…" and appropriating the people's appreciation for himself by saying "I did it." If others respond to him by singing his praises, and if he welcomes these, it is a further degree of disrespect and moral corruption. Such an attitude is also a form of *ghulul*, a major sin, and betrayal of trust.

Working Hours of the Devoted Souls

Question: *How is the volunteers' understanding of working hours supposed to be? Will you share your considerations on how self-sacrifice relates to working hours?*

Answer: Our time spent working for the sake of Divine truths can be considered in the same category with money and possessions donated for the sake of God—or with *infaq* to use a general term—with respect to their essential philosophies. Particularly in the conditions of the Meccan period, the issue of *infaq* was taken in the absolute sense: "*...and out of what We have provided for them, they spend (of wealth, knowledge, power, etc., to provide sustenance for the needy and in God's cause, purely for the good pleasure of God and without placing others under obligation)*" (al-Baqarah 2:3).

As it is seen, God Almighty encourages us to spend as much as we can out of the blessings He provided us. In the same way, acting with a complete spirit of devotedness and spending our time on the righteous path with the absolute understanding of the Meccan period is a consequence of such horizons of self-sacrifice. However, one important point should not be overlooked. In order to motivate the volunteers, we can make statements like "They should spend as much as they can" or "They should run like noble steeds until their heart stops..." As such a style can be adopted for the sake of encouragement, some situations may truly necessitate one to give whatever one possesses and run breathlessly until he or she perishes. However, considering everybody in general, it is necessary to take human nature into consideration both regarding spending for the sake of God and planning the hours of working. That is, we are human beings, we have families to support and other responsibilities, and thus expectations from us should not be beyond what we can bear. There can be exceptional figures who do keep running until they perish. However, such sacrifice should not be expected from everyone, and such performance and program should not be taken as the basis for everybody. We need to make our plans by taking general facts into consideration and present our issues accordingly.

Following the Way of the Noble Prophet in Programming Our Lives

In a *hadith* we can relate to our subject, the noble Prophet, peace and blessings be upon him, stated: "Indeed, this religion is easy, and no one will ever overburden himself in religion, except that it will overcome him."[45] That is, religion in its essence is not something beyond people's power to carry out. By planning our time, putting things into order, and receiving support from one another we can easily carry it out. However, if one makes religion unbearable, that person should not forget that he or she will be overcome. One should take the issue in such a way that they will be able to carry out their practices during their youth, maturity, and old age alike; so that they can practice religion not as an individual, but as a family and a society. There can always be some people who totally dedicate their entire lives to serving in the name of righteousness and Divine truths, who totally forsake the world and are totally indifferent to anything other than serving faith. If such people do not try to impose their subjective case on others around them, there may be no harm in their preference. Among Sufis as well, there were the Halwati dervishes, who spent their lives as hermits. They completely closed their doors to the world in order to avoid any distractions that might avert their gaze. However, it should not be forgotten that this is not what is expected

---

[45] *Sahih al-Bukhari*, Iman, 29; *Sunan an-Nasa'i*, Iman, 28

from the inheritors of the noble Prophet's tradition. We meet those people's greatness with respect. However, as the Messenger of God, millions of peace and blessings be upon him, conveyed the Divine teaching to his followers, he stated that being among people and putting up with the troubles they cause is better than living alone in retreat.[46] In this respect, everybody is supposed to fulfill some responsibilities for the sake of their people and what befalls an ideal believer is to carry out that responsibility in the best way one can. Elevating oneself in a way depends on the people's and future generations' elevation. Therefore, one should develop wide-scale projects that take the relevant needs of society into consideration and then make the necessary efforts to realize those projects. In addition to doing that, they should plan their time without neglecting their personal religious life and spiritual progress, along with serving in the way of God to the best of their powers. Then everybody should fulfill their duty so as not to leave a gap in any part of life. They should efficiently plan their time and their divisions of labor; whoever can do what in the most perfect way, they should try to perform efficiently.

As Abdullah ibn Amr ibn As was an outstanding Companion with respect to his piety and God-consciousness; he was also one of the people who listened to and understood the noble Prophet in the best way. This blessed Companion would spend his nights standing at Prayer and spend his days fasting. Sometimes, he would not eat anything for two or three days in a row. Imagine what happens to a person who observes such a life of devotions. If he is married, he neglects the rights of his family. For example, a man who stands in Prayer until dawn may not have the opportunity to see his children and have a talk with them. He may be neglecting other responsibilities as well. Hence, on hearing about the situation of his Companion, the Messenger of God told him to sleep for a part of the night and pray during the rest, to fast on some days and not to fast on others; then he warned Abdullah that in addition to God's right of worship, there are other owners of rights upon him, such as his own self, his family and guests, and

---

[46] *Sunan at-Tirmidhi*, Qiyamah, 56; *Sunan ibn Majah*, Fitan, 23

that every rightful one should be given their rights."[47] With this warning, the beloved Prophet not only draws attention to the significance of objective responsibility that one can handle, but also to the necessity of good time management and putting things to do into order.

Getting back to the initial question, we need to be balanced in our understanding of service and notion of *infaq*. Imagine a factory owner who came to a charity organization and said, "I would like to donate my factory altogether. You can use it as you wish." And let us say that some 10 other factory owners did the same. It causes a serious problem of handling things. Can the staff of that charity organization run those factories or not? Can the people who donated those factories give the donation they planned to make every year? You must take all of these into consideration. Acts of goodness should be realized in such a way that the business can continue running and the owner should be able to make a contribution every year. Otherwise, one who gives away everything will simply watch while others keep giving the following year.

What Good Time Management Promises

In addition to a spirit of self-sacrifice, one must manage their time well to serve on the righteous path. As conveyed by the final verses of the chapter Al-Inshirah in the Qur'an (94:7–8), it is possible to take an active rest and use time efficiently by alternating between acts of worship and worldly tasks. We need to eliminate spiritual tiredness with physical activity, and physical tiredness with concentration of the spirit. This way, it is possible to have a body and spirit of strong, sound, and dynamic structure.

In different countries, there are altruistic guides and teachers serving at schools and cultural institutions; they serve their people and the whole of humanity, and expect nothing for their person. What is expected from people working at those institutions is different—be it a small salary like the scholarship of a student, a decent salary, or whatever payment they need to get by. After having maintained the

---

[47] *Sahih al-Bukhari*, Sawm, 54; *Sahih Muslim*, Siyam, 181

livelihood of their families, they are supposed to give 30–40 hours of lessons, attend to their students night and day, if necessary, and even to provide them guidance during the weekend. How I wish those self-less souls could help with the studies of their students with a Prophetic determination, share their troubles of any kind, and even show a motherly care for their boarding students who stay at the dorm. With only such an understanding of work can we find an opportunity to order our life of knowledge and wisdom, which has been in ruins for such a long time. However, before expecting such a degree of self-sacrifice from individuals, we first need to tell about the necessity of understanding work, offer due rehabilitation, make people accustomed to it, and after all of these, entrust the notion of self-sacrifice to their freewill. Let me add that while doing all of these, there is nothing to be gained by using coercion.

The Language Olympiads and the Working Hours Factor

If we expect to get good results from our services, we need to devote a serious amount of time to it. Let us suppose that you are a guide or administrator at a school. In addition to carrying out the administrative responsibilities during the school day, you should supervise the students and fulfill their needs concerning where they should or should not go. Your effectiveness will be in direct proportion with your devotion of time and effort. I think the fruitfulness God Almighty granted to the works of volunteers is in a way related to their surpassing the notion of time and exerting themselves to the ultimate degree. Take the language Olympiads, for instance. Some sing the praises of this beautiful activity which serves as a conveyor of language and culture; some express their admiration and appreciation; and some cannot hold back their tears of happiness. But it should not be forgotten that all of those achievements are Divine favors granted in return for making serious efforts and working diligently, night and day, with an understanding of work surpassing the norms. May God grant success to those good people who carry out the activities that mean much for their people and humanity and let them keep on with such an understanding of work, may He enable them to love their work, and plan their time wisely, and may He continue showering His blessings on us!

Correctly Understanding the Laws Prevalent in Creation and Making a Work Plan

In his works, Bediüzzaman refers to time management as one of the important essentials of progress, and states that this can be realized by following the Divine commands, piety, and sound adherence to religion.[48] *Taqwa* (piety) includes avoiding what is forbidden, observing all of the *fard* (obligatory) responsibilities, fulfilling the *wajib* (necessary) acts in a flawless fashion, and keeping away from dubious things. In this respect, a person's careful observance of his lawful rights, his ability to use his time effectively, concentrate on his work, and fulfill his duties in the best way, are responsibilities directly related to *taqwa*. For this reason, if a person commissioned to a duty does not fulfill his responsibilities, he will be called to account by God, and will have let down the institution for who they work.

As it is known, *taqwa* has one more dimension: complying with the laws of creation in addition to observance of religious laws.[49] For example, making your activities run smoothly by using your time very well, must be done in accordance with taking into consideration the developments in the world and the various hostile individuals or circles likely to impede your activities; it is the worldly aspect of *taqwa* that necessitates many of our responsibilities. If a person harms his or her people, and the circle of service they are affiliated with, for God's sake, what can this be called other than sin? As time management is a religious commandment, it is a very important means to lead us to success. It is necessary to plan very well when to have a rest, when to work, what will be gained through what means, when to receive spiritual nourishment and when to give it... all of these should be well planned. One needs to be prompt and follow the planned hours carefully.

---

[48] Nursi, *The Gleams*, p. 171
[49] Nursi, *The Words*, p. 750

Division of Labor and Doing Things on Time

On the other hand, not only planning the working hours but also choosing the things to do is very important. Who will do what, and the duties individuals are likely to succeed better at, need to be chosen correctly. This can be fulfilled well by truly competent leaders. A different depth of the Prophetic perspicacity of God's Messenger was that everybody he commissioned for a certain duty proved to be the precisely perfect choice. There was no need to change any of the people he commissioned; each of them succeeded well at their duty. This depends on gaining insight into people, testing them well and discovering their characters very well before commissioning them. Within the conditions of our time, fathoming individuals' abilities well and commissioning them correctly depends on collective reasoning and consciousness.

I would like to make one final point here: Different programs and meetings are held at certain intervals in state institutions or private establishments. It is absolutely necessary to be prompt about timing, because time is very precious. Nobody has the right to waste and kill other people's precious time. God will bring people to account for such irresponsible behavior. Particularly for some tasks, your half an hour delay can cause failure; a little delay might cause serious losses and negative consequences. On the other hand, agreeing for a certain meeting at a certain time and place is a kind of promise. One who does not comply with it should fear the Divine admonition, "*Why do you say what you do not do (as well as what you will not do)?*" (Saf 61:12). Although the verse conveys a wide range of meaning, when we study the reason for its revelation, we see that it was a case of not keeping one's promise.[50] For this reason, a person who promised to join a meeting must do one's best in order to be there on time. When needed, they should even go there some time before and wait at the door. Instead of making others wait for us, we had better wait for others. If one faces a problem that causes them to be delayed, then it is necessary to phone right away to apologize and give notice, so that others do not come early and waste their time. In addition, matters

---

[50] Fakhruddin ar-Razi, *Mafatihu'l-Ghayb*, 29/270; Al-Baghawi, *Ma'alimu't-Tanzil*, 4/337

to be discussed in the meeting should be put in order beforehand, serious notes should be prepared to present the issue, and no place should be left for disorganized speech depending on what comes to mind at that moment. The matters we noted regarding sound mind, feelings, and heart are very important for us; we can keep the issues we discussed within frame this way. Otherwise, somebody makes a remark, another gives a reply, somebody brings up some other issue, emotions and feelings arise, and thus the main issues can be lost. However, the notes we take beforehand will draw a frame for us. Notes we take with a sound mind will help us keep on task and time will not be wasted.

Another issue I tried to warn my friends of is not unnecessarily prolonging phone conversations. Sometimes, they prolong issues so much that expressions like "err..." or "I mean..." make up most of the talk. However, if one chooses to take notes before speaking, they may avoid unnecessarily wasting time. Sometimes you see that a matter to be presented in two minutes takes half an hour owing to lack of preparation and talking in a disorganized fashion. Doctors warn that talking on a cell phone for too long might lead to a brain tumor. Thus, we need to take their advice and be careful about using such phones; otherwise, we will have committed a sin. In conclusion, believers need to be well organized in all of their actions; they should behave in a disciplined way, talk in a disciplined way, and continue their lives within the Divine discipline and rules.

Sacrifice: A Means of Closeness with God and People

Question: *The devoted souls take the opportunity of the (Eid of) Sacrifice, which is a means of closeness to God, and go to different corners of the world, particularly poor regions like Africa, and build bridges between hearts. Could you share your considerations on such activities during the Eid of Sacrifice and recommendations for bettering them?*

Answer: Everything commences with a small angle at the starting point. Those who come later give support, shoulder that task, develop new ways and methods, and generate different alternatives. This is what happened with the sacrifices in Turkey. While people used to offer their sacrifices as an individual responsibility and shared the meat with their close surroundings, they first started to share it with people in other regions in their country, and then with people in different regions of the world; eventually it became an important means for warming hearts.

Sacrifice and the Virtue of Altruism

At the beginning of the second chapter of the Qur'an, God Almighty states: *"Those who believe in the Unseen, establish the Prayer in con-*

formity with its conditions, and out of what We have provided for them they spend" (al-Baqarah 2:3) and point out that He is the true owner of everything but we people are only temporary attendees. That is, "He" is the real provider of what we seemingly provide for the needy. By stating *"We"* have provided, He also reminds us that there is no need to worry that we might be deprived by spending for God's sake. This fact is explicitly stated in another verse: *"Surely God—it is He Who is the All-Providing, Lord of all might, and the All-Forceful"* (adh-Dhariyat 51:58). Actually, believers' sharing the means—be it alms or sacrificial meat—they possess with others is the minimal degree of the issue. (That is, if you neglect doing even this much, you can hardly be called believers.) Another verse points to the maximal degree as follows: *"...and in their hearts do not begrudge what they have been given, and (indeed) they prefer them over themselves, even though poverty be their own lot"* (al-Hashr 59:9). Individuals acting with this spirit will use everything they possess—such as time, opportunities, knowledge, wisdom, fortune, horizons of thought, or everything God gave them—for the sake of humanity to the final degree; they will share with others what is in their hands.

During the time of the religious festival, Muslims will conquer hearts with their generosity and share their sacrificial meat with others. As it is stated in a *hadith*, on the Day of Judgment, God Almighty will turn the sacrificed animals into steeds for the use of the ones who offered them, at a time when they are in dire need of help.[51] In the face of such a situation, people will fill with admiration and wonder, asking themselves, "Which one should I ride?"

Another *hadith* demands everybody who can afford to offer a sacrifice: "Who has the means to offer a sacrifice but does not, let that person not approach our place of Prayer!"[52] Since this *hadith* conveys an intimidating message for those refusing to offer a sacrifice, scholars of the Hanafi school ruled that it is no less than *wajib* (necessary) to offer

---

[51] *Kanzu'l-Ummal*, 5/88, 1274
[52] *Sunan ibn Majah*, Adahi, 2

a sacrifice.[53] As it is obligatory to give *Zakah* for everybody who is wealthy enough, it is similarly necessary to offer a sacrifice for those who can afford it. Given that it is a *wajib* act of worship, then every believer should fulfill this responsibility. Nobody wishes to be deserving of the address, "Let that person not approach our place of Prayer."

The stated condition "who has the means" suggests that some people in the society may not afford it; in that situation, those who have the means will not forget the fact that they are supposed to support poorer ones who have a right to benefit from their wealth.

Another verse encourages giving from what people love: "*You will never be able to attain godliness and virtue until you spend of what you love (in God's cause or to provide sustenance for the needy)*" (Al Imran 3:92). Then one had better choose the sacrificial animal, which will become a steed on the way to Paradise, from robust ones. The religious rules for offering sacrifice already necessitate the animal's being a healthy one without defects as a broken horn and the like. Everything done here will appear to us in the Hereafter with their true reflections. As we cannot how things will be in the next world, we cannot really imagine how they will return to us. Who knows, maybe they will appear like a plane, ship, boat, or like a good horse. If we look at the issue by considering the immensity of God's graces and the truthfulness of His promises, we can say that they will definitely return to us somehow.

According to a report by our mother Aisha, God's Messenger distributed two-thirds of the animal he sacrificed to the poor and left the one-third for not depriving his family of it.[54] This is the criterion for one who wishes to distribute the meat in compliance with the example of the noble Prophet. However, if there are different animals for different members of the family, then it is also possible to follow a different pattern. For example one of the animals, half of it, or one-third of it can be spared for home and the rest can be given away. By

---

[53] As-Sarahsi, *Al-Mabsut*, 12/8; Al-Marghinani, *Al-Hidaya*, 4/70; Ibn Nujaym, *Al-Bahru'r-Raik*, 8/197

[54] *Sahih Muslim*, Adahi, 28; *Sunan Abu Dawud*, Dahaya 9, 10

making such a distribution, one will let the members of the family—who will naturally wish to taste the meat—have their share, lend a helping hand to ones in dire need, and build bridges of love and compassion between different sections and societies.

Ingraining Noble Qualities in Oneself

As stated at the beginning, people in Turkey used to sacrifice their animals, leave some of the meat at home, and distribute the rest to neighbors. There came a time when the sacrifices became means of helping the needy over long distances and those who could afford it made due promises. Some of those munificent people did not suffice with only one; some of them donated two, three, and even ten, twenty, or thirty sacrifices. This was an indication of a noble character ingrained in those people together with the feeling and thought of giving. In addition, doing it openly served as encouragement for others to join. Thus, the sacrifices were a form of support to the poor in different regions of the country. Having seen that it worked on the small scale, they decided to have a try by God's grace in a larger scale; so what started with a small angle at the center became huge in the periphery. Those selfless souls went to almost every country in Africa, since dire poverty exists rather broadly in that region. People who live there probably cannot eat meat even once a year. So the altruists who knew that started donating sacrifices and taking them to those places.

It was not only Africa. They offered sacrifices in different parts of the world and distributed the meat to the people there. Such an act was very appealing for people of different cultures and understandings. Offering that sacrificial meat to those people—in cooked or uncooked form—was something completely new for them. They had no such practice in their world; in lands where people do not offer a cup of tea without guaranteeing to receive two, this attitude was a novelty. Through this means, people recognized the beautiful values that affected it. They witnessed the generosity of Islam, the bountifulness of Muslims, the spirit of altruism, and the feeling of letting others eat instead of oneself. In consequence, they began to feel warmth and love toward the essential dynamics behind this philosophy. In my opinion, such activities are important factors in terms of building bridges of love and dialogue between different cultures in a globalizing world. The activities done in this direction came to a certain level. As not trying to improve what is in hand is a kind of lethargy, our ideal should be to constantly keep running for higher goals.[55]

Another aspect of the issue is that you had better bring a new spirit every year to the activities you carry out by adding new hues and patterns to them. For example, in addition to giving meat, you may collect clothes and other things people do not use, store them in available places you find, and then distribute them to the poor. In some areas of the countries the volunteers go, people do not even have decent clothes to put on. You see skyscrapers on the one side, and miserable shanties on the other. There are poor countries in Africa that are so poor that a bit of help there will mean very much for the needy. In short, you should seek new ways of making people happy by adding new hues and depths to your acts of goodness. Their smiling faces will make us smile happily too. We do not even know how God's graces come and what other doors of goodness He opens as a result of those efforts. For this reason, with a slight change of format and adding some originality every time, we should continuously try to build up love in hearts. God knows the rest. With the approach of Bediüzzaman, we carry out what befalls on us, and do not try to interfere with the dealings of our Lord.[56]

The Surprises That Come through Sacrifices

As a matter of fact, seeking closeness to God in all acts of worship, saying "O God, I did this for Your sake only," and having the same feeling inside must be the basis of our actions. It is necessary to lead one's life oriented to this thought. In this respect, while carrying out the worship of sacrifice, we need to keep up our purity of intention, which we describe as "what the heart means to do." One should be so sincere as to say, "O God, you demanded me to sacrifice an animal, and I am car-

---

[55] "... contentment with what one already has is not desirable contentment; rather, it is lack of the necessary endeavor." Nursi, *The Words*, p. 749

[56] Nursi, *The Gleams*, p. 180

rying out the command. Had you commanded me to sacrifice myself instead, I would gladly do so. If it is necessary to form a circle for the sake of my faith, chastity, person, property, and country, I am ready for that also." That is, when giving from one's belongings, which people do not wish at all to separate from, it is necessary to remember other things one can possibly give and show their obedience to Divine orders. As a matter of fact, the situation of Prophet Abraham and his son Ishmael shows they grasped the gist of the secret of worship and obedience to orders: *"Then when both had submitted to God's will, and Abraham had laid him down on the side of his forehead"* (as-Saffat 37:103).

If a believer begins the worship of sacrifice with such a sound intention from the very beginning, then all of his or her acts will be counted as worship and other things done for the sake of this good deed will return to that person as rewards for the Hereafter. That is, buying an animal from the market, tying it up somewhere, feeding it, attending it for some time if necessary, taking it to the slaughter house by car, and then distributing the meat... shortly everything will be included in the believer's record of good deeds. On the other hand, fulfilling the commands in spite of drawbacks to make you pity the animal such as its resistance, shedding its blood, and the like, will bring you extra rewards for your consciousness of obedience to the command.

You may even see such things you carry out as unimportant. However, when their truth is revealed to us in the Hereafter, they will make us say in surprise, "O God, how bountiful You are! You have taken those little things, made them bloom, flourish, transform, become eternal, and now You are offering them to us!" In this respect, a person should fulfill the worship of sacrifice with an inner richness and contentment of the heart. The following verse also conveys this point: *"(Bear in mind that) neither their flesh nor their blood reaches God, but only piety and consciousness of God reach Him from you"* (al-Hajj 22:37). If a person carries out this worship, taking it as a means of connection with God Almighty and holding such considerations in the heart, then he or she will meet very different riches and surprises in the next world.

Sacred Values and Wakeful Eyes

Question: *A hadith mentions two kinds of eyes that will be free from Hellfire; one of them refers to a guard keeping watch near borderlines. What does "wakeful eyes" mean, and what is the message to be drawn from this notion with respect to the present conditions?*

Answer: This term is used for valiant soldiers vigilantly keeping watch near borderlines against possible violations. They keep watch until the morning for the sake of their country, faith, children, future and the like. As it is mentioned in the question, the *hadith* gives glad tidings: "Two kinds of eyes will never be touched by the fire of Hell; an eye which weeps out of fear and awe of God and an eye which spends the night alert, keeping watch for the sake of God."[57]

The Danger within and Early Recognition

This statement of the noble Prophet gave significant glad tidings for the people on guard duty in those days' conditions. It served as a great source of motivation for those keeping watch for the sake of their country and faith. However, dangers threatening today's believers have assumed a different dimension. There are such dangers and threats in Muslim lands that people live together with them. The sinis-

---

[57]   *Sunan at-Tirmidhi,* Jihad, 7; Abu Ya'la, *Al-Musnad,* 7/307

ter plots that insinuate through some hypocritical means target our spiritual heritage and cause serious destruction. Suffering with concern for one's country, ideals, people, and faith, and thus losing sleep over the fear of a new wave of spiritual degeneration, fall within the meaning of "wakeful eyes" mentioned in the *hadith*. As such eyes are constantly watchful and vigilant, they try to detect dangers as early as possible and take due precautions. They build up not only one protective wall, as in the castles of the past, but many alternative walls against dangers. They build up such walls that when attackers bring one down, the next one stands against them; if they bring that wall down too, they find another insurmountable wall before them.

Blindfolded Eyes and Manipulated Societies

I seek refuge in God from casting aspersions on our predecessors. The Messenger of God advised Muslims to remember deceased people not for their negative sides, but always for their good sides.[58] This is what we try to do today as much as possible. Together with that, I cannot help but express one truth here. It is so sad that Muslims came under domination owing to their dissociation from the world during a certain period. This happened as a consequence of indulging in heedlessness and comfort. There were no projects about opening up to the world; even those who extolled the virtues of their nation did not come up with any serious, permanent, long-term project. It was a period of dissociation, when people lived for quenching their appetites. This state gave way to a paralysis of enthusiasm and lofty feelings as well. If there had been wakeful eyes to detect the dangers at an early period, then it could have been possible to let everything undergo renewal and to take due precautions against the dangers sneaking in. If this could have been done, the consequences may not have been so disastrous. If it had been possible to understand the world better and detect the dangers at an early stage, and most importantly, to build alternative barriers against them, then the situation could be very different today.

---

[58] *Sunan at-Tirmidhi*, Janaiz, 34; *Sunan Abu Dawud*, Adab, 42

Even though some efforts are made for the sake of sharing the values of our spiritual heritage with the world, it is a reality that circles of schemers do not wait passively. Almost the entire world is turbulent. In some countries, people are trying to topple over the tyrants in power. However, it should not be forgotten that if a society underwent certain degenerations and deformations, the means and methods for restoration must be planned very well. It is not possible to turn everybody into upright ones all of a sudden. People have been estranged from religion and are virtually numbed by a secular lifestyle; rehabilitating them to recognize the unique potential granted to humanity takes a certain process and time. In this respect, all of the projects targeting such guidance must be reckoned very well from beginning to end. Particularly on a crucial issue as faith in God, if you cannot deal with the problem of raising individuals with sound morality, Mephisto will play his game one more time, and humanity will lose against him one more time.

Chaos and Confusion Do Not Lead to Order

Revolts in a society are mostly helter-skelter reactions. There may be lots of people acting with good intentions. However, you never know where such kind of events may lead. For this reason, I always hold doubts about helter-skelter movements.

Returning back to our main subject, everything happened as a result of acting like sleepwalkers, and our inability to grow aware of things going on and evaluating them with closed eyes. So the owners of wakeful eyes within a society are the ones who envisioned oncoming menaces and knew how to take precautions. For example, Sayyid Qutb spent his life in struggle; he was already born into a home where the idea of struggle reigned. His father, mother, and brother all had this idea. When you look at his works as In the Shade of the Qur'an and Social Justice, you see a man ready to die for his ideals. Indeed, before his death, Abdel Nasser's men told him that he could avoid execution if he apologized to their ruler, but he turned down the offer by saying that a believer will never apologize to an unbeliever. He walked to death with dignity and became a martyr. In spite of spending a life of struggle, in one of his final letters he wrote in jail, he made a self-criticism and expressed his regret for neglecting the issue of faith. He confessed: "The prescription of faith was the real cure for the troubles of society. This is what we failed to see," and drew attention to a truth: Restoring individuals with their own spirit and building them anew is the issue of top significance to deal with in order to bring a society into a more desirable form. In other words, if a real change is to be realized, the issue must be taken up with all its aspects. All parts of a body need to be healthy so that the body can function properly; in the same way, bringing social life to a desirable form necessitates approaching all of its units. If you leave a gap somewhere, you fall down, just like a paralyzed limb. If you do not make your plans with sound reasoning, judgment, compassion, and insight, then your actions will be lost in chaos. For this reason, we need to ask "what" should be done and "how"? We must ask, "Are the roads safe to travel or are there possible traffic problems along the way?" We need to ponder deeply over these questions.

It is possible to understand "wakeful eyes" in a general sense to cover all of these meanings. Therefore, we can say that as the eyes shedding tears night and day for the sake of God will not see Hellfire, the owners of wakeful eyes who are vigilant against such attacks targeting their faith and spiritual heritage will also be free from Hellfire.

Question: What is the relation between wakeful eyes and suffering?

One may be suffering for personal or familial problems, or suffering for problems related to the neighborhood, town, or the country. Feeling such suffering in one's conscience is a necessity of being human. However, true suffering is a loftier feeling related to being concerned about the problems of all of humanity, seeking solutions for them, and opening's one's arms and heart to the whole of humanity. If you really have this kind of suffering, then it causes you to lose sleep and you will not feel comfortable even while lying in your bed. If you are unable to tackle existing problems and cannot come up with alternative ways for solving them, then you will probably throw aside your quilt and pace around in an almost delirious state. Such suffering will not let you sleep and cause you to become an owner of wakeful eyes. However, I find it necessary to remind that the real source of suffering is sound faith in God. That is, in order for a person to feel such suffering in one's conscience, he or she needs to know what Paradise or Hell really means, and to know the path of the noble Prophet. One who says "I wish I could embrace the whole of humanity! I wish I could breathe my values into people of all levels! I wish I could pour the inspirations of my soul into their hearts!" and feels due suffering will not be able to sleep, and such a person will keep making new plans and seeking new courses of action. That person—excuse me—will be preoccupied with seeking solutions even while returning from the lavatory. When some good idea comes to his mind, he will note it down or immediately call by phone people related to the issue and share the idea with them. Sometimes, such sudden ideas will even make him stop his ablutions or Prayer halfway; because he acts like a doctor in the face of the different social problems and is continuously seeking ideas about the right cures. A suffering person who sees that the prescriptions he tried do not work and wonders what else he can do will immediately put to practice any useful alternatives he can find. Such suffering does not let one sleep, and makes him walk around deliriously.

Functions of the Mosque

Question: *What were the functions of the mosque during the time of the noble Prophet? How can it be possible to re-vivify mosques with respect to both architectural features and their place in social life?*

Answer: Those blessed places are referred as "cami" in Turkish, which means "one that gathers together." There is also the original Arabic word *masjid*, which means "place of prostration." Mosques are not named after words related to bowing or standing. Although these are among the essential movements in Prayer, they can never be compared to prostration, which is a person's closest state to God as stated by the noble Prophet himself,[59] because prostration combines both meanings of expressing God's greatness and admitting one's own pettiness. When these two considerations unite, they form the closest state to God. They complete one another and bring the person closest to God. When a servant prostrates oneself in modesty, humbleness, and humility, with the intention of placing one's head even lower if possible, it results in closeness to God. In other words:

> *Head and feet both on the ground, the Prayer rug kisses the forehead.*
> *Closeness to Him is through this road.[60]*

---

[59] *Sahih Muslim*, Salah, 215; *Sunan Abu Dawud*, Salah, 148; *Sunan an-Nasa'i*, Mawaqit, 35; Tatbiq, 78

[60] Gülen, M. F., *Kırık Mızrap*, p. 382.

In this respect, we can say that "mosque" is the name of the blessed place where those who put an end to separation and seek closeness to God—ones who take this closeness as an elixir—run to be discharged from strain and find relief; it is a place of spiritual recharge for them.

Matters Resolved in the Embracing Atmosphere of the Mosque

As we have stated above, a mosque is a place where believers gather together. However, understanding this "gathering" only as praying in congregation will mean narrowing the issue. We need to understand the purpose of the mosque in a wider sense. Naturally, in order to understand such functions of the mosque, it will be wiser to take a look at the time of the Messenger of God, peace and blessings be upon him. When we view that golden age in this respect, we see that the noble Prophet gathered his Companions in the mosque for different purposes, like consulting on certain matters, putting his decisions to practice, and finding alternative solutions to a problem. Therefore, in addition to its function of bringing people together for Prayer, it was a place where different matters were resolved. According to need, that blessed place can serve as a school, a Sufi lodge, or a place of worship. In addition, a mosque is a place people use for spiritual retreats as *itiqaf*, a place where—in the words of Bediüzzaman—people leave aside their animal side and physicality, ascend to the life level of the heart and spirit, and continue their journey accordingly.[61] In this respect, the mosque is not a place exclusive to men. As far as the proper manners and conditions are maintained, mosques are blessed places of worship for ladies as well; this was the case during the Age of Happiness.

Let us elaborate these points further: In the Prophet's Mosque, people gathered in circles for the remembrance of God Almighty through different Divine Names. In addition, they also gathered to listen to the talks of the blessed Prophet. A newcomer would be included in the circle right away. The Messenger of God would sit at a spot where every-

---

[61] Nursi, *The Gleams*, p. 189

one could see him easily. Even seeing him effected relief in souls; seeing him is a part of *insibagh*—taking on the spiritual hue prevalent in the presence of a true guide.[62] The Pride of Humanity had such seriousness, such stance before God Almighty that an unbiased person could accept his being God's Messenger immediately upon seeing him.[63] His Companions, who were well aware of this fact, would eagerly follow him attentively, even noting the slightest movement of his eyes. The noble Prophet would pour the pure inspirations of his heart into those souls turned to him. God's Messenger gave so much importance to the talks that he once expressed deep appreciation for a man who did not give up until finding a place and joining the circle; he stated that it was indolence to take a back seat. He warned his Companions about the situation of a man who went away after not finding any place for himself: "He turned away, and God turned away from him."[64]

Foreign Delegations Accepted in the Prophet's Mosque

Besides what we have mentioned, the Messenger of God, peace and blessings be upon him, accepted envoys in the mosque. Groups of people came from all corners in order to see him, listen to him, understand him correctly, and directly witness his virtuous character. Although he had declared Medina as an area of sanctity,[65] the noble Prophet accepted foreign envoys and delegations there. As mentioned in most reliable sources of reference, the noble Prophet accepted a Christian delegation from Najran and they stayed in the mosque for days.[66] The Christians from Najran ate and slept there, and they also offered their worship in the Prophet's Mosque.[67] This way, they had an opportunity to observe how that blessed one spent his night and day, and recognized him better. Although they did not become his followers, the

---

[62] Nursi, *The Words*, p. 507

[63] *Sunan at-Tirmidhi*, Qiyamah, 42; *Sunan ibn Majah*, Iqama, 174; *Darimi*, Salah, 156

[64] *Sahih al-Bukhari*, Ilm, 8; *Sahih Muslim*, Salam, 26

[65] *Sahih al-Bukhari*, Jihad, 74; *Sahih Muslim*, Hajj, 475

[66] *Sahih al-Bukhari*, Fada'il al-Ashab an-Nabi, 21; Maghazi, 72; *Sahih Muslim*, Fada'il as-Sahaba, 54–55

[67] Ibn Hisham, *As-Sirat an-Nabawiyya*, 3/112–114

noble Prophet succeeded to soften their hearts and they appreciated his teaching. Eventually, when he suggested praying together[68] with their women and children, and invoking God's curse upon those who lie, they could not accept the challenge but preferred to depart with the promise of not confronting him.[69] Later on, they also joined the growing number of Muslims. As it is seen, the Mosque had a very extensive function during the blessed Prophet's time. It was the place of learning the Qur'an and Sunnah, of developing the thought of Islamic jurisprudence by reasoning and deductions, and of germinating Islamic thought. There, a drop grew into a sea, and an atom transformed into a sun. Unfortunately, we closed the gates of mosques over time and only opened them during the Daily Prayers.

An Architectural Understanding Welcoming All

I meet all works of the Ottomans with appreciation; they served very well for the sake of believers for ages. On the other hand, I think they lacked an architectural philosophy to let everyone, women and children, easily offer any kind of worship in the mosque. I wonder why those mosques lack the facilities to let women act comfortably without worrying about their privacy. I wonder why women have been deprived from such services. During the time of the noble Prophet, women would join the Prayer in the mosque at the rear.[70] I presume none of us can claim to be more sensitive than the Companions at practicing religion. The dirtiness to be witnessed in the markets and streets, together with the spiritual life of Muslims contaminated and darkened there, gives us a sufficient idea of the present. In my opinion, not considering women's needs in mosques in every respect is a serious lack in terms of the completeness of the mosque. For this reason, fascinating beauties of our mosques should be accessible to beholders, including visitors from other faiths. Everybody must be able to savor those blessed places' dizzying material-spiritual beau-

---

[68] See Al Imran 3:61.

[69] Fakhruddin ar-Razi, *Mafatihu'l-Ghayb*, 8/71; Az-Zamahshari, *Al-Kashshaf*, 1/396

[70] *Sahih Muslim*, Adhan, 132; *Sunan at-Tirmidhi*, Salah, 97; *Sunan an-Nasa'i*, Imamah, 32

ties, aesthetic aspects, and architectural perfection. In order to realize this goal, it is necessary to form the suitable grounds for thinking and discussing the architectural philosophies behind mosques and the meanings conveyed by domes, vaults of Prayer niches (*muqarnas*), decorations, and lines.

Going to the Mosque and Manners to Be Observed

As a matter of fact, the address of a verse in the Qur'an alludes to the fact that doors of mosques must be open for everyone: *"O children of Adam! Dress cleanly and beautifully for going to the mosque, and (without making unlawful the things God has made lawful to you) eat and drink, but do not be wasteful (by over-eating or consuming in unnecessary ways): indeed, He does not love the wasteful"* (al-A'raf 7:31). As we see here, the address is not directed to "Muslims," "believers," or "those who observe the Prayers" but to all people as conveyed by "children of Adam." Preference of such general address via the name of Adam can be taken as a sign to open the doors of mosques to everyone, including non-Muslims. This way, it will be possible for some people who hold biased opinions against religion, religious people, and mosques to be freed from their negative feelings by the charm of the mosque; they can love that beautiful place and melt in its warm and welcoming atmosphere. The verse continues with the demand for taking care of one's clothing while going to the mosque, a place of gathering. As also required by the prevalent understanding today, people do not attend a meeting with their daily working clothes, but dress more elegantly. When we view the *hadiths* related to the Friday Prayer, we see that the issue is given further care. The Messenger of God advised Muslims who will go to a Friday Prayer to have complete body ablution, brush their teeth, put on a fragrance, and dress for the Prayer.[71]

If we take the issue from the perspective of another *hadith*, some people from the Mudar tribe came to the Prophet's Mosque one day. They were clothed in wool out of poverty in spite of the hot weather.

---

[71] *Sahih al-Bukhari*, Jumu'ah, 2; *Sahih Muslim*, Jumu'ah, 1–12; *Sunan Abu Dawud*, Salah, 219

As they perspired, the heavy odor began to spread in the mosque. The Messenger of God was moved to tears, and he asked the Companions to support them to change such clothes with more suitable ones.[72]

As mosques are places of gathering, one should avoid from going there in a state to disturb others. What befalls believers is to put up with some occasional inconveniences like odor of sweat or bad breath. On the other hand, we need to avoid leaving others in such situations. How much sensitivity does this issue take? Excuse me, but if there is any disturbing odor caused by a health problem like chronic pharyngitis or another, one should seek ways for treatment and find a solution without losing time. Nobody has the right to disturb a fellow Muslim standing beside them. Such factors can distract others who are concentrated on the Qur'an and worship. In this respect, people going to the mosque should put on the cleanest and best clothes, put on a fragrance if possible, and go there in a pleasant condition. Such behavior conveys respect for fellow believers as well. On the other hand, it is unbecoming to go to the place of prostration, a person's closest state to God, with bad odors and dirty clothes. We tidy up ourselves even before going to the presence of an important person; Prayer means standing in the presence of God. After all, it is a form of the Ascension (*Miraj*).[73] Is not somebody making such an important journey expected to show utmost care out of respect for God Almighty? The verse also makes a warning about wastefulness. That is, put on your clean and beautiful clothes when you go to the mosque; be in your best-looking form. On the other hand, do not be wasteful about clothing, eating, or drinking, and keep up moderation. As in everything else, God does not like wastefulness in these issues either. For example, thoughts as "I will put on a new coat every day," or "I will iron my clothes every day for going to the mosque," can be counted as excessive. So the verse warns us about the issue of eating and drinking along with the issue of clothing; it tells us not to give up moderation and always keep following the Straight Path.

---

[72] *Sahih Muslim*, Zakah, 69; *Sunan an-Nasa'i*, Zakah, 64; Ahmad ibn Hanbal, *Al-Musnad*, 4/358

[73] Fahruddin ar-Radi, *Mafatihu'l-Ghayb*, 1/214; As-Suyuti, *Ash-Sharh as-Sunan ibn Majah*, p. 313

The Relentless Enemy of the Devoted Souls: Satan

Question: *It is mentioned that Satan harries everybody in accordance with their level. Could you explain this fact?*

Answer: Satan is a creature that does not have the slightest inclination to goodness, one totally fixed on malice and full of evil feelings. From the moment he rebelled against God Almighty, he has been humanity's greatest enemy. In order to understand this, you can imagine a furious man who is like a bomb ready to explode—though man cannot completely become like Satan. You sometimes see such people around you. If the wishes of such a person are not satisfied, you might witness wild behaviors, like yanking the cloth off a table and bringing everything crashing down, utensils and all, or like kicking a nearby chair, or knocking picture frames off the wall. If you try to mention the virtues of mildness at such a moment, you might get punched, since that person is not of sound mind. Such rage is a fit of delirium, which entails disastrous consequences.

As for Satan, he is full of rage toward humanity, carrying all evil feelings like jealousy, disdain, grudge, and hatred. He is so vengeful toward humanity that he will not feel satisfied even if he leads all the children of Adam astray. As a matter of fact, with the creation of Adam, Satan revealed all of his disdain and jealousy toward him, and rebelled against God with the insolent words: *"Then (I swear) by Your Glory, I will certainly cause them all to rebel and go astray"* (Sad 38:82). As it is stated in another verse, he declares his hatred and animosity by saying, *"Then I will come upon them from before them and from behind them, and from their right and from their left"* (al-A'raf 7:17). From these expressions, it is understood that he wishes to misguide people in different ways such as arrogance, hopelessness, bohemianism, and unbelief. It is for this reason that the noble Messenger of God sought refuge in God against all of these dangers in his morning and evening prayers: "O God, Protect me (against dangers) from in front, from behind, from my right, from my left, and from above, and I seek refuge in Your greatness from being swallowed by the earth beneath me."[74]

Satan takes most benevolent people as his target in order to inflict the greatest harm against humanity, which he loathes so much. It seems understandable that an evil being like Satan, who was created from smokeless (fusing flame of) fire,[75] holds animosity toward Adam, the pure one of God,[76] and one of the best servants.[77] The animosity Satan feels toward humanity's great guides is much greater than toward ordinary people. His animosity toward Moses and Aaron is very different from that toward the misguided Samaritan and Korah. In short, the closer one is to God through their actions, the more Satan opposes them.

Bridles Satan Uses and Idle People

The great scholar Abu'l-Lays as-Samarqandi has a work titled *Tambih al-Ghafilin* (Advice for Heedless Ones), which is a book of spiritual refinement (*raqaiq*). When I was about 15 years old, and in my broken Arabic, I gave courses to the people of the village of Korucuk.[78] The first chapter of this work is on sincerity. The next chapter is about

---

[74] Sunan Abu Dawud, *Adab*, 110; Ahmad ibn Hanbal, *Al-Musnad*, 2/25

[75] See Ar-Rahman 55:15.

[76] Abu'sh-Shaykh, *Al-Azama*, 5/1596; As-Sa'labi, *Al-Kashf wa'l-Bayan*, 6/51

[77] See Al Imran 3:33.

[78] This remark rather reflects the humble attitude of Gülen, who actually had very good knowledge of Arabic.

Paradise and Hell. After a few other chapters that evoke spiritual refinement, As-Samarqandi relates Satan's meeting with the noble Prophet, peace and blessings be upon him, in the final chapter. Although the parable is not related in the primary sources of *hadith*, the fact that an important figure like As-Samarqandi relates such a parable makes it noteworthy with respect to the message it conveys. So the parable contains an important point related to our subject: When the Messenger of God asks Satan, "Who is your greatest enemy?" Satan replies, "You!" without hesitation.[79] It makes perfect sense that the accursed one, who claims to be the deity of darkness, is an enemy to the Innocent One, who brought down oppressors with a single move and brought light to the pitch-dark world. For this reason, those who uphold the Divine teaching and represent it as they should are the prime targets of Satan. Bediüzzaman says, "Satans strive very much against those who try to do these works."[80] In other words, Satans attack those who devoted themselves to faith and beneficial services.

Let me elucidate this further with a parable: A man who did not observe Prayers passes from the garden of a mosque. He sees someone waiting with a lot of bridles in his hands. The man goes near that person and asks who he is. The latter replies, "I am Satan." Then the man asks what the bridles are for. Satan replies, "There are worshippers in that mosque who gave their hearts to God. I intend to use these bridles in order to take them away from that atmosphere in my footsteps." The man wonders whether there is a bridle for him and asks, "Which is my bridle then?" Satan says, "There is no need for a bridle for you. You already come running after me with a simple beckoning!"

For this reason, whoever gives his or heart to God and resolves to revive the Divine teaching and is dedicated to serving on His path, Satan will devote more of his energy to dealing with that person. Satan does not waste his energy with poor ones indulging in intoxicants or prostrating themselves before idols, since he is a professional corrupter, tempter, and deceiver.

---

[79] As-Samarqandi, *Tanbihu'l-Ghafilin*, 763
[80] Nursi, *The Gleams*, p. 226

Satan and the Family

Satan harries everyone in accordance with their capacity. He primarily deals with people who are held in esteem by a certain number of people. He tries to conquer the top first. He rejoices at success since it pleases him to spread evil on earth. In a relevant *hadith*, the Messenger of God stated: "The Devil sets his throne on water: Then he sends his forces here and there to do evil." Some of them succeed at making people become involved in usury, some provoke the eye to look at forbidden sights, trigger bohemian feelings and make people act upon their lust. Some of them control the mouth and make it lie, backbite, or slander others. It can be said that each one of his aides does what they will according to their special ability to tempt. *"The nearest to him in rank are those that cause the greatest dissension. All of them go to the Devil to tell him what they did. One of them comes and says: 'I did this and this.' But the Devil tells him, '"You have done nothing."'*

Actually, the Devil is pleased with every sin committed, for in every sin there is a path to unbelief. Every sin brings about a dark spot on the heart. At the same time, a person committing a sin is taking a step to distance him or herself further from God. However, the Devil expects more from his aides. "Then one of them comes and says (something about a common problem in our time): 'I did not spare such and such man until he broke up with his wife.' The Devil calls him to come nearer and compliments him: 'You have done well!'"[81]

What is it that makes Satan rejoice like this, and why did he make such a hearty compliment to his aide? Because the home is the molecule of a society; disintegration begins there. It is beyond our power to correct anything in society that is corrupted at such a level. When all of these are taken into consideration, we see that Satan ranks the evils he will do according to their degree of importance. In his strategy, he first tries to topple "heavy-weight" people who have influence on others. When he succeeds at toppling these people, those in the lower category become easier prey for him. Some of them will already come running with a simple beckoning. For this reason, Satan harries the

---

[81] *Sahih Muslim*, Munafiqun, 67; Ahmad ibn Hanbal, *Al-Musnad*, 3/314

respected Prophets first, and then the scholars of purity (*asfiya*), the reputable saints (*awliya al-fiham*), and the great scholars of sound judgment (*mujtahidin al-izam*). Those devoted to glorifying the Name of God are also among his primary targets.

He will not leave them alone and keeps striving to make them dizzy, avert their gaze, and busy themselves with unnecessary things.

Historic Figures Subjected to Attacks

Just like devils, their human accomplices inclined for corruption also target friends of God most of all. For instance, you see in a television series that a great figure, like Suleiman the Magnificent, who spent most of his life on horseback, is reflected as a person who spent an immoral life in the palace. Without basing the character on any reliable source, they introduce him as drinker, as someone who led a bohemian life. We seek refuge in God against such considerations. The late Malek Bennabi, who was a great Algerian writer and philosopher said, "If it weren't for the Turkish society in the North of the Islamic world, there would not be an Islamic world at all today. If it weren't for the Turks, there would be no Islam on earth today." Those who make offhanded remarks about that great sultan do not know that he was the person who helped people across such a wide region to live in peace during his nearly half century of rule. Today's ills, like incitement, terror, and unrest, were prevalent in those days, too. However, such leaders sacrificed their comfort, stood up against danger, and overcame all of these problems. Imagining the limited troubles that accost me from within, I try to imagine the troubles those great sultans faced, and I try to figure out their condition. I guess what I suffered for a lifetime only amounts to what they suffered overnight; most of us do not go through such pains for an entire life. Some things are easier said than done. We ordinary people would probably be crushed under those troubles had they befallen us. Due to its leaders' fortitude and character, certain saints mentioned the Ottoman state—before it came to existence—and stated that it ranks after the period of the Righteous caliphs with respect to its level of importance.[82] However, some TV programs produced by those unaware of the time's worth present a completely distorted image of those great figures. May God enable us to see truths and save everybody from wrongdoing and unfairness.

---

[82] Ibn Arabi, *Ash-Shajaratu'n-Nu'maniyya fi'd-Dawlat'ul-Uthmaniyya*, p. 37

Love of Knowledge and Research

Q uestion: *Is the transfer of knowledge an obligation for reaching the desired level in the field of science and research? What do you think needs to be done in order to establish an understanding of science based on the essential dynamics of Islamic teaching?*

Answer: The genuine source of knowledge is God Almighty's works. The lucid interpreter, clear evidence, and substantial proof of those works is the Miraculous Qur'an.[83] The interpreter and expounder of the Holy Qur'an is the authenticated Tradition of the noble Prophet. How the Prophet's Companions and the blessed generation after them understood the Qur'an is also an important criterion for us; the Qur'an was revealed in a language they understood well, and the noble Prophet also used a language that would suit their understanding. Thus, it is very important, first of all, to realize a correct and sound understanding of the laws of physics in the guidance of the Qur'an, authenticated Sunnah, and the perspectives of the generation of the righteous scholars after the blessed Prophet, and then to reach the horizon where those truths unify with the laws of religion. However, it should not be forgotten that this issue has been neglected for years and it is not possible to reach the desired level and the targeted horizon all at once. Love for knowledge and research in the

---

83   Nursi, *The Words*, p. 388

Muslim world received a blow in the fifth century after the Hijra (migration from Mecca), or nearly nine centuries ago. Together with that, the lofty meanings and truths that lead one to Divinity as a flourishing of knowledge in souls were excluded from the centers of Islamic education. As it was expressed in different talks, the madrasas did not only expel natural sciences, but also bolted up its doors to true spiritual experience.

The Dizziness Brought by Victories

At this early period, Muslims had both significant political and military successes, and strived for their faith seriously. Surely, it is very valuable in God's sight to protect believers against vicious attacks targeting the honor of their religion and their families. All of these deserve appreciation and praise. From the Seljuks to the Ilkhanids, from the Ayyubids to the Ottomans, different generations fulfilled the responsibility of bearing the flag. They upheld the crescent as a symbol of honor and chastity. However, as a person who concentrates on one field cannot be deepened in the same way in other fields, they fulfilled the task of bearing the flag, but neglected the issue of laboratories and research centers.

In the earlier centuries of Islam, knowledge was an issue of top importance and very successful scientists were raised. When you take Ibn Sina (Avicenna) for instance, you see that he was an expert in many fields. Along with philosophy and thought, he was also an important figure in physiology, anatomy, and medicine. He came up with certain solutions against viruses at a very early period. He also had some views on understanding the Qur'an. Besides, he took an interest in Sufism. It was not just Avicenna; in those times so many great figures were raised, from Muhammad ibn Zakariya al-Razi to Jabir, from Fazari to Zahrawi, and from Khwarazmi to Biruni... Those people took the guidelines for science from their religion, understood it very well as the unified point of truths revealed by sciences and those taught by religion. As a result of all of this, they did not feel an inferiority complex before others. Other people understood that this superiority stemmed from religion and they respected religion in those people. Unfortunately this love for knowledge and research, which continued until the fifth century of the Islamic calendar, lost speed and quality over time, and failed to fulfill the function expected from it. Possibly, the triumph that came with military victories, such as the conquest of Istanbul, may have made the Ottomans feel dizzy; gaining the caliphate may have contributed to that dizziness. These considerations should not be taken as a total denial of good works done in that period. The madrasas of Fatih and Sulaymaniya, and institutions like Enderun, the Ottoman palace academy, made important contributions to the development of knowledge. However, it is an undeniable fact that the flourishing and development of sciences up until the fifth century of the Islamic calendar was not seen in later periods.

The Book of Nature Studied Meticulously

It is a reality that the West came to a certain point of knowledge and science by scrutinizing phenomena with a serious love for research. We see it in documentaries. For example, they followed, for days, the lives of penguins in the South Pole or of wild whales in some other part of the world. A researcher says, "I have watched the life of cobras for 25 years." I guess those people do not even know what exactly they will obtain after so much effort. Still, they scrutinize "wild" nature as they call it. They undo, detach, and redo... they savor the pleasure of redoing. With all of this research and study, they try to get to somewhere.

Let me express another point here: Those people made a certain advance in the name of science but they tried to explain the results by attributing them to factors like natural instincts. Unfortunately they failed to take this one step further and ascribe the issue to the True Owner. They saw that every living thing virtually acts like a human being and that some were even more evolved when it came to certain functions that helped them survive. However, they failed to recognize the Creator behind such a magnificent order and harmony, and the laws He decreed. Since they were not thoroughly conscious of the gist of walking to God by starting from facts about humans and the phenomena around them, and since they did not own a perspective to guide them to such horizons, most of them—though we cannot say all—were stuck in naturalism, positivism, or materialism. Despite all of those studies, they failed to see that this universe, which resembles a great book, tells about God with its every letter, word, and paragraph.

Safe Routes That Lead to Truth

Getting back to our main subject, we unfortunately cannot see Western scientists' diligence in scrutinizing things in Muslim scholars and researchers, at least those who have come after the fifth century of the Islamic calendar. So if we do not focus on this issue and do not give ourselves to such research with the diligence they do, it is not possible for us to attain real success. First of all, we need a very serious thirst for truth. As there is no greater truth than God, there can be no greater truth than what God sees as great. Then we need a love for reaching Him. Then this intense love felt for the Truth of Truths will trigger a love for science. This love for science will lead some people to research; they will always seek ways for reaching Him through, varied new research in varied places.

Understanding the fact expressed in "The roads leading to God are as many as His creatures' breaths"[84] as only referring to different Sufi paths and schools of thought is a narrow perspective. Actually, there are many ways leading to God, through every being, from minute creatures to macro realms. So we are supposed to find these ways and try to form safe routes to save people from falling into valleys of misguidance and being stuck up there. We will be drenched in sweat exerting ourselves to the utmost degree, so that people can pass from those safe routes and reach God. For the sake of letting others live in the true sense of the word, we will give up leading an easy life of our own. On the other hand, at the points where people get stuck in naturalism, we will show how the issue connects to God, and try to see the

---

[84] Nursi, *Al-Mathnawi Al-Nuri*, p. 369; Ibn Arabi, *Al-Futuhatu'l-Makkiyya*, 3/549; Al-Alusi, *Ruhu'l-Ma'ani*, 1/396, 6/165, 14/160

works of His hand of power, encompassing knowledge and supreme will in everything. Effecting such a spirit in seekers of knowledge requires a very serious rehabilitation. Beginning with the primary school, if you do not rehabilitate all steps of academic life as oriented to this feeling, you cannot raise such a team from among them. If need be, you should give them prizes. Although in our philosophy, grace comes after attaining knowledge, we need to know that not everyone has or will have this virtuous feeling. In order to encourage attaining knowledge, you will offer prizes from the very beginning and assure the livelihoods of those who seek of material and spiritual knowledge. For example, you can say, "If you carry out such and such research, and gain insight into this matter, then we will guarantee your livelihood. In order not to busy your mind with material issues instead of knowledge and research, we will provide you with two apartments and give you a satisfactory salary." Actually, scientific research is a matter of love, a matter of completely dedicating oneself to that issue with a thirst for learning. However, inspiring such yearning depends on rehabilitating them.

The Transfer of Knowledge and What Really Matters

Walking toward the future, the transfer of knowledge is the first matter to be tackled. For this reason, it is possible to follow in the footsteps of the Japanese and the Chinese. As it is known, they took the sciences developed in the West and, by making some additions, they adapted those sciences to suit their worldviews and thus benefited from them. For example, China has become a world giant today by finding lower costs for using the knowledge and technology they transferred. Japan was demolished at the end of World War II with the atom bomb. In spite of it all, they walk far ahead of us in the fields of science and research. Germany was also demolished in World War II, then divided by powerful states. East Germany became subject to Russia and West Germany to the US. In spite of all those negative conditions, they got back to their feet and started to transfer workers from countries like Turkey. In this respect, it is also possible for Muslims to go through a period of transfer. First, it is possible to make good use of what is transferred from outside, and then to guide our people toward much loftier ideals. Some term it as the "Islamization of knowledge." Instead of saying so, I think it will be more appropriate to say, "Pinpointing the unification point of the legislative and creative commands, which are the source of sciences." Surely, it is not possible to reach such a point in a flash. Therefore, as you raise dedicated researches crying out for truth like a muezzin, you should not fail to keep pace with your age by following new developments and technologies.

To conclude, in order to have a mentality of science based on Islamic dynamics of thought, it is necessary to transfer knowledge, then to kindle love and zeal for deciphering, understanding, and interpreting phenomena. After that, it is necessary to let that knowledge meet with our own values, and then use those values to realize and adapt. Then, by looking at the accumulations they have made so far, we will do the same research after realizing there is nothing that stops us from it. That is, the transfer of knowledge is a process, and its adaptation is another process. What comes next is evaluating everything in accordance with their true natures, acting in line with the Divine purpose in creating this universe like a book for us to read, and then studying the fact that the Qur'an is its lucid interpreter, clear evidence, and substantial proof pointing to its Maker. After attaining a sound perspective, you will begin to see the same truth by looking at those two books of God Almighty. The Qur'an will seem like a universe, and the universe will look like the Qur'an to you. On the other hand, you will begin to see humanity as an index of this universe, and the universe an unfolded human. Eventually, you will cry out, affirming all of these matters with the attestation of your conscience.

Getting to See Important Responsibilities as Mundane Tasks and the Qur'anic Method of *Tasrif* (Renewal of Format)

Question: *Concerning the duties we are responsible for, we are sometimes taken by a feeling of carrying out a mundane task. What are your recommendations for breaking this feeling?*

Answer: Even at actions and services that take start with the deepest love and enthusiasm at the beginning, people will be doomed to monotony and doing things in a spiritless fashion, if works and activities carried out are not revitalized by bringing new aspects and depths to the project. This can be done with new hues, patterns, and designs. In such a situation, even if the task you carry out is a vital one, it will seem to you as ordinary, and thus you will try to finish it quickly, in a careless fashion. For this reason, if you have a noble ideal, such as making people love God and His Messenger, then you need to continuously make variations, not let people be weary due to the same format, and not view your responsibilities as mundane activities.

Renewed Enthusiasm through Renewed Formats

It is possible to relate our topic with the revelation and message of the Qur'an, in terms of its method of *tasrif*—presenting a truth in renewed formats. When you study the miraculous Qur'an from this aspect, you see that the same concept and meaning are used in different parts in different styles and formats. For instance, the parable of Moses is repeated in different parts since it is a good example to help solve different problems, to show different ways out, and to emphasize a Prophetic determination and struggle. In spite of that, no parable of Moses is a copy of another one in a different part. Every time, the same parable comes up with different statements. In terms of voicing the same truth with different words, God Almighty changes the speaker to Moses, Jesus, and Muhammad, peace be upon them all. This is the meaning of *tasrif*, or presenting the message in varied forms.

Presenting issues in such a renewed form and voice has a refreshing effect on people. Giving your message in renewed forms will present their true depth and immensity, and also draws attention to those truths. This will evoke respect toward the matters you represent. The values in our hand are precious in themselves. Therefore, they should be presented not in a blacksmith's but a jeweler's shop. There are so many beautiful truths that they seem worthless in the hands of people who fail to present them as they deserve to be presented. On the other hand, so many pale truths gain a different majesty through the tongue of people who compose and present the matter very well and thus fascinate people. Sometimes, falsehood might gain acceptance through cunning rhetoric whereas truth may be deprived of the appreciation it deserves for not being presented successfully. For this reason, if the matters you are trying to tell are truthful—they definitely are—then you must evoke due respect in others toward those truths by the Qur'anic method of *tasrif*.

Being in Recognition of the Era

Another important means of avoiding exhaustion and always staying fresh is recognition and consciousness of the era. Given that believers are supposed to be "children of their time" then we need to know the requirements of our time well and follow appropriate methods. For example, if I start speaking today in the same way as I gave sermons in İzmir or Edremit some thirty or forty years ago, it would be too simple. Today's listeners are very different than those in the past; most of the current audience knows those matters already. What needs to be done today is to take the issues with their philosophical depths and show their reasonableness.

For example, if an Islamic topic you are going to tell is related to jurisprudence, you should be able to view the issue from Shatibi's viewpoint or discuss the issue within the frame of the ideas in Taftazani's *Talwih*. If you can do that, people will find it worthwhile to listen to you. Otherwise, they may not be willing to listen to the truths you are to tell. Given that God Almighty, the Eternal Teacher, shows us a way by using *tasrif* in the Qur'an, then we are supposed to utilize it well.

Having pointed out the importance of grasping the meaning of being children of our time, I would like to draw attention to another point that might be misunderstood. As it is not correct to be detached from the conditions of the time one lives in, it is also not correct to attach the issue completely to the time and dismiss everything with a historical approach as a thing of the past. If I give such a sense with what I have told above, I seek refuge in God from that; the eternal truths of the Qur'an never change. However, there are open-ended points both in the Book and the authenticated Tradition of the noble Prophet that are left to conditions of the time. So the children of their time are supposed to fill those points with due scholarly judgment and deduction (*ijtihad* and *istinbat*). In addition, choosing from judgments and rulings made in different periods to suit the needs of contemporary believers is another important issue to be considered. These are the fields where *time* becomes an interpreter. This is the meaning of Bediüzzaman's pithy statement: "Time is an important interpreter; it is not to be objected when it reveals its ruling."[85]

Self-Criticism and a New Revival

Another means of renewing oneself is making a critical evaluation of works and activities at certain intervals. I heard that Japanese people

---

[85] Nursi, *Münazarat*, p. 73

retreat together to a place for some time each year and then discuss what they did and what they will do. They say that in those meetings, things done in the past are conceptualized once more in imaginations, re-formulated, and new targets are also determined in order to prepare for the future and to keep up spiritual vigilance. If such programs are held, even for the sake of industrial and commercial life, then the constant need for rehabilitation on an issue as crucial as spiritual guidance, which concerns people's eternal lives, is obvious. Given that this is the case with worldly matters, doing the same for otherworldly matters needs to be seen as an absolute necessity of vital importance. For this reason, we can say that if journeyers on the path of spiritual guidance do not join a seminar to enrich their own capacity, to purify their minds, revise their past mistakes and take due precautions for the future, they keep repeating the same mistakes and cannot succeed at what they do.

This is the kind of rehabilitation we need. Because the responsibility we undertake is really serious and great. We are trying to be worthy of a trust from God and His Messenger. Let me clarify the situation with an example: The great scholar and Companion Ibn Mas'ud did not dare to report anything about the noble Prophet without displaying signs of serious concern brought by this heavy burden. He would pray to God for help and showed different signs of uneasiness due to the fear of saying something wrong. He was so afraid of saying something contradictory to the spirit of the matter because of his awareness of the gravity of his responsibility.

Sometimes, one word can destroy everything. Sometimes you see leading figures delivering great talks. But sometimes, they upset everything when they mix a raven's cry in between the song of a nightingale. People under responsibility can never talk in a carefree fashion. A patient can express certain considerations about his or her own illness, but a disciplined physician with ethical concerns who intends to abide by the Hippocratic Oath—will and can—never make casual statements based on hearsay. Otherwise, a wrong statement can cause much more serious complications for the patient he is supposed to treat. The gravity is obvious when the issue under question is religion, which regulates your worldly life and shows you the ways for eternal bliss in the next world, which lets you gain a sound conception of Divinity and Messengership. Such an important responsibility cannot be carried on without such rehabilitation and adding to one's previous knowledge.

Those Who Make Mistakes Most

Some may have been within a circle of ones who strive to serve humanity. However, if they did not feed the heart and mind efficiently, their level of knowledge could remain some ten years behind others who joined the circle later. The bitter fact is that, the earlier joiners do not realize this gap. For this reason, it is necessary to take a fresh start and consider, understand, and analyze matters anew. Otherwise, so many mistakes can be made without anyone being aware of them. Those who make the most mistakes are the ones who take confidence in their seniority. New ones make fewer mistakes in comparison; because as they get concentrated on what they will do with one eye, they watch the guide before them with the other. Whenever they begin to hold considerations as, "I have been included in this for years, after all, I have a certain degree of knowledge..." they should know that they are already out of the issue and are not really aware of what is happening. In order not to fall in such a situation, everybody should gather together once or twice a year, revise where they stand and reflect on the mistakes they have made. In order to not repeat the same mistakes, they need to take into consideration the precautions to be taken, and the tasks and projects to be done in the future.

The Purpose of Life

Question: *What are your recommendations for being able to take serving for the sake of God as the ultimate purpose in life?*

Answer: Adopting a task one is responsible for to the degree of seeing it as the purpose of one's life first of all depends on knowing its real value, significance, and worth. For example, if a person takes matters of faith as "An issue very important for eternal deliverance, one that cannot be done without," then that person will lead and weave his or her life according to this ideal.

God Almighty commands His Messenger to *"Convey and make known in the clearest way all that has been sent down to you from your Lord. For, if you do not, you have not conveyed His Message and fulfilled the task of His Messengership"* (al-Maedah 5:67) This warning addressing the blessed Prophet in the first place is true for his followers as well. As he cannot escape the responsibility he was assigned with, the same goes for today's believers.

The Sacred Positive Attitude

Given that God Almighty places His trust on the shoulders of trustworthy bearers, we should not dismiss the fact that there is a hopeful approach here. As one man can think positively and have a hopeful approach about another, the Divinity has such an exalted, supreme, and holy positive attitude toward people. That is, God Almighty takes us as trustworthy bearers of His Trust. Then nobody can escape responsibility by the assumption of their not being eligible for it. Otherwise, what excuse can we assert when we are brought to account before God? We will obviously be reprimanded for letting down such a serious responsibility. A true believer will take all of these into consideration and act accordingly.

In addition, it should not be forgotten that being included in the circle of volunteers is a special blessing. I guess it is possible to give such an example: There is a very wide gate near which thousands of people pass. At times, the gate is half opened, and the passersby at that particular moment are ushered in. Every volunteer can realize in retrospect that they once received such an invitation. However, some people might not be so fortunate to benefit from this blessing in spite of having stepped in through that gate. When he lived in Erzurum, Mehmed Kırkıncı—may God accept his good works—collected a large group of people in order to listen to a disciple of Bediüzzaman who had come to the city. When I left Erzurum, only one or two people from that first group were still within the circle. For this reason, staying inside after stepping in still depends on God's keeping, given that one uses the willpower in this direction. Then this is a special favor of God Almighty, and one should try to prove eligible for it.

On the other hand, good works done for the sake of God give a different kind of pleasure. I cannot claim to be the kind of person who has experienced this full delight. I can say that I am taken by weariness. I may even be holding within secret considerations of avoiding the responsibilities before me. I am fully convinced that I am not a good and useful person. I have faced different pressures and confinements throughout my life. Only God knows what I went through after the military coup in 1980. Even now, with respect to the circumstances I am in, I feel to be in a barrel of needles. Despite all of these I say, "No matter how shallow a servant I am on God's path, it is worth to undergo ten times worse troubles for this sake."

Even If One Remains Alone

There is an example of heroism narrated by the Messenger of God, peace and blessings be upon him. A soldier with deep faith was fighting in a battlefield and all of his friends fell, one by one. When he saw that he was the only one standing, he spurred his horse forth, never to turn back again.[86] This is the degree of devotion we need. Even if you stay on your own and the entire world is against you with their forces, you should still keep walking with dogged determination. God gave us stubbornness for wisdom; we are supposed to use it in the form of perseverance on the righteous path. One who sees things from this perspective sees sharing the truths of faith with the world as the most important issue. Such a person thinks that this is the very issue that gives meaning to his existence, and arranges his life accordingly. It is very crucial to make this issue into one's purpose of life. At every moment of life, one should have the idea "My existence has no meaning if I do not serve for the sake of God." Keep this in mind for some five to ten years, and even declare this pledge to your spouse and kids so that it becomes a responsibility expected from you. Some thirty or forty times, tell them, "Let God take my soul if I am not to serve for Him." If you show any signs of stepping back on your word one day, people in your family will remind you of your pledge and say, "Wasn't it you who would supposedly act in such a way?" And thus, with this pledge of yours, you will have both put yourself under obligation and taken support and energy from others, on a path you cannot stand alone. You will avoid the shame of going back on your word and keep walking as a matter of conscience.

For this reason, every believer should bind oneself to a noble goal—with fifty ropes at least—for the sake of making people love God. Until the last moment of their lives, they should do their best to remain steadfast in it.

---

[86] Ibn Hibban, *As-Sahih*, 6/298

"They Did Not Appreciate My Worth"

We should not forget that it is absolutely necessary to undertake a responsibility in order to feel a noble ideal freshly in one's heart all the time. Sometimes, one may not be given the duty he or she expected. For example, a man can be eligible for handling an entire company, but he can be given the duty to lead a single division of it. Even if he is capable of carrying out a higher responsibility, that person should try to fulfill his duty in the best way without complaining that they did not appreciate his worth.

Incidentally, let us add the fact that the people in administrative positions should discover the potentials of the individual they will employ very well and let him work in a field he is likely to succeed. When a person is successful, he will praise God, be happy with, offer thanksgiving, and feel motivated to do. In case of failure, it is necessary to provide people with the necessary grounds and opportunities to make up for their mistakes.

"They Must Definitely Ask Me"

The points we have mentioned have not become a discipline among Muslims yet. Unfortunately, narrow-minded perspectives still dominate our actions. Those in administrative positions hold an understanding as "They must definitely seek my approval and ask me what to do to solve matters." However, what befalls on good leaders is to test people they work with by giving certain duties first, and then let people realize their potentials by commissioning them in the fields they are likely to succeed.

The Messenger of God, peace and blessings be upon him, discovered latent abilities of people and employed them in unexpected positions. For example, the noble Prophet assigned Zayd ibn Haritha, who was an emancipated slave, as the commander of an army of three or four thousand at a very critical battle in Muta, and Zayd proved worthy of his mission.[87] Considering the prevalent culture, assigning an

---

[87] *Sahih al-Bukhari*, Maghazi, 44; Ahmad ibn Hanbal, *Al-Musnad*, 1/256, 5/299, 300

emancipated slave to command the army was a very important event. The Messenger of God both discovered a talent to give that duty its due and destroyed a mistaken understanding in that society. When his life is considered as a whole, it will be seen that he employed everybody in a position where they could realize their potentials in the utmost degree.

For this reason, it is necessary to offer everybody a duty that suits their level. It should not be forgotten that if you do not let people shoulder some task and give them important responsibilities, their potentials will never be realized. Then people will not carry out what they do with enthusiasm, they will grow weary, and this will result in a failure to uphold what is right and true. One of the most important dynamics behind the heyday of Muslims was employing everybody in the most efficient fields. For this reason, grasping this gist is crucial for the future of Muslims.

Heroes of the Heart and Spirit

Question: *You mentioned in different talks that those who practiced Islam in the best way were Sufis. Could you please elucidate this further and tell about the general characteristics of those heroes of the heart and spirit?*

Answer: Before answering this question, it will be useful to remind of one important fact. Whoever they are, nobody's practicing of Islam should be slighted. From the base to the top, everybody's good deeds can gain acceptance in the sight of God. The proclamation of faith above all is like a mysterious key to the gate of Paradise. The Messenger of God heralded the fact that everybody who sincerely says "La ilaha illa'llah" (There is no deity but God) will enter Paradise.[88] When this was mentioned during an earlier talk, one of the attendants asked, "What if there are no good deeds?" Since we cannot tell what is in someone's heart or tell that person's real intention and inner considerations, it is not appropriate for us to make a definite remark about that issue. We make our judgment by the apparent reality[89] and have a good opinion of a person who makes the proclamation of faith.

During a battle, Usama ibn Zayd was about to kill an enemy soldier but the man declared faith at the last moment. Taking it as a des-

---

[88] *Sunan at-Tirmidhi*, Iman, 17; Abu Ya'la, *Al-Musnad*, 7/9, 34; Ibn Huzayma, *As-Sahih*, 3/304

[89] Ar-Razi, *Al-Mahsul*, 5/538; Al-Amidi, *Al-Ihkam*, 1/343; Ibn Kathir, *Tuhfatu't-Talib*, 1/174

perate trick to survive, he still killed the man. It is out of the question for a great Companion like Usama ibn Zayd to kill someone out of personal feelings he cannot control. It seems that he had not grasped the gist of the issue. In those times, the Companions learned everything as a fresh principle and put to practice right away. How could they know without the Messenger of God telling them? When the blessed Prophet was informed about the situation, he reprimanded Usama ibn Zayd by repeatedly asking whether he had cleft the man's heart open to see his faith. This brave commander, who was the son of Zayd ibn Haritha, wished that he had become a Muslim after that event so that he had not faced that severe reprimand.[90]

Thinking Positively about Others

Evaluating the issue according to these criteria, we can say that those who somehow observe their responsibility of worship, God willing, will be saved. The Messenger of God stated that "Whoever prays like us and faces our *Qibla* and eats our slaughtered animals is a Muslim and is under God's and His Messenger's protection. So do not betray God by betraying those who are in His protection."[91] One who fulfills the deeds mentioned is never a person to be dismissed. On the other hand, some scholars deliberated the question whether faith by imitation is acceptable or not.[92] According to them, a true believer, whose faith is based on verification, approaches matters under the guidance of the conscience, relies on substantial proofs, and—as Bediüzzaman puts it—sees, hears, and feels everything with perspicacious wisdom and is able to consider matters of faith within that horizon. An imitator however, remains superficial. For this reason, they may have been referred to as people who are Muslims in theory rather than practice. Still, we had better prefer to think positively about them. For example, we see that some man scratched his head during Prayer or did

---

[90] *Sahih Muslim*, Iman, 158; *Sunan Abu Dawud*, Jihad, 95; Ahmad ibn Hanbal, *Al-Musnad*, 5/207

[91] *Sahih al-Bukhari*, Salah, 28; Adahi, 14; *Sunan at-Tirmidhi*, Iman, 2; *Sunan an-Nasa'i*, Iman, 9

[92] At-Taftazani, *Sharhu'l-Maqasid*, 2/265-271

something more complicated that will invalidate his Prayer. We should say, "Maybe I misperceived it." God might be testing us to reveal us the level of our positive thinking. We do not know whether we are being tested with some man's pulling up his trousers, moving the cap on his head or some other deed to invalidate the Prayer. For this reason, we should always try to take positive thinking as basis and should not hold negative thoughts about others.

Different Lines on the Spiritual Path

Getting back to our main topic, Sufism has different ways and lines; it has different spiritual stations and levels to pass. For example, a Sufi initiate may reach a certain point through spiritual journeying. Sometimes, people such as Imam Rabbani, Muhyiddin ibn Arabi, and Sheikh al-Jilani become aware of who they are and what their position is. For this reason, along with being very stern about making self-criticisms, they may say, "My feet are on the shoulders of other saints."[93] Such expressions indicate their being aware of their spiritual rank. This can even be observed in ordinary people like us. However, if one does not keep up a sound relationship with God, such awareness can—may God protect—lead one to egotism or egocentricity. Those who rise to the peak of spiritual perfection and are aware of their rank can maintain their position if they do not hold any ill opinions about others and not make a mistake such as disdaining others.

Nobody Is under Guarantee

Even if they reach spiritual peaks, nobody has a guarantee like "You do not need to fear anymore." When this is the case, how is it possible for a believer not to fear? As related to us by the beloved Prophet, God Almighty does not let his servants have one of the two feelings of security or fear in both worlds.[94] Therefore, it should not be forgotten that a person who feels secure in terms of faith in this world, is likely to face a fearful end.

---

[93] Al-Munawi, *Fayzu'l-Qadir*, 6/16; Ibnu'l-Imad, *Shazaratu'z-Zahab*, 4/200

[94] Ibn Hibban, *As-Sahih*, 2/406; Al-Bayhaqi, *Shuabu'l-Iman*, 1/483

The attitude of the Pride of Humanity, millions of peace and blessings be upon him, is an example to us. He was sent as a means of deliverance and rebirth for humanity. Thanks to his coming and the message he brought, humanity came to existence once more and broadened its horizons. He is the spiritual father of humanity. Who knows, maybe this is the meaning of the *hadith* that he was a Prophet even while Adam was in a state between (being) spirit and body.[95] That is, he was beyond Adam in spite of being one of the children of Adam. On the other hand, when we study his supplications, we can see how the noble Prophet feared God. In spite of being under guarantee[96] he sought refuge in God from so many things.[97] We can see it as a part of his duty to be our guide, and respectfully remark that he did it in order to teach us how to pray. Together with that, we need to see that those words were not merely uttered for the sake of others but he had a considerable share in them.

An Ordinary Person among Others in Spite of Being a Paramount Figure

Concerning the type of sainthood where the person is aware of the spiritual level attained, it is a very important essential and principle to see oneself as an ordinary person among others. Such people do not disdain anyone. Let alone disdaining others, they constantly face themselves and practice severe self-criticism. In this respect, this type of sainthood is more valuable than the other. Umar ibn al-Khattab told believers to constantly bring themselves to account before the Day of Reckoning comes.[98] Actually, everyone needs to confront one's shortcomings and weaknesses. One should recollect unpleasant considerations that passed their mind, polluted their dreams, and pierced their imagination like a spear, and say: "My God, how lowly a person I am.

---

[95] Ahmad ibn Hanbal, *Al-Musnad*, 5/59; Ibn Abi Shayba, *Al-Musannaf*, 7/329; At-Tabarani, *Al-Mu'jamu'l-Kabir*, 20/353

[96] See Al-Fath 48:2.

[97] *Sahih Muslim*, Qadar, 17; Abd ibn Humayd, *Al-Musnad*, p. 137

[98] *Sunan at-Tirmidhi*, Qiyamah, 25; Ibnu'l-Mubarak, *Az-Zuhd*, 1/103; Ibn Abi Shayba, *Al-Musannaf*, 7/96

Why did those ugly considerations visit my mind, which is supposed to be a pure place?" Everybody should watch oneself and see others as worthier. They should never say, "Such and such person remained at a superficial level, unable to go beyond the rudimentary knowledge." As Bediüzzaman expressed, "The carnal soul is lower than all, but the duty is higher than all."[99] Another saintly figure voiced the same truth as: "Everybody is good, but I'm rough; everybody is wheat, but I'm chaff."

Individuals who are occupied with their own mistakes will not disdain others and not develop ill thoughts based on suspicion. While looking at others, they will not be occupied with thoughts like "Why does he become concentrated in Prayer to the degree of forgetting to rise from prostration? On the other hand, he never forgets the fast breaking meal when it comes to eating." Those who try to practice their faith meticulously should say, "Actually, it was necessary for a person in my case to find what I found. But such and such person did not have the same means. He did not become soundly acquainted with the Qur'an, he did not reach the fount of spirituality, or own the effulgent books in my hands; they did not recognize great personalities like Abdul-qadr al-Jilani, Sheikh Shadhili, and Mustapha al-Bakri. Therefore, given that God Almighty showered His blessings on me although I was not eligible for them, I must offer due servitude to Him. If I behave otherwise, it will be my ruin!" If God Almighty let one advance up until the door of a private chamber for His special servants, then that person is supposed to observe subjective responsibilities by being more sensitive to servitude. In the chapter "On Sincerity" (Ikhlas), Bediüzzaman says "One who destroys this sincerity falls from the pinnacle of friendship. They may possibly fall to the bottom of a very deep pit. They cannot find anything in between to cling on to."[100] That is, responsibilities are proportional to a person's spiritual rank. One who steps to that private chamber and is blessed with certain spiritual experiences is not the same as others in the corridor or in the waiting lounge. If such a person does not give his or her position its

[99] Nursi, Şuâlar, p. 424

[100] Nursi, Bediüzzaman Said, The Gleams, New Jersey: Tughra Books, 2008, p. 229

due, they might be kicked out to the street. Therefore, sometimes God Almighty rebukes His Messengers, who are protected from sin, for the blessings they are bestowed are really great.

Willingness for Worship

Considering what we have told, the Sufi path is an important one. Those people feel the issue by practice. What we mean by practice is carrying out good deeds together with the spiritual dimension and feeling them in one's heart. For example, if devotions become a part of your character, you feel a desire toward them, as you desire to eat and drink. What we call "deepening in faith" can only then be realized. If matters of faith become a depth of your nature, then you feel them with due appetite, which is the truth of the matter. Bediüzzaman says, "... be freed from animality, restrict your carnal appetites, and enter the level of the life of the heart and spirit! You will find a broader sphere of life than your imagined world and a realm of light"[101] Then the heart and spirit will have a level of life superior to physicality and a body-oriented life. If such a superior life level is to be gained through reflection, deliberation, and practical deeds, it should not be neglected. So far, millions of saints made serious efforts for this sake with a Prophetic resolution, made due progress, and came to a certain level through spiritual journeying. By God's permission and grace, they reached the level of the most unshakable certainty (haqq al-yaqin)—if we except a different consideration by Imam Rabbani.[102] By putting the theory in practice, they did not only hear about the name of honey but tasted it and understood it. No matter how much they tell you what a wonderful delight it is to eat honey and milk cream, you can never know it for real without savoring it in your own mouth. For example, even if they make dizzying descriptions of Paradise to you and then say, "Beholding the Beauty of God for a minute is worth thousands of years in

---

[101] Ibid., p. 189
[102] Imam Rabbani, *Al-Maktubat*, 2/141 (Letter 100).

Paradise,"[103] how much can it really be understood without experiencing that for real? This is the case with matters related to the way of the heart and spirit. They can only be understood by experience. There is an Arabic proverb meaning, "One who has not tasted does not know."[104] For a real understanding, a person needs to orient his or her life to the heart and spirit. For this reason, heroes of the heart and spirit have been the ones who believed in the real sense. Let us state once more that what we have told so far does not express a disdain for other believers. No believer should doubt about his or her own faith. What we have told here aims to point out the depth and immensity of faith on the horizons of heroes of the heart and spirit.

---

[103] *Sahih Muslim*, Iman, 297; *Sunan at-Tirmidhi*, Jannah, 16; Tafsir as-Surah (10), 1; *Sunan ibn Majah*, Muqaddima, 13

[104] Al-Ghazali, *Ihya Ulum ad-Din*, 4/101

The Sultan of Hearts

Question: *Bediüzzaman states in his work Al-Math-nawi an-Nuri that the vast and supreme sultanate of Prophet Muhammad, peace and blessings be upon him, was not only an outward one. He has an inward sultanate in a wider and deeper sense because he attracted and summoned all hearts and minds toward himself.*[105] *Could you explain the "inward sultanate" of the Final Prophet?*

Answer: The noble Prophet established a system to take a place in the world's balance of powers upon the orders, commission, and message of God Almighty. This system answered individual, familial, economic, and administrative concerns. It answered all needs of people, as a consequence of his outward sultanate. On the other hand, there are the spiritual essences and depths upon which this outward sultanate was built upon: God Almighty sent His Messenger, who has risen to the station in which everything is seen as annihilated in the Divine Being, equipped with the necessary potentials for his mission. Through his hands, God Almighty established on earth a system beyond dreams, one sought in utopias.

---

[105] Nursi, *Al-Mathnawi Al-Nuri*, p. 21

A Manifestation of the Divine Name
Al-Batin (The Inward)

Outward deeds realized by our noble Prophet, the Perfect Guide, are manifestations of the Divine Name "Az-Zahir." Another Divine Name is "Al-Batin" (The Inward).[106] The system established by the Pride of Humanity on earth was one to make angels in heavens envious. As a manifestation of the Name Al-Batin, this system has its spiritual essences and depths. Keeping the system upright and fresh depends on a sound observation of the essentials of faith and Islam, along with a consciousness of *ihsan*—a constant consciousness of God's omnipresence. A legal or administrative system that neglects these essentials, that ignores the spiritual side of people and solely takes them at their physical dimension cannot succeed. It cannot put a stop to crimes, such as stealing, that upset the peace of a society and answer people's needs.

It is not possible for people to find true peace in a system which has no place for faith in God, angels, and resurrection after death. Faith evokes different things in the hearts and minds of different groups—in children who have fragile and sensitive natures, in young people who have stormy energies of feeling and passion, in patients suffering from different diseases, and in the elderly who are nearing the end of their worldly journey. Faith enables us to control our feelings like greed, grudge, and hatred. Thanks to faith, we walk on the path to eternity without giving in to despair in the face of death and the transience of things. Thus, making the essentials of faith and the perfect God-consciousness the pervading spirit in our lives constitutes the inward dimension of the blessed teaching of the noble Prophet. As we tried to point out at the beginning, this sultanate of the Pride of Humanity is based on Divine support. For various reasons—some of which we know and some we do not—God Almighty turned hearts toward him and He willed the beloved Prophet's charm to be a continuous one.

---

[106] In fact, the Divine Names Al-Awwal, Al-Akhir, Az-Zahir, Al-Batin are in a way like a sum of all Divine Names. In other words, all of the Divine Names are related to these two.

The transcendent attachment of the leading Companions—such as Abu Bakr, Umar, Uthman, and Ali, may God be pleased with them all—to the noble Prophet, and believers' continued loyalty to that blessed person in spite of ruthless attacks and destruction, could only be possible by God's support and believers continued faith in him. Even in such a corrupt era, most Muslims attach their hearts to the Messenger of God, peace and blessings be upon him, at a young age.

Beloved One of Hearts

I would like to relate a childhood memory of mine. When I was about 7 years old, my father said one day, "If you recite the Surah al-Ikhlas a thousand times on Thursday, you will see the noble Prophet in your dream." I cannot describe my considerations and feelings exactly, but I remember that I recited the Surah al-Ikhlas a thousand times until the morning with the hope of seeing the blessed face of the noble Prophet. If it did not happen, the next day, and then the next... I continued to recite the Surah al-Ikhlas. If some people still experience such an excitement in spite of their being raised in a spiritually poor environment and failing to recognize him with his true depths and to appreciate his works, the reason is nothing but his sultanate's continuity up to our day. God Almighty rendered him the beloved one of hearts and made his followers love him in a way that can be comparable to no other human being. In this respect, the prince of both worlds is not only the beloved one of God but also of God's servants. Aware or not, people feel seriously attracted toward him. Even the possible distortion of image in people's minds and hearts, owing to unbecoming claims fabricated by humans and jinn devils, fails to block the flood of love for him and believers feel earnestly attached to him without caring about any of these, because the matchless one of all times presented a perfect example of faith and good deeds, and led his entire life in perfect God-consciousness. In return, God Almighty implanted love for him in the hearts of dwellers of heavens and earth. There is no equivalent of that sultanate on earth. So it needs to be known that this happened thanks to the special support of God Almighty.

The sultanates established by ones devoid of Divine support are doomed to disappear with their persons. Indeed, it was the case with those of Caesars, Napoleon, Hitler and the like. As for the sultanates of the hypocrites that appeared within the Islamic world, even though they continued for a while, they were also extinguished like a candle in the end. However, the blessed light of the pride of this universe has been illuminating everything like a projector and will continue to do so. By God's grace and help, no opposing wind will manage to extinguish the love felt for him.

The Perfect Guide in Every Area of Life

Question: *It is revealed in the Qur'an that, "...God has done the believers a great kindness by raising among them a Messenger of their own, reciting to them His Revelations, and purifying them, and instructing them in the Book and the Wisdom; whereas, before that, they were lost in obvious error" (Al Imran 3:164). Could you explain the verse with respect to the noble Prophet's attributes cited?*

Answer: At the beginning of the verse, God Almighty draws attention to an important favor and kindness. The fact that God did not send an angel from the sky but a person from among people who was born as the child of his parents like the rest indicates God's grace to humanity. It is such a favor that this human Messenger shares the same feelings and thoughts with people, guided them on the path leading to God, came to the fore when they needed a leader, showed them in the best way how to be a commander ... in short, he provides guidance to people in every area of life at every moment they could need. Sending such a Messenger as a human being from among others is such a great honor! How can believers remain indifferent to such a significant blessing? Then it is necessary to offer due thanks.

Afterwards, the verse states that the Messenger of God, peace and blessings be upon him, recites them God's revelations. It is noteworthy that the Arabic word used here is "tilawah" (recitation) instead of "qira'ah," "ard," or "taqdim." "Tilawah" means reciting time after time, and continuously. The verb's being inflected in *mudari* tense puts further emphasis on continuity, which conveys the meaning of simple present tense. Accordingly, if we view the issue in connection with his blessed life, such a meaning can be drawn: in order not to let you feel contempt by familiarity, he constantly conveys the verses of God with the Qur'anic style of presenting subjects from fresh perspectives. In order to keep you spiritually alive, he presents matters time and again in different forms. There is also another meaning to be derived: As the Prince of both worlds recited God's verses in his own lifetime, he will continue to do so after passing away. This can be taken as an allusion to the fact that the Qur'an will remain protected. It is possible to take this point in relation with God's kindness mentioned at the beginning. In addition, He not only does this kindness, but also purifies you. Your spiritual purification—particularly by giving up arrogant considerations and always seeing oneself as blameworthy—then the refinement of you heart, and wandering comfortably over the emerald hills of the heart... all of it depends on His purifying, which becomes possible thanks to the Divine message.

Beholding the Existence from the Horizons of Wisdom

The Messenger of God teaches the Book and wisdom. His first and foremost teaching is the Qur'an the Miraculous Exposition. Verses of the Qur'an are the expounder, lucid proof, and clear interpreter of God's works. By reciting them continuously, the Messenger of God shattered veils of contempt bred by familiarity.[107] He makes everybody see phenomena with respect to their underlying truths, metaphysical sides, and spiritual depths. He teaches you wisdom at the same time. Wisdom has different meanings. In a way, it means gaining insight into the inward and underlying truth of phenomena. On the other hand, wisdom means

---

[107] Nursi, *The Words*, p. 155

grasping the wisdom and purposes of God's creation of the universe and humanity, and to see that everything in this universe is perfectly well-placed and that there is nothing useless in it. One other meaning of wisdom is the Sunnah, or tradition of the noble Prophet. All of the concise issues in the Qur'an, which is full of examples of wisdom to make reason affirm it, are expounded with the Sunnah—be them related to individual life, societal life, or the Afterlife.[108] Since the Paragon of Virtue, peace and blessings be upon him, clarified the concise, absolute, or general statements of the Divine revelation, in a way to leave no vagueness, some interpreted that "the book and wisdom" mentioned in the verse as the Qur'an and Sunnah, respectively.[109] At the end of the verse, it is stated: "Before that, they were lost in obvious error." Until the time these blessings of God came showering upon you, you were in obvious misguidance. You can name it as misguidance by being deprived of the Qur'an, of purification, Divine revelation, and wisdom, or misguidance by materialism and naturalism, which means attributing God's works to nature. Since some unfortunate ones devoid of wisdom view everything from the material perspective, their reason is reduced to their eyesight. However, physical vision is blind to spirituality. So the Qur'an removes the veil and reveals the truth of everything. In other words, the Qur'an does not leave the issue to mere eyesight, but provides insight. It does not suffice with mere reasoning but gives the reason under the heart's command and entrusts it to the appreciative scales of the heart. Thus, you become enabled to understand everything with their real nature and meaning. In other words, you are equipped to view phenomena from the horizons of wisdom.

All of these are only some drops from his spiritual kingdom. May peace and blessings be upon him, as much as the depth of our reason and immensity of our hearts allow. May God not deprive us from the sphere of His Messenger's kingdom in this world and the next.

---

[108] *Sunan at-Tirmidhi*, Fazailu'l-Qur'an, 14; *Darimi*, Fazailu'l-Qur'an, 1
[109] At-Tabari, *Jamiu'l-Bayan*, 1/557; Al-Baghawi, *Ma'alimu't-Tanzil*, 1/116–117

Steering Securely

Question: *What do you mean by the phrase "route safety"? What are the essentials of steering securely in terms
of both individual volunteers and their collective group?*

Answer: The word *güzergah* I use in that expression is a word of
Persian origin that means "road" or "highway," but it refers to a main
road that takes one to the targeted destination. These targets can differ as worldly or otherworldly. However, as worldly targets cannot be
real purposes for sincere believers, they make even worldly purposes gain otherworldly meanings.

Good Pleasure of God is the Sole Target

When a man with sincere belief takes responsibility as a village administrator, his purpose is not, and should not be, solely gaining an advan-
tageous worldly position. On the contrary, he strives for the village
people's happiness in both worlds for the sake of making God pleased.
He works night and day for the building of schools, mosques, libraries
and the like; he guides people toward noble ideals and benefiting the
whole of humanity, beginning with their own nation. Otherwise, what
can worldly positions and titles mean for a true believer? In terms of
its material aspect, the entire world is not worth a fly's wing. The
Messenger of God stated that if the world bore the value of a fly's wing
in God's sight, He would not let an unbeliever take a sip of water from

it.[110] However, the world bears great importance with respect to its being a road that leads to the Divine Names, the Hereafter, Paradise, the Beauty of God, and gaining the good pleasure of God.[111] In this respect, a sincere believer takes the good pleasure of God as the intended—and the greatest possible—target in all of one's actions and efforts. What follows next is introducing the Pride of Humanity—a means like a target in itself—to humanity and making people love his teachings, but even these two are means for gaining the good pleasure of God. Although they are important means we cannot do without, what really matters is God's good pleasure; all efforts made toward this end can be regarded as having reached their target. So *güzergah* is such a road that takes one to such a lofty target. In order to keep steering on that road without being taken by obstacles, one needs to adopt a holistic perspective from the beginning to the end, and envision dangers and risks beforehand. Thus that person ensures safe travel on his lane and does not give way to any traffic jam.

The Problem That Began with Satan

If a person realizes splendid acts of goodness and works wonders for the good of humanity, then he should be a more careful person. It is necessary to take into consideration that there will always be some who will not stomach the situation and fume viciously like magmas. Even people who run together for the same cause may not be able to stomach the other one but enviously think, "Why is it him, not me!" They might be influenced by the goading of Satan, act with feelings of rivalry, and see themselves more eligible for works to be appreciated. Actually, the first example of jealousy began with Satan, who showed his grudge, hatred, envy, and inability to stomach Adam. As Goethe also puts it, the Mephisto-Faust game is not over. It is the Devil on one side and humanity on the other. There are even human devils who completely surrendered to jinn devils. The Qur'an mentions *"devils of humankind and the jinn"* (al-An'am 6:112). This refers

---

[110] *Sunan at-Tirmidhi*, Zuhd, 13; *Sunan ibn Majah*, Zuhd, 3
[111] Nursi, *The Words*, p. 366

to people who completely act by the guidance of jinn devils and lead their lives accordingly.

Now if so many evil eyes, from the severest to the lightest, are on a person steering in pursuit of good acts, then what befalls on such a person is the need to check their course time and again. In other words, in order not to cause anything wrong to happen, they need to envision possible incidents. By taking care of how they proceed, they need to secure the good works they do or will do. So this means steering securely on the road.

The Greatest Trust

The Messenger of God stated that his name would reach everywhere the sun rises and sets.[112] Then it brings an important responsibility to sound believers. In comparison to such a responsibility, even an event like the conquest of Istanbul—heralded by the noble Prophet as definite to happen and celebrated annually with pompous ceremonies— will be a drop in the ocean. If bearers of such a trust act without caring to steer securely, it might mean betraying the trust. If they take it from a perspective of personal benefit and say, "Let me not suffer any damage and let me save the day," they will have upset the trust unawares, in spite of the seeming safety of their course. Sometimes you thunder against injustice as an outcome of your faith. Your thundering can be sincere and spontaneous. But if the works you are trying to do make noise and raise ill will, this also means harming the trust unawares. The Messenger of God stated that "Fitna (discord and ill will) is asleep. May God's curse be upon who wakes it."[113] For this reason, when the service of faith is harmed in certain respects, we need to make be self-critical, wonder what kind of a mistake we made and whether we led others to groundless apprehensions with our behavior. For this reason, the dedicated volunteers in our time must represent Islam in the best way, like the Companions of the noble Prophet, and show the perfect beauty of the truth in their hands.

---

[112] Sahih Muslim, Fitan, 19; Sunan at-Tirmidhi, Fitan, 14; Sunan Abu Dawud, Fitan, 1
[113] As-Sarahsi, Al-Mabsut, 10/124; Al-Ajluni, Kashfu'l-Khafa, 2/108

They must open up their hearts to the world and conquer others' hearts. Otherwise, claiming one's rights through violent means leads one to badness while seeking to do goodness. In spite of being treated so harshly in Mecca, the Messenger of God did not hit anybody even with the tip of his finger. Easier said than done: from the age of forty to fifty-three he spent a thirteen-year life of severe persecution in Mecca but put up with all of their torments. Nobody can say that he made the slightest harm to anyone; he would not hurt a fly. From the closest to the most distant person, he always inspired trust in all around him and never provoked anyone.

A Responsibility to the Degree of Obligation

When all of the above mentioned points are taken into consideration—though Islamic scholars of jurisprudence in our time may object—I see maintaining safe steering as a real obligation (*fard al-ayn*). That is, making the trust reach where it should securely is an important duty; if you do not reckon everything meticulously, consider every possible danger you can meet on the way, and do not make out the meaning on the looks turned toward you, then you will have failed to fulfill the responsibility of the trust. This is the degree of sensitivity it takes. This issue has no tolerance at all for populism, expressing oneself, or holding worldly expectations.

As the great spiritual master Bediüzzaman said "Said does not exist, nor does he have any power or authority. What speaks is only the truth, truths of faith."[114] In the same way, everybody should say, "I do not exist and neither does my personality. If my existence, considerations, worldview, and claims of selfhood are to do a grain's worth of damage to this cause, then let God take my soul.

But if I will serve faith in the least and realize that noble ideal, then let my Lord allow me to survive long enough to carry out that little amount of service. One must be fair enough to say that. A devoted soul should completely hold this consideration and act with utmost modesty, humbleness, and humility by nullifying the ego. It is a reali-

---

[114] Nursi, *Emirdağ Lâhikası-2*, p. 72 (Konuşan Yalnız Hakikattir)

ty that a person who keeps banging the drum for oneself and sounding out the same note as "Me! Me!" who always wishes to be the center of attention, and who tries to emphasize his or her personal worldview and philosophy of life can realize nothing good. Even though such people start quickly, it is inevitable for their efforts to end up in failure. For this reason, not only for a temporary period but from beginning to end, it is essential to be self-critical. Since making a mistake in this respect will mean betraying the trust, we will feel regret and embarrassment in both worlds.

Before completing my compulsory military service, I served as an imam at a very young age, although I was far beyond being eligible for such a duty. Afterwards, God Almighty enabled me to work as a preacher. In retrospect, I see the mistakes I made once or twice a week, though not every day. I say to myself "Shame on you! People came near the pulpit, sat there and listened to you. Why did you not use empathy and take those people's feelings into consideration? Why didn't you seek ways of reaching into souls through the way of people like Rumi? Why did you slam your words on heads with your rough style? Even though your word choice was not so, you made people feel so with the emphases you made..." This is how I criticize the past. I really blame myself so much, you cannot know. God will call me to account about all of those days. He might say, "I enabled you to give sermons in the mosque. People sat around the pulpit and I directed their hearts to you. Why did you not conquer their hearts? Why did you not make them love Islam? Why did not you make them crazy for God Almighty and the noble Prophet?" This has been a personal example, but every believer who bears the responsibility of reflecting the beauty of his or her faith must act very sensitively with respect to the responsibility and trust they bear. The Pride of Humanity states that saying "I wish," in the sense of criticizing Divine destiny is a disaster.[115] Such phrases of "I wish" are useless utterances a failure will resort to. In this respect, "I wish..." is an unbecoming expression forbidden to believers. There is another type of "I wish..."

---

[115] *Sahih Muslim*, Qadar, 34; *Sunan ibn Majah*, Muqaddima, 10

that deserves praise and these two should not be confused. For example, our master Abu Bakr expressed his wish that when he assigned Khalid ibn al-Walid for a certain duty, he should have assigned Umar ibn al-Khattab for another, so that he would have settled two different problems.[116] Some of the Companions made statements like "I wish I had asked such and such thing to the Messenger of God."[117] Such phrases of "I wish..." indicate that the speaker is a person who seeks to do the best. They reflect the speaker's good intention and God rewards them for that. The condemnable form of "I wish" is the one uttered as an arrogant reaction to cover up one's mistakes. These are words uttered by Satan's goading while referring to the wrongs Satan caused that person to commit.

In this respect, we need to watch our step today in order not to double the weight of our sins by saying "I wish..." tomorrow. Taking every step with the Name of God, sensibility, and prudence, we should start and do everything for the sake of God, and act with the consideration that the destination we target is His good pleasure.

---

[116] At-Tabarani, *Al-Mu'jamu'l-Kabir*, 1/62; Abu Ubayd Qasim ibn Sallam, *Al-Amwal*, p. 175; Az-Zahabi, *Tarikhu'l-Islam*, 3/118

[117] Abu Ya'la, *Al-Musnad*, 1/20–22; At-Tabarani, *Al-Mu'jamu'l-Kabir*, 1/62; Al-Hakim, *Al-Mustadrak*, 4/381

Philosophy of *Siyar* and the Peace Treaty of Hudaybiya

Question: *It was previously stated that it is definitely necessary to compare the time of the noble Prophet with ours, and find out the points that relate to our time. In this respect, could you evaluate the Treaty of Hudaybiya, in terms of the messages it gives for today?*

Answer: Muslims always need to refer to the discipline of *Siyar*, the biographies of the noble Prophet, as a very important source. It shows how the Qur'an should be understood and elucidates established principles in religion. The noble Messenger of God indicated by personal example—with his blessed life, words, attitudes, behaviors, and explanations—how to lead a life in compliance with the Divine revelation. His blessed Companions, each of whom was a master of language, interpreted these two holy sources correctly, conveyed their meanings correctly, and left a path for the later generations to follow. I think the deliverance of contemporary believers also depends on following their example, as stated by the noble Prophet as "My Companions are like stars; whichever of them you follow, you will find right guidance."[118]

---

[118] Aliyyulqari, *Al-Asraru'l-Marfua*, p.388

A Great Interpreter: Time

Although the events that occurred in the time of the noble Prophet were minor events on their own, they serve as a reference for all events in the greater scale that will take place until the end of the world. Every happening of that period bears some tips for solving the situations to be faced in future periods. People who take those tips as starting points can come up with solutions for the problems in their time, by taking into consideration the conditions of their own time and the cultural level of the people who lived in those days. This holds true for finding alternative solutions to the problems in today's rapidly globalizing world. In order to fulfill these problems in the best way it is necessary both to know the life of the noble Prophet well and to interpret and analyze the contemporary age well. It is possible to study all books of *Siyar* and to tell them to others. You may have gained very good insight into the events of those times, to the degree of feeling yourself like one of the actual characters of the stories, and feel due sadness or joy according to the narration at hand. However, if you simply suffice with that much and fail to grasp the open ends in them and to figure out how they can fill certain gaps in our time, then you gain nothing but a good narration of historical events. Naturally, along the course of fourteen centuries of Islamic history, certain points about the philosophy of *Siyar* are much referred to and some events in the time of the blessed Prophet were interpreted in terms of social history. It is a reality that there are very serious sociological differences between the conditions in those interpreters' time and the present. Some of the earlier philosophical considerations were put aside in time, some became outdated and new ways of thinking developed instead. For this reason, even though it is possible to benefit from earlier commentaries and perspectives, it is hard to claim that they suffice to shed light on contemporary issues. Only those who successfully take time, the greatest interpreter, into consideration can come up with a sound philosophy of *Siyar* for our time; they are the ones who deserve to be called "children of their time" (*ibnu'z-zaman*). When *Siyar* is viewed from such a perspective, it will be seen that it is such a pure and fresh fount of wisdom. Those who know how to benefit from it will gain very much from it. When we view the Treaty of Hudaybiya mentioned in the question, we see that it conveys so many messages of wisdom for our time.

The Sun of Mildness That Melted the Ice of Hatred

In the sixth year of the Hijra, the noble Prophet promised his Companions for *Umrah* (Minor Pilgrimage) and he set forth toward the Ka'ba in order to teach them how to fulfill *Umrah* in compliance with the essentials and spirit of Islam. However, the Quraysh tribe rigidly wished to prevent it. In the vicinity of Mecca, the Messenger of God sent a man to express that they only wished to make *Umrah*. However, some people from the Quraysh attempted to kill the envoy. After that, Uthman ibn Affan was sent, but they caught and imprisoned him.[119] Upon this, the Messenger of God, peace and blessings be upon him, gathered Muslims for a pledge of allegiance.[120] As a consequence of these events, the tension was high. The Companions had their hands on the hilts of their swords and were ready to react. The noble Prophet had promised for a pilgrimage and they had covered the 400 km distance under the conditions of those times, by riding camels and horses. They had come as near as Jeddah, but the polytheists prevented their advance. Had the blessed Prophet taken it as a matter of honor and gestured them forward, the Companions would not have feared the horsemen of Khalid ibn al-Walid, or the Meccan army of ten thousand armed soldiers. They would have fought their way on and reached the Ka'ba. However, such a course of action would not have been of help in terms of their noble ideals. There were so many people before them, who would hopefully, with time, believe in one God. The Messenger of God, who was an ever-sensible person, perspicaciously reckoned the likely consequences and signed a peace Treaty with the Meccan polytheists in Hudaybiya. As he had taken the pledge of allegiance from his Companions that they would fight until death if

---

[119] Ahmad ibn Hanbal, *Al-Musnad*, 4/323–325

[120] Ibn Hisham, *As-Siratu'n-Nabawiyya*, 4/283

necessary, he astutely turned that loyalty into a peace treaty.[121] People who swore allegiance under such a difficult situation would much more easily obey orders upon returning to Medina without confrontation. As this matchless perspicacity and sagacious attitude of the noble Prophet can be seen as a consequence of Divine inspiration, it can also be seen as natural outcome of his character.

The articles of the treaty were seemingly disadvantageous to Muslims.[122] First of all, 1500 people[123] whose hearts were burning with the desire to visit the Ka'ba would not go beyond Hudaybiya but return to Medina. Outwardly, it seemed to be a loss. However, these people, who found security thanks to the Treaty of Hudaybiya, would disperse to the region among different tribes and invite them to the verses of the Qur'an and beauties of Islam. At the same time, the peaceful atmosphere brought by the agreement began to transform the rigid attitude of the Meccans to a milder one. Within one or two years, very important personalities as Khalid ibn al-Walid, Amr ibn al-As and Uthman ibn Talha[124] felt the void of meaning on the side they supported, grew aware of the developing power before them, and came to Islam not by force but by their voluntary choice. Since they had not faced any coercion about accepting Islam, their hearts were not broken. It was not only these three people; there were hundreds or thousands of these converts in the same situation. Thanks to the blessed Prophet's mild character, the opposing parties came to their senses, one by one, within the peaceful atmosphere generated by the Treaty of Hudaybiya and they voluntarily accepted Islam. The Messenger of God, peace and blessings be upon him, who had envisioned all of those developments with a holistic perspective, did not give priority to reaching to the Ka'ba or even conquering Mecca, but he targeted conquering hearts. For this reason, he preferred peace even though the conditions were seemingly disadvantageous. At the same time, he did not let neighboring tribes say "Muslims entered the holy Ka'ba by blood-

---

[121] Ibid.

[122] *Sahih al-Bukhari*, Shurut, 15; *Sahih Muslim*, Jihad, 90–92

[123] *Sahih al-Bukhari*, Maghazi, 35; *Sahih Muslim*, Imara, 67–72

[124] Ibn Sa'd, *At-Tabakatu'l-Kubra*, 4/252; 7/395; Al-Waqidi, *Kitabu'l-Maghazi*, 1/748

shed." Mecca was conquered after a short while without bloodshed or disrespect to the holy shrine.[125] Only a limited group of people reacted during their entrance to Mecca, and they were people who had not grasped the essence of the issue.[126] However, it was a minor and exceptional situation.

Doors of Hearts Being Opened within the Atmosphere of Peace

This event, which we relate with its general outlines, has some points to provide today's people with inspiration. In today's world, where distances have become diminished through means of transport and communication, people with different faiths and cultures coexist. For example, when you visit a country in Africa you see that some people continue their tribal religions and some people follow Christianity. Some of these people are even more devout Christians than their counterparts in the West. On the other hand, some of them display a negative and biased attitude toward Islam. If any good relations are to be built with them, it is necessary to astutely analyze the present picture and act sensibly by calculating every detail well. The issue has no tolerance for offensiveness. You can never build good relations with an attitude of total disregard for their values. On the contrary, it is possible to build a warm relationship through dialogue, tolerance, respecting everybody's position, recognizing their being honored with the best pattern of creation, and acknowledging that every one of them is a bright mirror to the Divine, with respect to their essence and potentials. After gaining real insight into all of these aspects and saying, "I am a child of this time and living in such a society," it is necessary to determine a style. I think one of our greatest shortcomings is developing a universal discourse to embrace everyone. Just as there are dialogue centers, I wish there were centers of discourse development to let people of our time acquire a refined manner; I wish it would be possible to explain how to "establish dialogue with people from differ-

---

[125] Ibn Hisham, *As-Siratu'n-Nabawiyya*, 5/42–68
[126] Ibid., 5/66–67

ent cultural backgrounds and understandings without offending them." Muslims have two important sources in their hands, in the Qur'an and Sunnah. These can offer solutions for the problems of any era. Introducing their beauties to different societies and children of different cultures requires speaking the same language. Then it is necessary to understand others' feelings and know their sensitivities about issues such as language, culture and the like. Trying to voice one's own truths without taking these into consideration is a mistake. People who are solely concentrated on their own car cannot be good drivers. You need to watch others who steer on the same road and act accordingly. Speaking haphazardly with occasional outbursts of emotion can be grossly offensive if you do so unaware.

Getting back to our main subject, the Hudaybiya example provides a tip for this issue. We need to seek ways for peace in a smaller world, no matter what faith other people follow. To this end, it is possible for civil society organizations to sign treaties about relations between societies, such as a treaty of Africa, the Far East, or Canada etc. Against possible attacks or biased attitudes, we must find an opportunity to show that we intend no harm. This way, we can express ourselves better. As believers, we do not intend any harm to anybody at all. But we need to have a suitable ground to present our true character and let others listen to us. It is necessary to know that others will trust you as much as they recognize you together with your heart and inner world. In short, good developments in today's conditions can only happen within an atmosphere of friendship, alliance, and support. If we come together with people of different cultures and understandings, hold hands, eat at the same table and have the same tea, then we have an opportunity to know one another better. Others' knowing us with our own depths and cultural riches can only be realized thus. People who live in different cultural regions of our time can only rid themselves of prejudices through such interaction and dialogue.

Underground Riches and Responsibilities That Befall on Believers

Question: *It is reported that the Messenger of God said: "Seek rizq[127] in the depths of the earth."[128] What are the responsibilities that befall on believers as this saying signifies?*

Answer: After God Almighty created humanity, He did not simply tell them "Go and take care of yourself on the earth." On the contrary, He sent them to such a ground and such a place of learning that almost all things await them nearby. However, we are not supposed to sit at home and say, "Let everything come near us on their own within a hand's reach." Happenings in this world, which is the Abode of Wisdom, take place within the frame of causes (God Almighty acts behind the veil of cause and effect) and we are responsible for fulfilling what they necessitate. As for the Hereafter, it is the realm of Divine Power. In Paradise, something passing one's mind or something imagined can appear from nowhere. There is no need for the veil of cause and effect. In fact, the prayers God Almighty accepts in this world show some of its examples to us in a way. Sometimes we see that we are provided right away with something we prayed for. Similar to these

---

[127] *Rizq*: sustenance, what God provides for a living creature.
[128] Abu Ya'la, *Al-Musnad*, 7/347; At-Tabarani, *Al-Mu'jamu'l-Awsat*, 1/274

directly accepted prayers, dwellers of Paradise will see that things will come true as soon as they move their lips or think about them; the overwhelming power of God will overtly reveal itself there without the veil of causality.

Yet Unknown Materials and *Rizqs*

In many verses of the Qur'an, God Almighty reveals that the skies and the earth are made subservient to humanity. When we look around at trees flourishing, waters flowing, seas we benefit from, the living creatures they contain, or the light coming from the sun, we recognize that all of them hold different blessings for us. When we explore the earth and seas a little bit, we encounter amazing blessings. However, all of these blessings are enveloped in causes, so that the Divine Power is not associated with trivial issues in simple minds.[129] In order to reach those blessings, we need to tear those envelopes open. For example, you wish to harvest fruit of a certain kind. You first sow the seeds in soil or plant a sapling you find, and then prepare the suitable conditions for its growth. So the *hadith* mentioned in the initial question tells us to make an effort and search for the provisions and blessings God created in the depths of the earth. In fact, the significance of natural resources as different metals and energy sources is evident for everyone. In our time, scientists try to make some estimation about the reserves of those resources. But their work is limited to what is currently within our reach, as much as the available technology allows. There are such geological layers we have gained no access to yet. Let me give an example from a primitive tool: if you know that slamming a pickax will cause magma to burst on you, then you cannot dare search for anything in those depths. On the other hand, there is continuous metamorphosis occurring on earth, such as some creatures undergoing mutations. The Almighty Creator who makes those metamorphoses happen can also create new forms of provisions continuously under the earth. Who can claim that God will *not* create new certain things we think to be doomed to vanish? Who knows

---

[129] Nursi, *The Reasonings*, p. 55

how many times the earth underwent changes, how many times the poles changed place, how many times mountains left their places to seas and vice versa. For this reason, let us not forget that the claims made about the reserves of underground resources in certain countries can be serving speculative purposes and pulling the wool over people's eyes. By acting this way, some powers can be trying to delude the masses to suit their benefits.

Mother Earth, which Cuddles Humanity with Compassion

The initial question was related to believers' responsibilities signified by the Prophetic command to search for provisions in the depths of the earth. In the Qur'an, God draws the importance of the earth for humanity. *"Have We not made the earth as a cradle...?"* (an-Naba 78:6). This verse suggests that God Almighty did not leave humans, who are essentially impotent and weak like a baby, to mercilessness on earth, but He created the earth like a cradle for them, as if it were prepared by a compassionate mother who also placed the food by their side. Human beings, who receive such compassionate care in such a suitable place, can enjoy all of God Almighty's blessings on earth by giving their willpower its due. Since their available means blind them to the rest, they fail to see the blessings exhibited in this planet. If they can look around with a serious feeling of impotence and helplessness, with a mood of suffering in dire need, then they will realize the presence of so many blessings they had been unable to see, and different dimensions and depths they missed in those blessings. Great Messengers of God encouraged people to find the coded keys of the blessings in the universe and then enjoy them. At the same time, they pointed to the Divine messages like the Qur'an, Torah, and the Bible and told us to use them as keys. Therefore, we Muslims have a key like the miraculous Qur'an in our hands, which can help us enjoy all the blessings on earth. It is such a sad fact that we have been unable to use this key for the last few centuries and could not find the way to enjoy those blessings. Instead, we have been afflicted with illnesses that paralyze the willpower, such as arrogance, boasting about the past, pursuing carnal desires, and seeking personal benefit. In the meantime, motives like wishing to rule the world and gaining economic power triggered some others' desires and made them take action. As they searched for a certain metal, they came across other elements in time and they kept discovering new things as they explored nature with a zeal for scientific exploration. As a result of this, they spotted the locations of oil reserves and important underground resources in different regions of the world and made plans for seizing those places. Later, those powers decided to put an end to the Ottoman state and thought that each of them could get a good share if they shattered the Ottoman lands. They would divide the land into different states and benefit from the riches therein. It is arguable whether the Ottomans were really aware of this situation in those days; there was an undeniable reality that they faced a serious shortage of intellectuals to generate new thoughts and take due action. On the other hand, the West was going through a new revival and industrial revolution. The West had undergone great changes and set about discovering the world. They started scrutinizing phenomena with a serious zeal for research. In the meantime, Westerners occasionally met some surprises. They found gold while searching for silver, amethyst while searching gold, and rubies while searching for amethyst, etc. All of these led them to new formations and new considerations.

The Islamic World is in Dire Need of Lovers of Truth

Today as well, there are different powers resorting to every legal or illegal means to seize natural resources in different regions of the world. For example, certain field experts claim that in some areas of Turkey there are enclosed areas, which could be containing reserves of oil, gold, silver, and other materials. Thus, failing to give the willpower its due about this issue and leaving those riches to exploiters will inevitably mean loss and grief, yet again.

Energy resources have become a major need of modern life, similar to food and shelter. In a way, everything somehow relates to the issue of energy. From lighting to vehicles on roads to planes in the air, so many things depend on energy. Since energy is of such vital importance, we can talk about a serious focus on energy almost everywhere. By God's grace, the people of Anatolia have begun to be appreciated in the region again. Nowadays, they are building bridges of friendship with different countries in very different lands; they establish new business and economic relations. At this point, what we will need more than anything is scientists and seekers of truth, people determined to find out the truth and relate it to an eternal meaning. Naturalism and materialism can take people only so far. These systems are bound by the limits of matter. Therefore, researches cannot extend beyond that point. On the other hand, seekers of the eternal, who are always thirsty for deeper meaning, can carry on. With this broad perspective, believing scientists and researchers will meticulously scrutinize the depths of the earth with the labs and research centers allocated to them, reach down into the earth's heart, bring out anything beneficial for humanity hidden in these underground layers, benefit from the earth, and try to serve humanity with their new findings.

The Elixir to Eliminate
Heedlessness: Remembrance

Question: *What is heedlessness? Can we talk about different types of remembrance (dhikr) which can be recited to disperse the heedlessness that enshrouds us?*

Answer: The word "ghaflah" (heedlessness) conveys meanings like being absent-minded, careless, failing to see what goes around, not knowing the true nature of phenomena, and failing to see and feel as one should. To put it differently, as a religious term, heedlessness means failing to thoroughly discern what one is supposed to do in the journey of this life, and living oblivious of, and unconcerned about, one's end. It is possible to talk about many important elixirs to eliminate heedlessness. For example, deliberation, discussion, and reflection on matters of faith can alleviate heedlessness. If you refer to the works of Bediüzzaman, you find them full of such advice to eliminate heedlessness. Whichever of his works you refer to, they take you to different valleys of reflection. What you read opens new horizons before you, and you begin to see and judge correctly. Your feelings and senses extend to the depths of your heart; latent potentials virtually resurrect, and your conscious faculties become activated.

Sincerely offered acts of worship are among the important means of eliminating heedlessness. For example, a call to Prayer made with the voice of one's heart eliminates heedlessness, turns your gaze to the sky, and prepares you for the Prayer. Thus, you walk there with enthusiasm. Sometimes the ablutions you make in the garden of a mosque, or a heartfelt *iqamah* announcing the beginning of Prayer, or sometimes a sincere *takbir*, and sometimes an imam leading the Prayer with a voice coming from his heart, can make you feel moved and draw you into a different world. You will feel as if you stepped into a different dimension of the world you live in. Therefore, all of these disperse the clouds of heedlessness before individuals' eyes and make them meet their own essence.

Latent Feelings and Sharing Enthusiasm

In addition to all of these, one of the most important means of eliminating heedlessness is remembrance of God. In Sufi tradition, people gathered in circles for remembrance and recited God's different Names and Attributes. Every order has their special ways and formats. It can be said that these different ways and formats have their influence on people of different characters. For example, some hold hands and sit so close in a circle that their knees touch one another. The leader of the circle joins them and they start the remembrance. Some others also form such circles but they rather prefer saying the words of remembrance covertly. As people say "La ilaha illa'llah; Subhan Allah; Alhamdulillah" their locked hands become a means of sharing their enthusiasm.

Let me point out that the same situation holds true for the Daily Prayers offered in congregation: if an imam can put his heart to the recitation of the Qur'an during Prayer and become oblivious to anything but God, and give himself to a flood of ecstatic feelings, then this state of his will pass to the people behind him, to a certain extent. In the same way, one sob by a worshipper in the ranks, whose heart has established a connection with God, may pull at everyone's heartstrings. The crying of such an excited soul resembles, in a way, a warning to them. It says, "Wake up! Make up your mind and rid yourselves of this heedlessness!" Therefore, what really matters is the quality and depth of the act of remembrance. When remembrance of God is made sincerely, it affects other individuals as well; it takes those people from the three-dimensional realm we live in to a different one. They virtually feel they are walking on the streets of Paradise, wandering on the skirts of Firdaws, and beholding God on the hills of Friday, and they almost hear the most honorable Divine address: "I am well pleased with you!"[130] All of these shatter the layers of heedlessness and let people see and hear what they should, and open the door to a person's knowing oneself and realizing the truth of human essence. Surely, remembrance does not solely mean habitually repeating certain things with the tongue; it is also an act of reflection by bringing certain things to mind. In this respect, remembering the heroic Companions such as Mus'ab ibn Umayr and Sa'd ibn Muadh is also an act of remembrance in the religious sense. Such remembrance will eliminate heedlessness and help the believer come around and discover oneself, discern and interpret oneself correctly with respect to his position, and thus soar toward knowledge of God; everything oriented to deepening in reflection and wisdom can be considered among acts of remembrance.

Remembrance by Reading Circles

The Messenger of God gave the following advice to believers via the person of Abu Hurayra: "Control and renew your ship once more, for the sea is truly deep. Take your provisions perfectly, for the journey is truly long. Keep your load light, for the slope before you is truly steep. Be sincere in your deeds, for God, who scrutinizes everything, is aware of what you do."[131] Given that God Almighty is omnipresent and sees us all the time, a wise person should do everything for the sake of God. It is very important for man, whose every act God sees and will treat accordingly, to be saved from heedlessness on such a vital issue. One should never forget that death is destined for everyone. It is not possible to keep anybody in this world for good. The journey of this world is a long one where a person passes at different stages from childhood to old age, and from there to the grave, to the

---

[130] *Sahih al-Bukhari*, Riqaq, 51; Tawhid, 38; *Sahih Muslim*, Iman, 302; Jannah, 9
[131] Ad-Daylami, *Al-Musnad*, 5/339

intermediary realm of *barzakh*, Resurrection, the Bridge, and then to Paradise or—God forbid—to Hell.[132] While such a hard journey awaits them, it is surprising how people can give in to heedlessness. Concerning this issue, the Qur'an commands the noble Prophet: "*But remind and warn, for reminding and warning are of benefit to the believers*" (adh-Dhariyat 51:55). This verse also commands "dhikr" to the noble Prophet, but it does not refer to repeating words of glorification on one's own. Rather, it refers to reminding this truth to believers in different styles and methods. Then it is stated that this reminding will be of benefit to believers. Believers always need such reminding. You can take up the issue within the context of groups of religious talk and say that we always have a responsibility to remind each other of certain truths, and that it is possible to attain very important results by fulfilling this responsibility. Such reminding, which will serve as encouragement to not waste time on amusements and actualities, is of great benefit and importance. Actualities and useless issues pleasing to the carnal souls are like whirlpools. If you let yourself into them, they take you away from yourself. When this happens, you face the threat of the Divine command "*And do not be like those who are oblivious of God and so God has made them oblivious of their own selves*" (al-Hashr 59:19). In a way, the verse tells us that our own selves are a means of viewing our own essence. By using it like a telescope, we are supposed to behold the splendid works of God Almighty, mirrors of the Divine Names, and the spectacles of their manifestations. However, some give in to heedlessness and become oblivious of God, and He makes these people forget about their own selves and condemned them to their own narrowness of thought, reasoning, physicality, and body. For this reason, believers should take reminding as a duty, and help one another with continuous warnings. If we consider that, after the command to remind and warn believers, God Almighty states: "*I have not created the jinn and mankind but to (know and) worship Me (exclusively)*" (adh-Dhariyat 51:56), then the actual point that needs to be reminded becomes clear. That is, attention must always

---

[132] Nursi, *The Words*, p. 342

be turned to servitude and knowledge of God. It is necessary to pave the way for every individual to deepen their knowledge of God by personal experience in accordance with their ability and potentials, and to let everybody differently view and consider phenomena according to personal level. To put it straightly, it is necessary to let every single person put aside their own narrowness and recognize the horizons of being conscious of seeing, hearing, holding, and feeling through God's being the true agent.

Types of Heedlessness
That Impede Serving Faith

Q **uestion:** *Could you explain the different types of heed-lessness that might impede the devoted souls on the path to serve their faith?*

Answer: It is important, particularly now when some misunderstand Islam and misinform others about it, that we let hearts feel the truth of Islam. It is our greatest responsibility. We must share the beauties of the teaching of the noble Prophet with others, and strive to let Islam be understood correctly, trying to show the beauty of its besmirched face; it is a necessity of being a believer and a duty Muslims owe their religion. In other words, we must represent the genuine Islam in the best way as practiced by the blessed Prophet and his Companions—like presenting a new gift to humanity. This should be the goal of our lives. Indeed, four corners of our world are caught in a fire with respect to faith in God. Individuals, homes, and in a way, places of worship, schools, and administrations, are all burning... In short, not only Muslim regions and but other parts of the world are virtually in flames. For the devoted souls to ignoring this miserable human condition of humanity and to not have the sensitivity to share their suffering is heedless. Wherever the fire is, the volunteers to serve humanity need to respond sensitively to it, as if their own children were suffering. This depends on having a Prophetic spirit and upholding the issue with a Prophetic will, resolution, and altruism. As it is known, no new Prophets will come, and it is not possible for those who follow their example to become Prophets. However, it is always possible to target being adorned with their high virtues. As God Almighty favors the Prophets among all people, He will not let down those who try to follow in their footsteps. For this reason, it is necessary to seek proximity to the noble Prophet by being adorned with his virtues. The Pride of Humanity was a paragon of virtue;[133] he was a living example of the high virtues described by the Qur'an,[134] which we can refer to as Divine morality. As his followers, Muslims can only find their true value, discover their depths and feel their true identity by following his example. I think that only those adorned with these high virtues can journey on the path of the blessed Prophet and share his feelings as much as their capacity allows; he will not leave such people halfway. The Messenger of God, peace and blessings be upon him, will never leave the devoted souls suffering for the troubles of the Islamic world - those exerting themselves to find solutions, and continuously generating plans and projects to reach into hearts. At the moment you say, "It's over," I swear by God, he will extend his hand of light to you. Maybe he will tell you to carry on in your dream, maybe his blessed spirit will walk among you and somehow raise your spirits. When you have him on your side, other blessed figures behind him will also be with you, his blessed family (*Ahl al-Bayt*) being the first.

Heedless Ventures

Getting back to our main subject, another type of heedlessness putting those journeyers on the righteous path at risk is being reckless on duty. This has different types as well. For example, acting casually, not using diplomacy when one should, acting without taking evil into consideration, doing wrong things for the sake of adventure, giving in to popular considerations, doing things solely to impress others, ven-

---

[133] Al-Qalam 68:4

[134] *Sahih Muslim*, Salatu'l-Musafirin, 139; *Sunan Abu Dawud*, Tatawwu, 26; *Sunan an-Nasa'i*, Qiyamu'l-Layl, 2

turing into some task without taking the consequences into account... these mistakes are different forms of being heedless on duty. Actually, each one of these types of heedlessness can suffice to topple a person. People overcome by such forms of heedlessness not only fall on their own, but they also make other people coming after them sink, like a heedless captain who ends up taking his entire ship to the bottom of the sea.

On the other hand, there are very important essentials for those volunteers on the righteous path: not offended anybody, approaching everybody with compassion, running to the help of others like a fireman, seeing all of God's manifestations—troubles and joys—as equal yet only treating others benevolently, being conscious of their own impotence and neediness, maintaining their zeal to serve God with gratitude for His blessings, and continuously feeding their spirituality through reflection and wisdom. The devoted souls should act in a chivalrous way and judiciously reckon the results of their actions. They need to appraise every step they take—whether it will leave behind grudge, hatred, and rage... or love, affection, and care. In short, they need to act very carefully and wisely regarding everything they do in order not to disappoint people who view them with hopeful eyes.

The Misconception of Causality

Laying too much importance on causality by ascribing everything to causes and being oblivious of the "Causer of causes,"[135] and ignoring Him, is another type of heedlessness. In the *Risale-i Nur* Collection, Bediüzzaman tried to open the door to recognizing the Causer of causes. Here is one thing he pointed out on the wisdom of causes' existence: "God's Dignity and Grandeur require apparent causes to prevent complaints and to hide, from those who reason superficially, the hand of Power's involvement in certain seemingly insignificant or vile things and affairs. At the same time, God's Unity and Glory require that these

---

[135] Causer of causes: *Musabbib al-Asbab*, or God Almighty.

apparent causes have no part in either the creation or disposition of things."[136] At another place, he makes a similar point:

"As befits God's Oneness and Majesty, causes have no real and creative effect in creation and the universe's functioning. But in the outward (corporeal) dimension of existence, causes function to veil Divine Power's operation so that certain seemingly disagreeable or banal entities and events might not be attributed directly to It."[137]

Causes are not the real doer. If causes have any true value, they take it as being projections worked by the Beautiful Divine Names and passed through many veils. Therefore, if causes are to be given any value at all, it should be done in connection with the Divine Names. On the one hand, a total disregard of causes is wrong, since it means fatalism. On the other hand, a person who sees causes as the real doer of everything is heedless of the Causer of causes. To give a concrete example, let us say that one of the volunteers goes somewhere and his efforts become fruitful: roses bloom in all the fields of thorn and nightingales start singing; that place virtually turns to Paradise. In such a situation, if another man remarks, "All of these would not have happened, if it weren't for such and such friend of ours," and attributes all of the good works to that person, then that man becomes heedless of God; he puts his friends under the same risk with such remarks. If that man is not capable of dismissing such remarks, then praising him will mean breaking his neck, as stated by the Messenger of God, peace and blessings be upon him.[138]

Ascribing the good works realized by a group of people to a single person is another type of such heedlessness. Ascribing the victory of an entire army to a commander means being unfair to his soldiers;[139] the fruits attained by concerted efforts of many people cannot solely be seen as achievements of the person who guides them. In addition, it should not be forgotten that what invites the Divine providence is those people's collective spirit of unity. That is, God Almighty bestows

[136] Nursi, *Al-Mathnawi al-Nuri*, p. 4

[137] Nursi, *The Letters*, p. 446

[138] *Sahih al-Bukhari*, Shahada, 16; Adab, 54, 95; *Sahih Muslim*, Zuhd, 65

[139] Nursi, *Şuâlar*, p. 349

them success if He is well pleased with their harmonious collaboration. If they work together despite the fact that every one of them has their personal arrogance and pride, He is pleased. Attributing that success to a single person, or failing to see the Causer of causes is heedless.

The Insolence of not Knowing One's Limits

When the issue is considered on a larger scale, you see that there are dangers facing a group of people, too. For example, if those who are affiliated with a certain movement ascribe to themselves the fruits of certain good works they tried to do in service of faith and humanity, they are being heedless. This situation depends on the existence of so many factors: having favorable conditions, the inability of misguided ones to disrupt good works in spite of their enviousness, hearts opening up to His volunteers with love, the world's general atmosphere being peaceful... and maybe fifty other factors should be included. If we calculate the probabilities, the chances would be around one in a million. When this is the case, why are the present good works reduced to the consequence of a few simple causes? Even if such a thought crosses your mind as a momentary idea, you need to ask forgiveness for it. Once, when I wrote something like[140] a couplet, which was to be published on the outer cover of the *Sızıntı* magazine, it occurred to me that my words were somehow well-chosen. Immediately, I repented and asked forgiveness from God saying "O God Forgive me please! Take the life of this donkey and do not let him feel pleased with what he did!" In this respect, a thought as "The speech I made really touched hearts and made people take action" is an insolence by not knowing one's limits; such a consideration ascribes the existence of an entire picture that depends on thousands of variables to one simple cause.

There is another side of this issue. As we have mentioned, being oblivious of the Causer of causes is an example of heedlessness. On

---

[140] It is typical of Mr. Gülen to refer to things he personally did with such expressions out of his humble attitude. For example, he says "I was giving *something like* a sermon..." to imply that "An incompetent person like me cannot really give a sermon."

the other hand, not raising morale for those who strive on this path and causing them to lose enthusiasm is a different mistake. Instead, it is possible to pray for them by saying "May God be pleased with you forever. God Almighty is making you realize such good work. If He had not valued you, He would not have given this role as a part Divine destiny and used you in the cast. Then God has favored you. May He continue His favor upon you!" This can help raise their spirits without ascribing Divinity to causality. At this point, there is a principle we should observe: instead of attributing lofty attributes, such as sainthood, to people who serve on this path for some thirty or forty years, and who seem on the fore of this movement, we can reflect our good opinion of them in the form of being very much loyal and faithful to them. Even if we see them fallen, we need to hold them up right away, raise them up from where they fell, wipe away the mud on them, and embrace them. For this reason, acknowledging the Causer of causes does not necessarily mean refusing to see the ones striving to serve humanity; but this seeing should be done within a logical frame.

Failing to interpret the creation, to derive truthful meanings from phenomena, and to find God through them is a significant type of heedlessness. In a verse relevant to our discussion, God Almighty reveals: *"How many a sign there is in the heavens and earth that they pass by, being unmindful of the signs and giving no consideration to them"* (Yusuf 12:105). Every one of the types of heedlessness we mentioned can be more important in comparison to others. In other words, their degree of importance can show difference according to personal aptitude and abilities. Any of them can be a serious component of testing for different people. If we look at the issue in terms of Islamic faith, every type of heedlessness is a satanic idea and must be expelled. Getting rid of them depends on deeds and actions of the heart and spirit such as always acting with insight, being sensitive, trying to see the truth of phenomena, always keeping the "eyes of the heart" open, seeing while looking, listening while hearing, feeling while contacting, and making the conscience feel all of these.

Keeping Up the Ideal State in the Face of Social Changes

Question: *Ahmet Cevdet Pasha divides Ottoman history into a few stages and remarks that Ottomans became truly civilized only after the time of Suleiman the Magnificent. In addition, he sees the corruption in the final years of the Ottomans as a natural process a society goes through.*[141] *How do you evaluate these views?*

Answer: Actually, the views of Ahmet Cevdet Pasha are more or less shared by historians, sociologists, and philosophers of history. Researchers such as Gibb and Renan, who lived in the recent past, also expressed this thought. I think Ibn Khaldun was the first to voice such considerations. The overall point they make is that, societies come to existence, mature, get old, and die just like people do. That is, all societies are destined to be buried in a grave awaiting them, sooner or later. If we apply this understanding to the case of the Ottomans, we can see their early period as an unsophisticated one. However, taking the Ottomans' qualities into consideration, it is more suitable to refer to this period as their "semi-civilized" stage. In my opinion, their early period was a period of pure belief. People were pure and plain in terms of their feelings and ideas. They did not hold any hid-

---

[141] Ahmet Cevdet Paşa, *Tarih-i Cevdet*, 1/124–125

den expectations for what they did. They simply walked on the path before them as their ideals required and tried to reach the target with determination and efforts. So those people were so pure and plain; they were free from considerations of worldliness and intent on seeking the good pleasure of God. Whatever ideal they pursued, they exerted themselves for the sake of realizing it.

The Will to Keep up the Desired State

Different nations have their glorious periods in history. The Ottomans signify such a period in the history of the Turkish people. The first period, of one and a half centuries, was a particularly magnificent one. The founder of the Ottomans, Osman Ghazi, spent a humble life in tents and he gave his last breath in a tent. While he could enjoy a life of ease with the victories he won, he always preferred a simple life. It can be said that he followed the example of the first four caliphs Abu Bakr, Umar, Uthman, and Ali, may God be pleased with them all. So when the path taken is the same, then the result is the same. Osman Ghazi's son Orhan Ghazi was no different than his father with respect to his zeal for serving the truth, spirit of striving in the way of God, and preferring simplicity. He almost spent his entire life on horseback. Sultan Murad I (Hudavendigar) was martyred on the battleground. Before he gave his last breath, he told his soldiers not to dismount; instead of making personal demands, he wished his soldiers to carry on with their responsibility without losing time for him. His example reflects a spirit of selfless devotion to the cause. That great sultan was not only a statesman and commander but also a saintly figure with a heart awakened to spiritual realms.

During that period of great figures, Ottomans presented a brilliant picture with flying colors in the history of humanity. This period, which we can see as the "youth" of the state, lasted until the conquest of Istanbul. After the conquest, the Western world referred to the Ottoman state as an empire. It would be too exaggerated to say that the inner purity and simplicity at the beginning was completely lost after that date. However, it is a reality that the victories won did have a dizzying effect on people. We should pay tribute to Sultan Bayezid II, who lived like an ascetic and tried to keep up the purity and simplicity of the early period. Then came Selim I, who tried to establish justice on earth and become a factor of balance among world powers. He represented the resolution, selflessness, and self-sacrifice required by such an ideal. After that great ruler, there came another important figure who kept up the state in the best way possible during his 46-year rule, with a speed coming from the centrifugal force of the action his father, Selim I, realized. However, when we take a close look into those periods with respect to social life, we will recognize the beginnings of a negative change. Apparently, the centrifugal force of the purity at the beginning had yielded a magnificent state admired by kings. On the other hand, it is a reality that a process of decay had also begun within. As a matter of fact, after Suleiman the Magnificent, neither Selim I nor Murad III nor others—with some exceptions—commanded the army. When Sultan Reşad (Mehmed V) visited the Balkans, the people rejoiced by taking it as a great event. A sultan's living among the people and leading his own army bears great importance in terms of their morale. At the same time, it presents a powerful stance against possible enemies waiting for the right time to attack.

However, it is very difficult to go on a campaign on horseback for those who run to bed as soon as they feel a bit sleepy, who have their breakfast as soon as they wake up, then have some snacks and have a lunch, and who want to be with their family all the time. One becomes an addict of such habits in time. Since these cannot be done on horseback, they chose not to be their soldiers' leader. Therefore, all of these signify a period of gradual decline. Actually, it is really so difficult to keep up the desired state at such a period when pleasures of the world smile at you invitingly. Maybe the Ottomans' most fruitful achievement for keeping up the desired state was to raise people of deep spirituality in the Sufi lodges. At the same time, the powerful chief religious scholars (sheikhulislam) they educated were also important factors. It seems that if it weren't for them, the process of decay may have started much earlier.

The Efforts for Elongation

The above mentioned considerations should not be taken as an allegation against the Ottomans. Such a process can be described as "conditional determinism." Such periods of decline seem inevitable for societies. A matter of extending life is always possible in the hands of able physicians. Then God Almighty may change His decree about the issue, depending on effective measures taken by people. This may be the very point Ibn Khaldun and other historians missed. Now let us clarify the point we made: God Almighty decrees a certain time period for the revival, rise, and decline of societies. But we cannot know the exact length of the period decreed. For example, take the volunteers devoted to reviving hearts, who say "If we cannot revive others, we will have no share of a revival." This may represent the first stage of a movement. As we cannot know the time limit decreed for them by Divine destiny, we cannot make a remark whether the movement will last for fifty years or more. Destiny is a manifestation of the knowledge of God, and we cannot know what this knowledge contains. Then no matter whatever stage we are going through, what befalls on us is to give our willpower its due and to try to make the good things in that period last longer. For example, there may be a decree about us as "If you behave such and such a way, you will experience a serious disintegration and will not be able to get back to your feet again." And let us also assume that the first signs of a decline have appeared. On the other hand, you really did your best and presented an ideal state. For instance, in spite of the fact that high worldly positions—as an undersecretary, minister, or a general director—were offered to you, you said, "How strange, I only seek God's good pleasure and try to glorify His Name, but these people are making irrelevant suggestions to me." Let us say that you presented such a dignified stance as a requirement of your sincerity. Thanks to the effort you made for keeping up your true spirit, the Divine Decree about you will be changed by another Divine Decree and thus you experience a new period of revival during what had previously been a process of disintegration. I just tried to elucidate the issue; let

nobody think that I take those positions lightly. They surely are important positions for a society, definitely needed in a state mechanism.
However, those devoted to a very important ideal should never expect
certain titles and worldly or otherworldly gains in return for the services they made; they should never leave a crack against such offers.
As long as people keep up their ideal state and spirit, they can keep their
vitality and add to the duration decreed as a certain society's lifetime.
For example, you witness the period when the devoted souls set
about their marathon, and thought to yourself that "With such performance, these people will continue this task for fifty years at least,
by God's grace." But if they keep up their state, receive good and correct spiritual nourishment, continuously attend contemplative dialogues, become oriented to seeking the good pleasure of God, and
retain their heartfelt trust in God, then the fifty years may extend to a
hundred. If their enthusiasm continues and their lives become pervad-
ed by a spiritual vigilance it can even be a hundred and fifty years.
Further than that, even at a period when the devoted souls become
engaged in economic, political, and cultural life, and worldliness
become dominant in different ways, as a period of culture where people seek consolation in arts and other activities, if people can still
retain their state to a certain degree, then they can even survive—
though sometimes by limping and sometimes under intensive care—
for another hundred and fifty years. A new endeavor in this respect and
turning to God anew can be a means of a new bestowal of God
Almighty, and an extra blessing.

If we get back to the main subject, the case of the Ottomans, it is
worthy of surprise not for its collapse but for having survived for so
long, as a state surrounded by so many adversaries. Even the issue of
some terrorist groups in the mountains has not been solved for twen-
ty-five years. Imagine that the Ottomans were surrounded by adversaries from all sides, including the seas. It was very difficult for the
Ottomans to rise up again as themselves while struggling against all
of them. Against all odds, they continued their existence and fulfilled
their historical mission to a certain extent. Taking all of these into con-

sideration, we need to declare and confess the merits of the Ottomans, honor their memory, and ask forgiveness from God for them. As they were exposed to continuous attacks by their adversaries from the East to the West, being located in a very strategic location where so many routes intersected, their continuity for six centuries is a surprising fact, in my humble opinion.

Gentleness and Elegance in Interpersonal Relations

Question: *In our time, many people are devoid of mannerliness in the way they behave or talk. Can mannerliness be learned from books? What are your recommendations for making good manners an ingrained quality of our personality?*

Answer: Mannerliness requires being chaste, decent, kind, and respectful in interpersonal relations; it requires avoiding attitudes that might break others' hearts even in the face of bad treatment or sorrowful events, and also keeping their words and behaviors in line with the essential traits of elegance, gentleness, and sincerity.

The Islamic world, which once built a civilization of mannerliness and elegance that would have made angels envious, unfortunately lost this quality after a certain period, and instead virtually entered a new age of ignorance, like the pre-Islamic Age of Ignorance. Referring to this truth, "The Ignorance of the Twentieth Century" was even used as a book name in Egypt. As a Turkish poet puts it, all the values Muslims possessed came crashing down, one by one. The Twentieth century is a time period that witnessed a total destruction of values within the system of belief, a system upon which an entire spiritual heritage took root to Muslims practices of worship and understanding of mannerliness. As Muslims lost practical contact with their religion, they also lost the importance of values, discipline, and terminology about good manners; in interpersonal relations, they became alienated to their own world of thought and culture, including their manners and courtesy. For example, in the Ottoman times, when a man was to refer to the son of another person he addressed, he would rather choose the courteous word *makhdum* (a master being served). If it was a daughter then he would courteously refer to her as *karima* (honored and treasured one). When the speaker had to refer to himself, he would humbly say "your slave." And when two people addressed one another, they would use phrases of respect like "your high person" or "my master." Such a style was not at all artificial. On the contrary, it was a natural outcome of people's cultivated manners. Today, we sometimes witness people using these courteous words mistakenly by referring not to others' but their own children. One thing I never forget is that, a university professor referred to himself by saying, "*My high person thinks thus at this issue...*" When I heard this, I did not know what to say. How did these phrases, which were an outward reflection of humbleness and spiritual refinement, come to be misused? It happened because we had not practiced courteous manners for a few centuries and failed to have them as an indispensable dimension of our lives. If you drive these cultivated manners, together with the morality and values they are based upon, out of practical life, then the words become dry forms devoid of meaning, condemned to oblivion. When you try to use these words abandoned of meaning and content as fanciful expressions, it will be inevitable for you to make such mistakes.

The Core of the Issue is Respect for the Human

Then what is it that needs to be done? First of all, we need to show the due respect the human essence merits, for God reveals that He created humanity as an honorable being of transcendent value: "*Surely We have created the human of the best stature as the perfect pattern of creation*" (at-Tin 95:4). This is the scale of human potential value. As it is known, the Messenger of God, peace and blessings be upon him, stood up out of respect when he saw a Jewish funeral passing.

When others reminded him that it was a Jewish funeral, without talking long, he reminded them that it was a human being.[142] Therefore, even if somebody shows disrespect toward you, you should never give up your respect for the Divinely honored human essence. If others scorn your values and present disrespect against God and His Messenger, then you should respond to them within the frame of your cultivated manners, which you should consider as your honor. You should not forget that you are Muslims and are equipped with the manners of the noble Prophet and the morals of the Qur'an. Then how can you possibly act like some others? Some might use ugly expressions, some might litter the places they pass and—if you excuse me—bare their teeth toward everyone. But you can never act like that. Even in the worst situations, you have to present your special and positive difference.

As a matter of fact, if somebody is a believer in the true sense of the word, their heart should miss a beat in the face of profanity against God and His Messenger. But an exemplary believer responds with careful manners and gentleness, saying "As a requirement of the cultivated behavior I learned from the blessed Prophet, I had better respond to them within such and such a frame," and they put up with negativities solely for the sake of God and His Messenger. On the other hand, they do not neglect to explain the truth of the matter to them in a soft and gentle style that conveys love and compassion. Thus, it is necessary to take "respect for humanity" as the basic idea and show respect toward all people in accordance with their degree. For example, you can show respect toward a person who does not share the same beliefs with you for being a servant of God, or toward another for being a believing servant. You may show respect toward another as for being a servant who accepts God in the right way, or toward another for being a servant who shares the same destiny with you and runs toward the same ideal. This way, the respect you show toward others grows into an immeasurable value by multiplying many times over. But first, this respect needs to emerge inside us.

---

[142] *Sahih al-Bukhari,* Janaiz, 50; *Sahih Muslim,* Janaiz, 81

Then our manners should reflect this feeling, and then by working through this issue continuously, it should become an ingrained part of our nature. As a part of established manners in a certain family, I knew some brothers who addressed one another by adding the respectable title "effendi" to their names. Be it the elder or younger brother, human essence actually deserves such respect. So you should accept this truth first, so that you can reflect it.

To give an example, the staff of a certain TV channel adopted a different attitude than the common one and started addressing one another with titles as "Mr…" In time, this became an established form of address and nobody found it unusual. It may have sounded a bit artificial at the beginning, but this consideration disappeared over time. In this respect, we had better try to revive all of our values that convey respect, one by one, and transfer them into practical life. Then we will be able to feel our identity as it is, and express ourselves comfortably in that atmosphere of respect. Therefore, nobody will encounter unpleasant expressions that will hurt them.

It Is High Time for Making a New Start, Be It with a Few People Only

Acceptance and internalization of such a code of manners takes a certain period of time; we are talking about a society exposed to a severe storm of disrespect for a long time. People usually talk without observing a certain measure or code in our time. It can be said that a kind of slang pervades the entire society. As for the language used in media, it is even worse than the society's. If you refer to dictionaries for the meanings of certain words used in media, you find notes stating that they are rude and slang expressions. In this respect, we should make a new start and undertake an effort to revive feelings of respect. At the beginning, only a few people will observe this code sensitively. Even if it remains limited to a certain circle at the beginning, they will make a positive difference with their manners and attitudes, and thus present a good example for others to follow.

As a matter of fact, volumes of works were written on good manners in Islamic culture. They can naturally be referred to. But it needs to be remembered that acceptance of matters only mentioned in books depends on their being practiced in specific circles. At a certain period in the past, people learned so much from the attitudes and behaviors of imams and muezzins while they preached in mosques. The society gained various beauties from the mosque. On the other hand, people in Sufi lodges gave a separate lesson on manners. Their relations were always centered on respect and reverence. Since life always continued with respect, it became an ingrained quality of people's nature. Therefore, people behaved in a respectful and mannerly way very spontaneously and without any artificial efforts. In the past, you would come across fifty of those blessed places. You would see fifty different sages teaching the beauties of this spiritual heritage. The people who visited those places would definitely receive their shares from these lessons. Now the streets are going through a dreadful shortage in this respect. Some establishments have lost their fruitful characters and some do not exist at all. In addition, there are no persons to teach the high moral code of Islam to others. This is why I pointed out the necessity of reviving these manners among a limited number of people in certain circles. A group of friends staying in an apartment can say "Bismillah" (In the Name of God) and start reviving such respect and manners with a resolution to attain this character. Although the issue of manners seems secondary in comparison to crucial issues such as faith in God, the Prophets, resurrection, and offering the Prayers seriously, these disciplines should not be neglected. The Pride of Humanity, peace and blessings be upon him, stated that faith consists of more than seventy subdivisions, and that the foremost one is faith in God whereas the pettiest one is to remove things on the way that will bother people.[143] This pettiest subdivision of faith is a kind of good manner as well. In the same way, smiling at a believer one meets,[144] or giving the water one pulls out of a well to another

---

[143] *Sahih Muslim*, Iman, 58; *Sunan at-Tirmidhi*, Iman, 6; *Sunan Abu Dawud*, Sunnah, 14

[144] *Sahih Muslim*, Birr, 144; *Sunan at-Tirmidhi*, Birr, 36, 45

person,[145] are also included among the subdivisions of faith and they should never be seen as unimportant.

As a final point, let me state that all subdivisions of faith and deeds related to them are complementary components. If you practice certain manners for seeking the good pleasure of God, they also serve as reminders of God, His Messenger, and Judgment Day to you. A single moment of remembering God and togetherness with Him for a split second is worth thousands of years spent without Him. Then, even though they seem to be petty, such matters are so great with respect to the meaning they stand for. For this reason, no matter what others do, we need to revive our own understanding of refinement, by referring to the manners of Islam and the Qur'an.

---

[145] *Sunan at-Tirmidhi*, Birr, 36; Al-Bazzar, *Al-Musnad*, 9/457–458

Invitation for Divine Providence

Question: *It is stated that believers are supposed to present a Prophetic diligence, on one hand, and to see the totality of their own efforts merely as a subordinate act to succeed at gaining the good pleasure of God, serving humanity, and making an invitation for Divine Providence. Could you please elucidate this consideration?*

Answer: Believers should be devoted to a noble ideal with respect to the intentions, efforts, projects, and plans they make; they should be ready to give everything if necessary. It is possible to describe this as a Prophetic diligence. Because, the way to make a lasting influence on hearts depends on possessing the lofty characters of the Prophets, the true guides of humanity. Their attributes such as innocence, trustworthiness, perspicacity, and conveyance of Divine truths are different spiritual profundities of those distinguished figures of the skies of humanity. These lofty attributes constitute their spiritual make-up. By the entirety of these virtues, God granted them perfection; a perfect religious teaching could not be established by imperfect ones to represent them. God Almighty decreed, *"This day, I have perfected your religion for you and I have completed My favor upon you,"* (al-Maedah 5:3) and He did it through the hands of His Prophets. Then the journeyers on the path of the Prophets are supposed to seek perfection in faith, practicing Islam, sincerity, and zeal.

"If I Am to Act Arrogantly..."

The Messenger of God appointed Abu Bakr as the imam after him, on the night prior to the day he passed away. Just as it was an important merit for Abu Bakr, may God be pleased with him, to welcome his new duty,[146] it was another merit for the congregation to welcome him as their imam. The broad horizons of the Companions enabled them to pledge allegiance to their new leader without much difficulty or confusion. In the meantime, the noble Prophet drew the curtain aside and saw his followers praying serenely behind their blessed leader and closed the curtain, smiling with the contentment of having fulfilled his duty.[147] The curtain was closed against the world as well. But the Pride of Humanity, peace and blessings be upon him, was glad while leaving this world; the distinguished group of people who would shoulder the cause of faith stood in the Divine presence with a spirit of unity. As this had been the goal of his blessed life, the Prince of both worlds closed the curtain on this world in serenity and contentment. We see the same noble thoughts and feelings after his meeting with the jinn to convey the Divine teachings to them. Abdullah ibn Mas'ud narrated that after this meeting, the Messenger of God stated that he had received the promise that people and jinn would accept faith, that people believed, and now the jinn also accepted faith; thus, the promise came real. Therefore, his mission was over and implied that he was soon to depart from this world.[148] The Prince of both worlds took his mission as the very goal of his staying in this world. As soon as it was over, he wished to be freed from the prison of the body and meet the True Friend.[149]

As a matter of fact, such a lofty thought should be the goal of every individual in love with the Qur'an, of everyone who seeks to realize a new revival for humanity. A hero of revival must dedicate his or her life to working for this noble ideal. They should even be able to say,

---

[146] *Sahih al-Bukhari*, Adhan, 51; *Sahih Muslim*, Salah, 90–97

[147] *Sahih al-Bukhari*, Adhan, 94; Amal fi's-Salah, 6; Maghazi, 83; *Sahih Muslim*, Salah, 98

[148] At-Tabarani, *Al-Mu'jamu'l-Kabir*, 10/67

[149] *Sahih al-Bukhari*, Fazailu Ashabi'n-Nabi, 5; Maghazi, 83–84, Da'awat, 29; Riqaq, 41; *Sahih Muslim*, Salam, 46; Fazailu's-Sahaba, 85

"My God, so far you have honored me by letting me serve on Your path, which is a means of agreement and unity between people. After this day, if I am to act egoistically and cause disagreement and conflicts because of my selfish concerns, please take my soul to Your side, so that You save it from toppling over and falling into ruin." One should adopt this noble approach all the time and pray to God after going to bed every night with the consideration: "If I am to serve faith in any way, then my staying in this world bears a meaning; otherwise it doesn't." What becomes a believer is to make a resolution to become like the Prophets; a believer should seek to be equipped with the noble ones' virtues, saying "My God, You can make potentials develop further. You have the absolute power and Your decrees can change anything destined;[150] bestow us unbound potentials, and grant brand new realizations to our potentials! Make us succeed in interpreting and evaluating everything more correctly!"

Unless Divinely commissioned, no person can attain the level of the Prophets, who are bestowed special abilities so that they can guide humanity. It is even very difficult for an ordinary person to equal the levels of the great imams such as Imam al-Azam Abu Hanifa, Imam Shafi, Ahmad ibn Hanbal, Awzai, and Sawri. The imams of the four Sunni schools are figures of particularly exceptional standing, even surpassing great saints (aqtab). In addition to realizing a very important revival with the books they wrote and the disciples they taught, they fulfilled a very important duty by maintaining a continuity of the feeling and thought of revival.

Given that We Manage to Eliminate Our Ego

Even trying to follow the footsteps of the Prophets (in a secondary sense) is too difficult a task for ordinary people like us. But against all odds, believers should always aim for very high horizons regarding their relations with God Almighty and serving on His path. While ask-

---

[150] The original phrases (qadar, qada, ata) Gülen uses are related to destiny in Islamic Theology. As destiny belongs to God, he can bring decreed things to existence (qada) or change something destined to happen (ata) as He wills.

ing for these high virtues from God, it is necessary to carry out what we must do with sincerity. The efforts made for walking on the path of the Prophets, and other great guides that followed them, can be seen as an invitation for Divine providence. This can be compared to the situation of a person who does not know how to swim but still jumps into the sea and exerts himself there. Those who witness that will naturally say, "Look at that man! It seems he doesn't know how to swim. Let us save him." In the same way, such a person trying to walk on the path of the great guides can say, "My God, it is beyond my power to give this path its due, but I have set forth for this sake. I see that all of the Prophets and saints were able to swim in this sea. Even though I cannot swim, I am resolved to follow their example." Having made this intention, jumping into the sea will be an invitation for Divine providence. God Almighty does not let down those who turn to Him so sincerely and saves them from drowning. Then He opens new horizons before them, making an atom into a sun, and making nothing into everything for those servants of His... given that we eliminate our ego with this consideration, given that we rid ourselves of arrogant claims. As it is known, zero has no value on its own. But if somebody puts a figure near it, then it suddenly gains tenfold in value. For this reason, believers should exert themselves, but they should also stay humble, recognizing their true position, and watching their steps carefully. They should never lay claim to beauties bestowed upon them, and should never forget that they are not the original source but only serve as a conveyor for those blessings to the rest of the world. No beauty bestowed upon us is an essential property of ours. Like bubbles on water that show a reflection of the sun, beauties are sometimes manifested on us and sometimes not; all of them belong to the Creator of all beauties. People with such consciousness can make their efforts truly fruitful. They witness the realization of the command "*If you are thankful (for My favors), I will most certainly give you more*" (Ibrahim 14:7), and enjoy more and more Divine blessings.

Baseless Negative Opinions and Envy

Q uestion: *Baseless negative opinions and envy are referred to as spiritual diseases. What are the causes of such problems? How can they be treated?*

Answer: Holding baseless negative opinions about others and envying them are both grave sins. One gives way to another. Someone who views another person through a lens of negative opinion begins to develop hostile feelings toward that person unawares, as a consequence of attaching a bad meaning to everything he or she does. Similarly, somebody can have negative impressions stemming from even the most innocent attitudes and behaviors of a person whom they envy and feel hostility toward. For example, the person they envy can be a man who strives to serve in the path of God; but the envier sees that man as one who tries to show off by proving himself, and thus always attaches a negative meaning to all of his acts In short, these two sins form a vicious cycle that feed one another. However, believers should seek not a vicious but a righteous cycle. That is, they should always seek righteous conduct so that everything they do paves the way for other good acts. Thus they will be seeking to do another good act as soon as they finish one.

Sparkle and Fire

Actually, baseless negative opinions and envy emerge as little deviations at the beginning. However, if one does not give the willpower its proper due and take necessary precautions, those inclinations transform into spiritual diseases over time. In other words, a crack at the center becomes a huge chasm on the periphery. For example, an envious person becomes unable to tolerate even otherworldly acts— like Prayers and pilgrimage—of the person they envy. This envy becomes so grave that this diseased mood transforms into intolerance to the degree of unbelief; this causes them to make wishes hardly compatible with faith such as "I wish he breaks his arm or has a plane crash and thus will not be able to go to pilgrimage." For this reason, it is essential to take action from the very beginning against such feelings that appear as small seeds in the heart. One cannot let them grow into invitations for much greater sins. It is easier to deal with them at earlier phases. If those symptoms are not removed with repentance and asking forgiveness (*tawbah* and *istighfar*) as soon as they make their first appearance, but are allowed to grow, they might darken the entire heart and cause it to be sealed up, as a sign of having lost its ability to believe. Bediüzzaman refers to this fact in "The Second Gleam": "Sin penetrates to the heart, darkens and hardens it until it extinguishes the light of belief. Each sin has a path that leads to unbelief. Unless that sin is swiftly obliterated by seeking God's forgiveness, it grows from a worm into a snake that gnaws at the heart."[151] The Messenger of God, peace and blessings be upon him, also referred to this truth. Accordingly, when one commits a sin, a dark dot is placed on his heart. When he gives up, asks forgiveness, and repents, his heart regains its luster. But if he persists at sinning, then the dark dot grows and covers the heart. This is the rust God mentions as "...*what they themselves have earned has rusted upon their hearts (and prevents them from perceiving the truth)*" (al-Mutaffifin 83:14).[152]

It is understood from the explanation of the noble Prophet that sins do not leave a stain on the physical heart but our spiritual life. Every such stain is an invitation to another. As a germ that settles on your tooth calls other germs for damaging the tooth and gums, the stain on the heart does not like to remain alone. As stains follow one another, they become a manifestation of the truth stated in the

---

[151] Nursi, *The Gleams*, p. 12
[152] *Sunan at-Tirmidhi*, Tafsir as-Surah (83), 1; *Sunan ibn Majah*, Zuhd, 29

Qur'an: *"What they themselves have earned has rusted upon their hearts."* After such darkening, it is not possible to see clearly what is right and wrong. For this reason, that person walks on the wrong path by mistaking it as the righteous one.

Attending the Circles of Contemplative Dialogue on the Beloved

The most important and efficient way of ridding oneself from this danger is to renew faith, every day, by forming the circles of talks on the Beloved—even if only with a few people. Diseases of this kind can only be treated with the truths of faith people freshly feel in their consciences all the time. For this reason one should be able to view faith from a different perspective every day, and be able to say, "My God, I did not know you this way, I now see that there was so much that went undiscovered. But now, I feel you with a much different profundity in my conscience," and thus they awaken to a fresh horizon of faith and knowledge of God.

The belief in resurrection must be approached the same way; the awareness of being called to account on the Day of Judgment must play a determining role on our actions. Attaining eternal bliss in Paradise depends on passing successfully through the grave and the following process of reckoning. If we cannot—may God forbid—then the end will be terribly grim. For this reason, we need to know matters of faith like we know the alphabet and try to feel it anew in our consciences every day with a new hue, pattern, and articulation.

In addition to belief in the Afterlife, belief in the message of the blessed Prophet must also be handled with the same degree of importance, and it should be presented in such a way that people should not be able to help but sigh deeply[153] at the very thought of God's Messenger. We must believe in the Divine decree and destiny in such a way that even in the face of great misfortunes, we are able to say "Goodness is in what God decrees"[154] or "All praise and thanks are for God for

---

[153] The original phrase is literally translated as "yearning to the degree of feeling a spasm in the nose bones."

[154] Aliyyu'l-Qari, *Al-Asraru'l-Marfua*, 196; Al-Ajluni, *Kashfu'l-Khafa*, 1/478

every state, save unbelief and misguidance."[155] We should be able to say, "There must be some goodness, underlying wisdom in it. So it seems that God is warning us." As it is very important to concentrate on truths of faith, it is also very important to observe Islamic essentials impeccably, with a sound consciousness of obedience to Divine orders. Grasping the essence of how to obey the orders is more important than the personal judgment of a thousand intellects. Satan used his magnificent intellect and went astray. As for Prophet Adam, peace be upon him, after a temporary lapse, he grasped the essence of obeying the orders, rose back again, and even excelled angels with his incredible progress. In the name of making all of these real, those who have a bit of useful knowledge and are able to talk must become mobilized for such lessons. Everybody must run from one session to another, and orient matters to the Eternally-Sought Beloved. Just as medical precautions are taken against seasonal infections in fall, precautions against spiritual diseases, which are much graver than physical ones, must be taken by developing due plans and projects. Physical diseases might cost a temporary life, at the most. But spiritual ones not only kill the heart in this world but they also ruin an eternal afterlife. In this respect, early intervention is crucial.

On the other hand, I doubt whether those in a position to provide spiritual guidance to others can treat such problems as jealousy and the inability to stand others' merits successfully; it is God who decides whether to remove any rust or seal on individuals' hearts. Anyway, what befalls on us is to do our best, in compliance with the Divine decree: *"And that human has only that for which he labors, and his labor will be brought forth to be seen"* (an-Najm 53:39–40). A true believer should strive to make up for the cracks and fissures that appear in individual and societal life, to cure those who suffer from disease, to lend a hand to those shaken or stumbling, and to remove negative considerations that pollute people's minds. This is the faithfulness a believer owes to humanity; its opposite will be a grim indication of unfaithfulness, and a loss of one's humane sensitivity.

---

[155] Nursi, The Gleams, p. 15

Benefiting from Contemplative Dialogues and Counsels

Question: *Could you explain the essential principles to be observed in order to benefit from spiritual advice in the best way, with respect to both the speaker and listener?*

Answer: *Nasihah* (advice) means living with the idea of doing good to others. The manner of doing good and the relation between the speaker and the listener might show differences according to different persons or societies. Some try to do good to others by counseling, authoring books, preparing brochures, and different other ways as their position and means allow, and thus appeal to their spirit. Spiritual advice is a very important need for everybody, no matter their walk of life. The Qur'an draws attention to this important point with the command, *"But remind and warn, for reminding and warning are of benefit to the believers"* (adh-Dhariyat 51:55). The act of reminding and warning mentioned in the verse has differing degrees of meaning that refer to faith (*iman*), Islam, and *ihsan*,[156] deepening in faith, and inviting someone to comprehend Islam as a whole. The inflection of the original Arabic word (as *dhakkara*) is noteworthy, for it denotes the significance and continuity of reminding. This form (of *taf'il*) denotes

---

[156] *Ihsan*: consciousness of omnipresence of God, or perfect goodness.

abundance in quantity. Accordingly, the verse commands continually reminding and giving advice. In other words, do not give up giving advice by saying, "I have said what needs to be told two or three times already, but people keep living in obdurate heedlessness;" instead, keep reminding as a continuous responsibility, for it will definitely be beneficial to believers.

The Messenger of God, peace and blessings be upon him, pointed out this truth with his invaluable words of wisdom that religion is sincere counselling and good advice.[157] Giving advice is an essential aspect of practicing religion in individual and societal level. If this duty is not fulfilled, then the religion is destined to fall, sooner or later. As a matter of fact, the blessed life of God's Messenger was centered on advice. He would sit at his mosque in Medina at certain times of day, and the Companions formed circles around him. Some would ask questions about worship, some about his statements they could not understand, and some would ask about the meaning of certain verses in the Qur'an. He never turned down any of them. In his entire lifetime, he only retreated to a corner away from his wives at one occasion; no other such case is reported during his mission.[158] He would stay among his Companions, explain verses of the Qur'an, answer their questions, and settle their problems. This is how most of the verbal statements in *hadith* sources were made. As for his exemplary behavior, recorded in *hadith* sources as "af'al an-Nabawi," or "acts of the noble Prophet," they constituted the practical aspect of his tradition. In addition, his keeping silent before practices he witnessed was taken as "approval," which constituted another aspect of his Sunnah. In other words, the silence he presented served as a criterion about states and behaviors acceptable in religion. In accordance with that, the Companions decided whether something was acceptable. These were the three ways in which he continuously conveyed what needed to be taught.

---

[157] *Sahih al-Bukhari*, Iman, 42; *Sahih Muslim*, Iman, 95

[158] At-Tahrim 66:1–5; *Sahih al-Bukhari*, Ilim, 27; Sawm, 11; Mazalim, 25; Nikah, 83, 91, 92; Talaq, 21; Ayman, 20; Sahih Muslim, Talaq, 30

Talking according to the Needs of Listeners

If both the speakers and the listeners are sincere, a question-answer format can make a religious talk more efficient. Otherwise, a speaker who does not take listeners' feelings and needs into consideration may think he delivers great speeches, but the matters he tells will not be of any permanent benefit for them. For this reason, like a teacher who follows a school curriculum by distributing subjects to different weeks and months, and teaches them gradually in a way to suit the level of the students, a religious instructor must convey what he or she will tell within a gradual plan that suits the capacity and knowledge of their audience; this will help them digest and internalize the issues being told. However, only those who can behold the issue with an overall view can present the subjects like that. As for the topics to be told by those who try to save the day, they will fail to make up a harmonious whole, and thus not yield the desired benefit for the listeners.

In this respect, what the society needs should be determined well. For example, if the Daily Prayers are not observed as they should be, the program needs to have the truth and essence of the Prayers at its core. If the Messenger of God, peace and blessings be upon him, is not properly known in a way that exemplifies his true worth, then he should be introduced with all of his aspects in order to work heartfelt love for him into souls. In the meantime, it will be wise to give the listeners an opportunity to ask the questions in their mind and thus allow deeper comprehension. Thus, like releasing a bucket into a water-well possessing good potential and bringing it into life by drawing out more and more, the questions they ask will help the speaker to expound on the issue better. The listeners gleaming knowledge from the speaker determines whether a talk is nourishing or not.

Self-Effacement

On the other hand, the speaker needs to be sincere, and the listeners need to be willing to benefit from what is told, so that the advice can be helpful. Since religion is a Divine system decreed by God, it definitely needs to be told with a consciousness of a dynamic relation with

Him. Besides, instructors must enter the subject through utter self-effacement, virtually becoming one of the characters being depicted. While telling about a hero such as Hamza or Anas ibn Nadr, they must virtually become that person and leave oneself to the flow of the subject. You can compare this to the Sufi way of becoming totally oriented to, or annihilated (*fana*) within, a given ideal, and refer to it as becoming "annihilated" in the religious talk. If the instructor tells the subject so deeply he merges with it, his or her crying, smiles, or speaking emotionally depend on the unfolding of the subject. Acquiring this state depends on a person's believing with heartfelt sincerity in what he or she tells. As for those who listen to this interaction, they should be able to enter into the subject together with the teller. For example, if a battlefield or ascension to spiritual realms is being depicted, the audience must be right there with the teller of the story, insofar as their imagination and conception allow.

Every Prejudice Is a Barrier

It is essential for listeners not to hold negative opinions about the instructor. They must be ready to welcome what is being told. If the words being uttered are not only to reach the ears but also the hearts of listeners, and be successfully processed in different mechanisms of consideration, the listeners have to be free from prejudices.

In addition, in order for a person to properly benefit from a talk, he or she similarly needs to be free from feelings like jealousy and covetousness; they must not make egocentric emphases, and avoid showing off their knowledge about the subjects being told. Even if some of the points being made do not sound totally agreeable, the listener should say, "We can discuss and settle this point after the session," and listen attentively in spite of all, keeping one's mind and heart constantly receptive to the message.

If there is a flaw about any of the points we have mentioned, it is inevitable there will be a breakdown of communication between the teller and listener. While listening, if we are including our own grudges, biases, egotism, arrogance, or boastful knowledge, then the emphasis we try to lay on our own person becomes a barrier against benefiting from the other person. Even if individuals in such a mood listened to the great masters such as Imam al-Ghazali, Imam Rabbani, or Bediüzzaman, and even if they had the honor to listen to the blessed Prophet himself, they still could not benefit from the talk. As a matter of fact, so many people like Abu Lahab and Abu Jahl did listen to him without benefiting. Today as well, many of their counterparts listen to the Qur'an and Sunnah, or hear the talks of truthful guides, but they do not benefit from these at all.

Let me express as a final point that just as achievement or authority are elements of being tested, knowledge is also a means of testing, and it causes most people to lose. The thought of "I already know" becomes such a screen that it prevents people from benefiting from a religious instructor. It might also be a factor in distancing that person from the Divine's teaching completely. God Almighty makes a warning in this respect: "*When an affliction befalls human, he calls upon Us (to save him). Then, when We (from sheer grace) have bestowed a favor upon him from Us, he says: 'I have been given this only by virtue of a certain knowledge that I have.' No, indeed... Rather, this (favor bestowed on a human) is a trial, but most of them do not know*" (az-Zumar 39:49). In fact, any blessing that distances a person from God is nothing but a "misfortune in disguise." Blessings that arrive as different positions and titles at different universities or administrative units stand for nothing but a curse as far as they cause people to become oblivious of God. The way to be protected from such danger is that, both the listener and the teller must approach the issue solely for the sake of God's good pleasure and the compass of the heart must always be oriented accordingly. Both the speaker and the audience need to go through a personal process of internal orientation at the very beginning. Fifty times at least, they need to slam a hammer on their carnal soul by not siding with it, by not holding themselves pure to be purified of evil attitudes.[159] If there is such essential preparation and initiation to the issue with sincere intention and inner purity, by God's grace, spiritual advice and talks will be much more efficient, fruitful, and beneficial.

---

[159] Nursi, *The Words*, p. 495

The Most Exalted Purpose and
the Feeling of Curiosity

Question: *In our time, the feeling of curiosity is often directed toward daily news, political polemics, or the lives of celebrities. What is the Divine wisdom behind equipping humanity with this feeling?*

Answer: The feeling of curiosity is an important factor that triggers a thirst for knowledge and a zeal for exploring other lives. One should use such an important dynamic for the sake of an exalted and noble ideal. What can be the most exalted ideal for a person? I think the most important ideal is to recognize and know the Almighty One, Who brought us into existence from nothing, Who rendered us the most honorable one among all of creation, Who laid this world before us as a corridor to Paradise, Who beautified the universe with manifestations of the Divine Names as an arable field for the Hereafter, Who sent us perfectly dependable guides to let us see beyond the veil and the truth of everything. For this reason, one must prepare for a lifetime of curiosity, using it to seek to know the Divine Essence as best as one can, beyond all forms and measures.

The Divine Essence is Absolutely beyond Comprehension

At this point, one statement of God's Messenger is an important criterion for us: "Reflect on God Almighty's works of blessings and power!

But do not ever attempt to reflect on the Divine Essence, for that issue transcends human conception."[160] Some people may have sensed and felt certain things related to the Divine Essence, in accordance with the immensity of their conscience and depth of their feelings and senses. However, these truths cannot be generalized for everyone. For this reason, what befalls on believers is to comply with the limit set by the Pride of Humanity, peace and blessings be upon him, and circulate within the sphere of Divine Names and Attributes. The Qur'an also points out this fact: *"Eyes comprehend Him not, but He comprehends all eyes"* (al-An'am 6:103). The Divine Essence transcends everything and it cannot be comprehended; something that absolutely encompasses everything cannot at the same time be encompassed by cognition. Given that He is the One that encompasses everything; the ones encompassed cannot encompass the One that encompasses. For this reason, people need to be aware of what they can know, to what extent, and how they should know, and then try to learn what they can within the allowed fields.

Gaining knowledge leads to loving Him, and the more seekers love Him, the more they wish to know about Him. Bediüzzaman also draws attention to this lofty truth, which is the real purpose of human existence, through the following words: "Belief in God is creation's highest aim and most sublime result, and humanity's most exalted rank is knowledge of Him. The most radiant happiness and sweetest bounty for jinn and humanity is love of God contained within knowledge of God. The human spirit's purest joy and the human heart's sheerest delight is spiritual ecstasy contained within love of God"[161] Here, in addition to asking for knowledge and love of God, Bediüzzaman refers to spiritual ecstasy or delight as an objective. But if you wish, you can ask for it to be spared for the afterlife, as well. However, it should be known that spiritual delight is not something to be dismissed. Who knows, when spiritual delight is manifested within, you will perhaps ask for more and feel eager to make deeper quests.

---

[160] At-Tabarani, *Al-Mu'jamu'l-Awsat*, 6/250; Al-Bayhaqi, *Shuabu'l-Iman*, 1/136; Abu'sh-Shayh, *Al-Azama*, 1/220

[161] Nursi, *The Letters*, pp. 239–240

If we can know God Almighty in such an immensity of knowledge, I think we will plan our lives accordingly, always try to walk in that direction, and will hardly be able to contain ourselves with the enthusiasm of making others feel what we experienced. I guess a similar immensity and depth of knowing God lay behind the relevant zeal and enthusiasm of the Companions of the noble Prophet and the Apostles of Jesus. They knew God so well, felt and sensed Him very well in their consciences, and thus their faith continued to deepen. As a consequence, this provoked such an enthusiasm in them that they maintained a spiritual vigilance with the consideration of "We should mention about the All-Holy Who manifests Himself all the time." In addition to faith in God, as believers get to gain insight into other articles of faith and essentials of religion with their true nature, they will begin to feel a deep interest in them. For example, when one feels curious about the worth of the Prince of both worlds in the sight of God, and what the message he brought stands for within humanity, then that person sets about to know the noble Prophet in the way he should be known. Thus knowing more about him evokes further love and respect for him. In time, the journeyer virtually witnesses the blessed Prophet as a guide who shows the way regarding everything. Deepening the essentials of faith and religion helps us better know their beauties, and allows our nature to conform to them. A person who feels all of these in their conscience will not be able to help but say, "My God, we are infinitely indebted to You! It is so glad that You enabled us—in spite of our own narrowness—to recognize and know You and Your Messenger. You have bestowed us the blessing of Islam, which is so crucial for our lives, and which helps us gain proximity to You. My God, thousands of praises and glory be to You! Then like Bediüzzaman's journeyer through the universe in "The Supreme Sign,"[162] he or she will ask for more and try to dig a bit further into the ground of knowledge of God. If you stand beside a well and set about drawing up water from it, I think the water will come out more as you draw more. As the water of the well gushes forth, it will spur

---

[162] For *Ayatu'l Kubra* (the Supreme Sign), see "The Seventh Ray" in *The Rays*, Bediüzzaman Said Nursi, New Jersey: Tughra Books, 2010.

up your enthusiasm to draw more. So you feel excited every time, with an insatiable zeal, and become an "asker for more."

Curiosity Is the Teacher of Knowledge

Curiosity is a very important factor in terms of reading this universe like a book of wisdom. In the words of Bediüzzaman, "Curiosity about something leads one to learn about it."[163] Knowledge (*ilm*) mentioned here does not refer to the narrow sense of knowledge, as in scientific knowledge. It refers to outward knowing, through theory, and inward knowing, through spiritual experience, which leads to knowing God through heartfelt love, and then to experiencing fervent love and enthusiasm for Him. Therefore, the knowledge referred to in the Divine command, "*Say: 'My Lord, increase me in knowledge'*" (Ta-Ha 20:114) is not an abstract knowing of phenomena; it is a knowing that yields spiritual insight, that leads to a "culture of the conscience," results in love of God, and extends to the depths of fervent love and enthusiasm for Him. So curiosity's being the teacher of knowledge needs to be taken in this sense.

In fact, some worldly people are curious, to a certain extent, about reading the universe like a book. Their curiosity is creditable. However, they view the issue with a materialistic perspective and from the limited frame of the laws of physics. Therefore, they find no prospect for metaphysical considerations. Some of those people may also have a potential for matters of spirituality. Moreover, some of them may have delved deep into immensities of parapsychology. For example, even while materialism was at its peak, communication with spirits and jinn was quite common. Even the famous Victor Hugo presented such weakness. When you study *Les Misérables* carefully, you can sense this sort of inclination in between the lines. It was not only Victor Hugo; many more who held materialist views sought consolation in such activities. However, most of those people who were engaged in secular sciences took a limited distance because of lacking a spiritual guide or the inefficiency of the religious teaching they followed; they were unable to go further beyond.

---

[163] Nursi, *The Letters*, p. 456

In spite of everything, their meticulous study and exploration of phenomena deserves appreciation. As I mentioned at an earlier talk, there are so many people among them who dedicated their lives to studying the life of a single animal species. For example, one of them states that he devoted an entirety of twenty years to studying the life of scorpions. Another one did that for a cobra. All of these are consequences of curiosity. However, as we have mentioned above, they were never able to go beyond the physical reality and open their thoughts to metaphysical considerations. Never able to reach into the realm of the heart and spirit, they failed to wonder at the splendid workings within and be curious about their true Doer and Causer. In addition, it is not possible to witness anything in the physical realm that corresponds to our inherent yearning for eternity or other human immensities. Then all of such human yearnings have their source in another realm, and they serve to orient the individual to another realm. So the scientists and researchers unreceptive to metaphysics were deaf and blind to all such messages. Even though they condemned themselves to a barren path devoid of wisdom and reflection, a believer should avoid it. Thanks to the facts revealed to them about truths of faith, it is always possible for believers to deepen their considerations on humanity, the universe, and phenomena; then they soar toward different horizons of thought by reflection, rumination, and pondering. Naturally, everybody has his or her own capacity of comprehension and knowing. Actually, the three levels of certainty in Sufism—based on knowing, seeing, or direct experience—points to this difference between people. On the other hand, as a believer might read the creational commands by means of science, they must constantly refer to the Qur'an, which is the everlasting translator, lucid interpreter, and articulate proof of the universe;[164] this will enable them to correctly interpret the seemingly vague points in the creational commands, as a requisite to save them from wrong interpretations while studying natural sciences. Thus they will not only understand what the creation tells correctly, but also have deeper knowledge and love for the Unique One all those sciences point to.

---

[164] Nursi, *The Words*, p. 388

The Greatest Help from a Fellow Believer to Another: Prayer

Question: *It has become a common demand for people to say, "Pray for me." This demand is often made lackadaisically. Will you share your considerations on how we are supposed to respond to demands for prayer?*

Answer: Prayer is very important, both in terms of how we servants relate with our Creator, and regarding His treatment toward us, His servants. Above all, praying indicates a consciousness of one's dependence and relation with God. Raising hands in prayer is an indication of a person's consciousness of coming into contact with the most exalted authority. God Almighty's treatment for those who establish such a relation with Him will be different. By accepting this much of an effort from the servant as a means, God treats people benevolently, as becomes His greatness.

A Mysterious and Pure Kind of Worship

On the other hand, *dua* (supplication) is the title for imploring God independently from causes. In this respect, it is a mysterious and pure form of worship. Other worms of worship have an explanation within the sphere of reasons, even if they are spiritual ones. For instance, observing the Daily Prayers and making ablutions have their aspects that are displeasing to the carnal soul. Similarly, fasting or going to

Hajj require taking certain pains. Therefore, these pains might lead worshippers thinking they are making demands from God in return for what they did. However, opening one's hands in prayer and turning to God wholeheartedly with a consciousness of one's helplessness and poverty (unless there is unceasing Divine help) through the tongue of need is such a mysterious deed of servitude to God that it actually is a very sincere form of prayer. In this respect, *dua* has a special place among other forms of worship. When we view the life of the Pride of Humanity in this respect, we see that he spent his entire life as a form of prayer and he always implored God Almighty night and day. While going to bed,[165] rising from bed,[166] mounting his ride,[167] attending a military campaign;[168] meeting people,[169] and suffering trouble[170]... he always kept praying and wove every moment of life with it. When we look at his blessed statements on praying, we see that they are so well-placed and are a guide on how to open up to God Almighty. As the noble Prophet, who was a monument of self-possession, knew God best, he was the one who also knew the best way to ask from Him. The excellence of his carefully picked words of prayer, down to their smallest nuances, is compelling. As it is very important to turn to God with appropriate words, we can do this by means of the blessed statements of the noble Prophet. For this reason, even if one says a thousand times at prayer:

$$\text{"اَللَّهُمَّ إِنَّا نَسْأَلُكَ مِنْ خَيْرِ مَا سَأَلَكَ مِنْهُ نَبِيُّكَ مُحَمَّدٌ صَلَّى اللهُ عَلَيْهِ وَسَلَّمَ وَنَعُوذُ بِكَ مِنْ شَرِّ مَا اسْتَعَاذَ مِنْهُ نَبِيُّكَ مُحَمَّدٌ صَلَّى اللهُ عَلَيْهِ وَسَلَّمَ"}$$

---

[165] *Sahih Muslim*, Dhikr, 60; Ahmad ibn Hanbal, *Al-Musnad*, 2/79

[166] *Sahih al-Bukhari*, Da'awat, 7, 8, 16; Tawhid, 13; *Sahih Muslim*, Dhikr, 59

[167] *Sahih Muslim*, Hajj, 425; *Sunan at-Tirmidhi*, Da'awat, 46; *Sunan Abu Dawud*, Jihad, 72

[168] *Sunan at-Tirmidhi*, Da'awat, 41; Ahmad ibn Hanbal, *Al-Musnad*, 5/83

[169] An-Nawawi, *Al-Azkar*, 180

[170] *Sunan Abu Dawud*, Witr, 26; *Sunan ibn Majah*, Dua, 17; Ahmad ibn Hanbal, *Al-Musnad*, 6/369

"My God, I am asking from you every goodness Prophet Muhammad, peace and blessings be upon him, asked from You; and I seek refuge in You from any evil from which he sought refuge in You!" (because God's Messenger never asked for anything out of the sphere of God's good pleasure).[171]

The Noble Prophet's Demand for Prayer from His Companions

The issue of demand for prayer is also very important for sincere believers. The Prince of both worlds asked so many of his Companions to pray for him. For instance, when he was ill, he made such a demand from his wife, Aisha, to pray for him.[172] Before the Messenger of God passed to the eternal abode, he was virtually made to go through the sufferings his followers would, so that his spiritual rank would rise, the truth of *al-Maqam al-Mahmud* (the Praised Position) would be realized, his sphere of intercession would grow, and he would become ready to be granted the means and authority to embrace all of his followers. As it is also pointed out in a *hadith*, the Prophets are the people who suffer most.[173] For this reason, the crown of all Prophets suffered in the iron fist of illness, particularly in his final days. So much so that in order to alleviate the severe ache, he would have his head wrapped tightly.[174] In order to help him with this suffering, the mother of believers, Aisha, held his hand and prayed for him. However, during his final moments, when she wanted to hold his hand again, he withdrew his hand and stated that he wished the highest company of God Almighty.[175] He had understood that God willed to take His Messenger to the realm beyond and he prayed thus.

---

[171] *Sunan at-Tirmidhi*, Da'awat, 88
[172] *Sahih al-Bukhari*, Fazailu'l-Qur'an, 14; *Sahih Muslim*, Salam, 51
[173] *Sahih al-Bukhari*, Marda, 3; *Sunan at-Tirmidhi*, Zuhd, 57; *Sunan ibn Majah*, Fitan, 23
[174] *Sahih al-Bukhari*, Jumu'a, 29; Manaqibu'l-Ansar, 11; At-Tabarani, *Al-Mu'jamu'l-Kabir*, 11/263; Al-Bayhaqi, *As-Sunanu'l-Kubra*, 6/371
[175] *Sahih al-Bukhari*, Fazailu Ashabi'n-Nabi, 5; Maghazi, 83–84, Da'awat, 29; Riqaq, 41; *Sahih Muslim*, Salam, 46; Fazailu's-Sahaba, 85

In another case, when Umar ibn al-Khattab asked permission from him for *Umrah*, he gave permission and added, "My brother, do not forget us in your prayers."[176]

In spite of the fact that he led a life under Divine protection in absolute independence from asking anything from anyone else, and that God Almighty accepted all of his prayers, he still asked Umar and other Companions to pray for him; this indicates that the issue is a very serious one that cannot be taken lightly.

The Fastest Accepted Prayer

In a *hadith* related to the subject, the Messenger of God, peace and blessings be upon him, stated: "The fastest accepted prayer is that which one makes for another in absentia."[177]

As Bediüzzaman tells the conditions for acceptance of a prayer in "The Twenty-Third Letter," he refers to this fact as well, and underlines that prayers made in absentia are hoped to be acceptable.[178] In addition, in many different parts of his works, he mentioned that "You (those who study the *Risale-i Nur*) are included in my prayers in the morning and evening. May you also please include me in your prayers. In this world, a believers greatest help to a fellow believer is through praying."[179] He went on to say, "... as for Said, your brother in faith, is together with you by means of praying at God's door in the morning and evening..."[180] and "... I am asking for prayer from you and from your mother, whom I consider as my second mother. Given that I include you in my prayers, you also pray for acceptance of my prayers please."[181] Lastly he said, "... I include them in my prayers, let them pray for me too..."[182] With such expressions, he indicated that this issue should not be taken lightly.

---

[176] *Sunan Abu Dawud*, Witr, 23; Ahmad ibn Hanbal, *Al-Musnad*, 1/29, 2/59
[177] *Sunan Abu Dawud*, Witr, 29; Abd ibn Humayd, *Al-Musnad*, 134
[178] Nursi, *The Letters*, p. 297
[179] Nursi, *Barla Lâhikası*, p. 234
[180] Ibid., p. 342
[181] Ibid., p. 267
[182] Ibid., p. 306

I would like to expound on one point underlined in the question: As the spirit and significant meaning of this issue becomes more common, people can use expressions like, "My brother, pray for us too," in a lackadaisical fashion. For this reason, the person who asks for prayer must be very sincere in the asking. They are not to be insouciant but serious. While making a demand for prayer, we always need to think, "God willing, he or she prays for me, and God willing, his or her prayers will be accepted," and believe that God will accept prayers made sincerely in absentia. In this respect, the dominant consideration in our mind had better be thus: "If it were not for righteous believers' prayers, which will be an invitation for Divine providence and due manifestation of help, I consider myself facing a great danger. God forbid, I am afraid of going astray into misguidance." With such considerations, it is possible to make a wish for prayers by saying, "My brother, if it is not going to be a burden for you, please, for the sake of God, while you pray for all of your fellow believers, if you can remember, also mention me in your prayers." A person who asks to be prayed for by someone else needs to be conscious of one's own impotence, poverty, and weakness, and see the prayer by someone else as a great means for Divine help.

Praying and Being Faithful

As one person demands to be prayed for with these considerations in mind, the person who is asked to pray should not neglect to pray for the asker as a faithful response. Upon such a demand, they can get up in the night, observe some Prayers—Tahajjud, Salatu'l-Hajah (Prayer of Need) or another—and then open their hands to God for whomever they wish, and then spare at least few minutes for the person who asks for being prayed for. Sparing such precious moments for another friend instead of praying for oneself—asking to be taken to Paradise once instead of five times—is an important form of faithfulness. This actually means, "My God, here I open up to you and seek refuge in Your faithfulness for a fellow believer." It should not be forgotten that nobody can be as faithful as God Almighty.

In the same way, let us imagine that they bring a list of a hundred names to a man and say, "These are the names of the devoted souls who travel to four corners of the world for serving humanity, who get by with a modest living and do not prove us wrong in our positive opinion of them. We are asking you to pray for them so that they stand upright where they go, their services become fruitful, and so that they do not face any obstacles." As a necessity of being faithful toward the people who hold such a positive opinion of him, the man must open his hands by taking good advantage of the invaluable hours of the night when God Almighty descends His mercy and graces to the heavens of the world and asks whether anybody prays to Him so that He will accept their prayers.[183] Then he must pray for the names on the list, whether the names are familiar to him or not.

Prayers That Receive a Visa of Consciousness

While doing all of these, it is important for the person who prays to utter every word by applying a visa of consciousness to them. The Messenger of God, peace and blessings be upon him, stated that God Almighty does not accept the prayers of one who is not aware of what he is saying.[184] For this reason, every word uttered while praying must be coming from the bottom of one's heart. By the way, let me point out the possibility of danger for the person demanded to pray. If a man lives within a circle of people who strive to serve humanity for the sake of God, the others may ask for that man to pray for them, purely out of the positive thoughts they cherish about him. It is natural for them to cherish such ideas, and it should never be taken lightly; underestimating such faithfulness will be a kind of disrespect toward God by underestimating His good pleasure. Anyway, if that man led an upright life for some fifty years, it is natural for his fellows to have a positive opinion of him. I do not care how profound that person is with respect to the shared ideals and whether he thoroughly fulfilled his responsibilities. By abstracting the matter from all of these, I look

---

[183] *Sahih al-Bukhari*, Tawhid, 35; Tahajjud, 14; *Sahih Muslim*, Salatu'l-Musafirin, 166
[184] *Sunan at-Tirmidhi*, Da'awat, 65; Al-Hakim, *Al-Mustadrak*, 1/670

at it in terms of his loyalty at waiting at a certain door and regard it as very significant. For example, the upright stance of Bediüzzaman throughout his entire life can be more important than reciting volumes of prayers. Thence, it is possible to demand prayers from such a person. However, that person should know his position as a servant of God, and know his limits; he should humbly say "My God, out of their positive view, they demand prayers from a person like me. Please do not prove them wrong in this positive opinion of theirs. I feel shame to be indifferent to their demand and turn it down..." after this humble consideration, he should ask for what he will. If the prayers are accepted, then it should not be forgotten that it is God who grants the good result, and this should be ascribed to the positive opinions of those who ask for prayers and their turning to God sincerely. Adopting such a view saves one both from deviations of thought by ascribing real power to causes other than God, and from growing arrogant by seeing himself as a blessed figure.

Everybody needs to watch their steps regarding this issue. If God Almighty grants someone healing through some person's hand, it must still be ascribed to Him from every aspect whatsoever. For example, you can put your hand over a patient's and say, "O God! Please consider Your beloved Messenger's hand also to be over this patient's, and let this person be saved from this illness. I know that such an outcome cannot be affected by my hand, but given that they have come here with a sincere positive opinion, do not turn this person down and grant healing out of Your grace;" one should acknowledge the actual power that operates, and abstract oneself completely.

We need to point out that there is no place in Islam for opening up some place for praying and other mystical purposes, and writing down spells for those who attend there. There are certain considerations on where and how to pray to God; but making it into a ceremony of visiting certain people puts one under the risk of losing faith in terms of attributing real importance to those people instead of God. Believers always need to act sensibly, see themselves as ordinary people, pray as ordinary ones, and spend an entire lifetime with such consciousness and sensitivity.

Human Weaknesses as a
Means of Spiritual Progress

Question: *How can we give advice to a person who says, "I have evil characters in my nature such as greed, hostility, and obstinacy and I cannot get rid of them in any way"?*

Answer: As human beings are created with comprehensive potentials, they are equipped with bodily and spiritual abilities related to both the mundane world and the heavenly one, respectively. Therefore, true human progress and deliverance depends on their using these latent potentials for the purpose they are created for. As members of humanity are honored with the "best pattern of creation" (*ahsan al-taqwim*), they can come into line with angels as far as they realize their otherworldly and spiritual side thoroughly, and lead their lives within the lawful sphere by giving their willpower its due, and resisting the negative feelings innately placed in human nature for different wisdoms. As Rumi also put it, humans stand at such a point that although carnal feelings and lust exist in their nature, they sometimes make angels envious by the good works they do; but sometimes they make even devils ashamed.

O Human! Read Yourself Correctly!

For this reason, people must first gain sound insight into themselves—their merits and weaknesses—and see certain negative feelings they have as a means for spiritual progress. If they can control those evil feelings and overcome them, and orient them toward goodness, then the seeds of Paradise within will begin to germinate. That Paradisiacal life experienced in the heart will turn the world into a corridor extending into real Paradise. In every part and every moment of such a world, a person can feel Paradise and witness its eternal beauties while in this world. It is also possible to voice this truth as follows: If the positive feelings in human nature are actuated well, they directly serve spiritual progress. As for the seemingly negative seeds, if they are taken under control by vigilance, watchfulness, and conformity to Divine orders, they become a means for different graces of God. In other words, your upright stance against those innate negative feelings will be counted as worship in the sight of God. For example, as the Daily Prayers are a very important form of worship that helps one achieve human perfection, defying carnal desires is no less important a form of worship. God Almighty points out this truth by the decree, *"But as for him who lived in awe of his Lord, being conscious of His seeing him, and of the standing before Him (in the Hereafter), and held back his carnal soul from lusts and fancies, surely Paradise will be his (final) refuge"* (an-Naziat 79:40–41). To reiterate, seemingly negative feelings can be turned to one's advantage if taken under control and channeled toward goodness, and become one of the most important means for entering Paradise.

People Become Truly Human by Actuating their Willpower

God did not create humanity within certain limits as he did animals. In other words, man is not a slave to a set of instincts. God granted willpower to humans and—in terms of the apparent reasons—He attached His blessings on the condition of giving willpower its due. For example, He could say, "When you lift your hand, I make the stars in the sky pour on your head." In such a case, we would seek no relation between moving of the hand and pouring down of the stars. Similarly, God Almighty grants favors and blessings in consequence of the worship people observe and the difficulties they forebear in the way of God, there is no point in seeking a relation of causality. Then God Almighty accepts the acts of individuals, which they do in compliance with the requirement of apparent causes, virtually as a seed, and He returns those acts to them as eternal blessings in Paradise.

Attacks from the Right and Left

We can compare the positive feelings in human nature as a person's right side and the negative feelings as the left side. I guess this can be better understood by Satan's threat as related in the Qur'an: *"Then I will come upon them from before them and from behind them, and from their right and from their left, and You will not find most of them thankful"* (al-A'raf 7:17). With his malicious joy, Satan is virtually saying: "I can come to them from in front and break down their hopes for the future and burn their bridges on the way to Paradise, and direct them to Hell instead. By coming to them from behind, I can show them the past as a dreadful grave, make them refuse to take a lesson from the example of their fathers and grandfathers... and make them fall for the delusion that life began with them. By approaching them from the right, I can deceive them even while doing acts of goodness and spoil their good deeds by showing off and taking pride in them. When they tell about God and the noble Prophet, or when they begin to write, I make them emphasize their own person and spoil even their good deeds. Finally, I approach them from the left and show forbidden acts as good, I offer them poisonous honey on golden trays and lead them astray."

In a *hadith* related to the subject, the Messenger of God, peace and blessings be upon him, stated that Paradise is surrounded with things unpleasant to the carnal soul, and Hell is surrounded with lusts that are tempting to the carnal soul.[185] Accordingly, what leads one to Paradise is difficult and unpleasant to the carnal soul. Believers will make their way to Paradise by passing them one by one. As for the way to Hell, it is engulfed by carnal feelings and lusts. In this respect, it is

---

[185] *Sahih al-Bukhari*, Riqaq, 28; *Sahih Muslim*, Jannah, 1

most likely for Satan to make one fall by means of indulging in food, drink, sleep, and living to fulfill one's carnal desires. Bediüzzaman points out the essential human weaknesses at the end of the "Twenty-ninth Letter." He mentions six human and Satanic intrigues: "love of fame and position, fear, greed, racism, egotism, and lastly, fondness for comfort and ease."[186] It is possible to count more. For example avarice, inability to stomach others, lascivious behavior, ostentation, and conceit are among other weak points through which Satan can find a way to defeat us.

Build up Walls around You with Prayers

Satan takes advantage of these weaknesses by approaching from the left. As he stated, *"Then (I swear) by Your Glory, I will certainly cause them all to rebel and go astray"* (as-Sad 38:82). The Pride of Humanity, peace and blessings be upon him, taught us this prayer to combat Satan: "O Allah! Conceal my imperfections and calm all my fears! O Allah! Protect me (against dangers) from in front, from behind, from my right, from my left, and from above, and I seek refuge in Your greatness from being swallowed by the earth beneath me."[187] He invited us to seek refuge with God against Satan by reciting this prayer night and day.[188] Satan is a professional; he knows such tricks that he toppled many giants far by using them. For example, if one tries to rise up in the night for Tahajjud Prayer, Satan uses various tricks and goading to prevent it. He will not stop even if he fails, and the believer leaves the warm bed in spite of everything. He plays a different trick on the way to ablutions and a different trick during the Prayer. For example, he tries to cause the worshipper to make noise, his aim to let the neighbors hear the noise and appreciate that person, so that the deed can be corrupted when the worshipper takes arrogant pride in his act. Satan has so many different tricks that it is really hard to overcome them; it takes serious determination and willpower along with continuously taking

[186] Nursi, *The Letters*, pp. 399–413
[187] *Sunan Abu Dawud*, Adab, 110
[188] *Sunan Abu Dawud*, Adab, 100; Ahmad ibn Hanbal, *Al-Musnad*, 2/25

refuge in God's help and protection. In this respect, what becomes clear is that a single wall will not suffice against Satan's tricks. We must continuously build new walls through more prayer. One cannot have too many walls. Before he retired to sleep, the Pride of Humanity, peace and blessings be upon him, recited the *surahs* Al-Mulk,[189] Ya-Sin,[190] As-Sajdah,[191] the Muawwizatayn[192] (Al-Falaq and An-Nas), and the last two verses of the chapter Al-Baqarah.[193] In addition, he sought refuge in God with prayers such as: "O Allah! Truly I have submitted myself to You, turned my face to You, entrusted my affairs to You, relied on You, there is no refuge or security except in You. O Allah! I believe in the Book that You revealed, and in the Prophet that You sent."[194] He also warned believers by saying, "Do not ever give in to heedlessness, always seek refuge in God against Satan."

What befalls believers is to see our weaknesses as a part of human nature and to constantly seek refuge in God against them, giving our willpower its due, and to thus make those negative factors into stepping stones for spiritual progress. At the same time, they need to make constant efforts to ascend to the life level of the heart and spirit by following true spiritual guides, and thus continue their journeying accordingly.

---

[189] An-Nasa'i, *As-Sunanu'l-Kubra*, 6/535
[190] Darimi, *Fazailu'l-Qur'an*, 21; Ibn Hibban, *As-Sahih*, 6/312
[191] Ad-Daylami, *Al-Musnad*, 5/411
[192] "The two means of seeking refuge in God," which refers to the last two *surahs* of the Qur'an. *Sahih al-Bukhari*, Fazailu'l-Qur'an, 15; Tibb, 39; *Sunan at-Tirmidhi*, Da'awat, 22; *Sunan Abu Dawud*, Adab, 108
[193] *Sahih al-Bukhari*, Fazailu'l-Qur'an, 10; *Sahih Muslim*, Salatu'l-Musafirin, 256
[194] *Sahih al-Bukhari*, Da'awat 6; Tawhid, 34; *Sahih Muslim*, Dhikr, 56–58

Helpless Ones in Dire Need and the Gates of Mercy Opened Wide

"He Who answers the helpless one in distress when he prays to Him, and removes the affliction from him, and (Who) has made you (O humankind) vicegerents of the earth (to improve it and rule over it according to God's commandments)? Is there another deity besides God? How little you reflect!" (an-Naml 27:62)

Question: *Could you explain the 62nd verse of chapter an-Naml with respect to how it relates to believers' individual and social lives?*

Answer: In the earlier verses of this chapter, God Almighty firstly asks: *"Is God better or all that they associate as partners (with Him)?"* (an-Naml 27:59) and then He places emphasis on the Divine acts in the universe and how they point to the omnipotent Creator: *"Or He Who has created the heavens and the earth, and sends down for you water from the sky?—We cause to grow with it gardens full of loveliness and delight: It is not in your power to cause their trees to grow. Is there another deity besides God? No, but they are a people who veer away (from truth)"* (an-Naml 27:60). Later in verse 62, God Almighty mentions it as another indication of Divine unity that it is nobody other than Him who answers helpless souls who implore to Him in distress. At first look, praying this way and finding a positive response can be seen as a rare case. However, those who examine their lives through the eyes of wisdom can find so many meaningful examples—particularly at times when they were completely helpless, deeply felt that God was the only true power, and wholeheartedly sought refuge in Him. In such situations, the light of belief in His absolute dominion, and the illusoriness of causality, lets them witness manifestations of His particular graces.

We implore Him so often in desperate situations, and He in return holds our hand, removes our trouble and grants us relief. Since we are not good at evaluating our experiences through serious reflection, we usually ignore such favors of Divine providence.

Causality at a Dead End and Divine Providence like a Bolt from the Blue

Whenever somebody turns sincerely to God, they can feel in their conscience that they received a positive response to their call. However, Divine aid for those in dire need comes in a more manifest fashion. For example, the brothers of Prophet Joseph, peace be upon him, left him to die in the bottom of a well. With respect to the apparent circumstances, there seemed no chance to be saved. However, God Almighty sent a passing caravan as a special blessing, and He took Joseph out of the well through the hands of those in the caravan. Afterwards, they sold him to somebody from the palace and Joseph was treated well in that new home. Later on, he faced a different kind of trouble: The lady of the house tried to seduce him. He gave his willpower its due, and preferred the prison over the palace as a hero of chastity. Thanks to his wholehearted devotion to God, Prophet Joseph received extraordinary Divine favors in the prison as well; he came out of the prison, reunited with his parents, and set a throne upon the hearts of Egypt.

God's help to Moses, peace be upon him, who was trying to safeguard his people form the army of the Pharaoh, is no different. The Qur'an describes their situation: "*When the two hosts came in view of each other, the companions of Moses said: 'We are certainly overtaken!' He replied: 'Certainly not. My Lord is surely with me; He will guide*

me (to deliverance)'" (ash-Shuara 26:61–62). They seemed completely helpless. There was the Red Sea before them and the Pharaoh with
his army behind them. In the words of Tariq ibn Ziyad, the sea before
them was like an enemy (blocking their way), and the enemy behind
them was (plentiful) like the sea. Right at such a moment, Prophet
Moses turned to God in wholehearted devotion and said: *"...My Lord
is surely with me; He will guide me (to deliverance)"* (ash-Shuara
26:62). God Almighty commanded him to strike the sea with his staff.
When he did so, the sea split in two, making way for him and his people to pass; they were delivered safe and sound by an extraordinary
favor from God.

At a point where no possible way out remains, the heart completely detaches from everything and turns to God, and very often, God
Almighty unexpectedly opens a new door. When you understand
through the light of faith that He is the Real One Who makes everything happen, then you are blessed with the manifestation of a particular Divine favor in accordance with the particular trouble you face;
Bediüzzaman calls this a manifestation of Divine Grace.

Inheritors of the Earth

In another verse, God states, *"... He Who has made you (O humankind)
vicegerents of the earth (to improve it and rule over it according to God's
commandments)..."* (an-Naml 27:62). Considering other examples,
Prophet David, peace be upon him, succeeded to kill Goliath in the
war against the people of Amalica. The Old Testament relates that In
those days, David was a young boy who shepherded goats and that
he killed the gigantic Goliath by hitting him with a stone he hurled
with his sling.[195] Without relating details, the Qur'an states: *"... David
killed Goliath, and God granted him kingdom and Wisdom, and taught
him of that which He willed... "* (al-Baqarah 2:251). At that moment
when David turned wholeheartedly to God, a particular favor of God
was manifested through the light of belief in Divine unity. Later, God
Almighty granted him rule and wisdom. In the same way, while the

---

[195] *The Old Testament*, Samuel, 1/17 (49)

Messenger of God, peace and blessings be upon him, was resting at his home before he left for Medina, the polytheists surrounded the house and no sign of hope remained. Then, as it is stated in Ya-Sin 36:9, *"And We have set a barrier before them and a barrier behind them, and (thus) We have covered them (from all sides), so that they cannot see,"* he virtually walked away through a different dimension they could not see. When the polytheists of Mecca finally entered the house, they found Ali ibn Abi Talib instead. God's Messenger, who was the paramount representative of faith in Divine unity and the illusoriness of causality, was in a state of dire need through which he turned to God in the purest faith; with extraordinary Divine graces and favors, the roads to Medina were cleared. When the Sultan of the Worlds arrived in Medina, roses bloomed all over. The Sultan of Roses initiated a new era of roses, and in a short time, Islam became a prominent balancing factor on the world scale.

You can consider the emergence of the Ottomans within the same perspective. As a consequence of the Crusades, the Seljuks had gradually been pushed to the verge of collapse. As a response to those with faithful hearts suffering in dire need, the Divine Providence paved the way for them to grow into the small princedom of the Ottomans, like a caterpillar metamorphosing into a butterfly. Nobody in the region expected a flourishing of that proportion. As a consequence of people's turning to God in dire need, the Sublime State (the Ottomans) arrived on the stage, and it served for centuries as a prominent factor in the balance power.

Suffering: The Form of Prayer Most Likely to Be Accepted

Be it on the individual or societal level, a state of dire need is a time when one feels suffering, which is the form of praying most likely to be accepted. Sometimes, there are such periods of suffering that individuals feel they are surrounded on all sides. Their insides are in agony. In such a state, if they do not complain but only petition God Almighty and implore Him, this will be best form of prayer. In these days, when the social situation is obscure, and when the cries of the oppresses sing out from all over the world, if God Almighty is to save believers from this misery and pave the way for becoming the inheritors of the earth, it will only be after they turn wholeheartedly to him in a state of suffering and dire need. Those who do not turn to him with pure faith might breach the trust to be granted them. That trust can only be placed on the shoulders of people who passed through different trials and who experienced suffering in a state of dire need. It is so very difficult to attain blessings obtained in a life of comfort. Folk wisdom voices this truth as "Easy come, easy go." For example, people usually squander inherited wealth, since they do not appreciate its worth. The believers of our time who wish to be trustworthy and serve humanity for the sake of God must be set on righteousness, as pointed out by the Divine command, "... *My righteous servants will Inherit the earth*" (al-Anbiya 21:105). Conscious of human impotence and poverty, and absolutely dependent on Him, they must implore God Almighty wholeheartedly with a spirit of dire need and sincere faith.

The Devoted Souls and Life Standards

Question: *Those who work at the establishments based on the philosophy of devotedly serving humanity, sometimes begin to develop expectations of a better payment and life standards, owing to factors like long working hours or having produced high quality work. Could you share with us your considerations on this issue?*

Answer: Let me first state one thing—that not all people will be on the same level of devotedness, as it is the case with other moral virtues. Even if a certain spiritual guide has an ability to make surprising impact on the hardest hearts, it is not possible for him to bring all of the people he guides to the same level of spiritual progress. As the guide is expected to give the message perfectly, those who are to receive the message need to be capable of receiving the message with their potentials and abilities. Let us say that you run to help a certain man with a water tanker, but he only has a bucket in hand. Even though you empty the contents of the entire tanker, the water will pour out once the bucket is filled.

When the Age of Happiness is viewed from this perspective, it becomes apparent that there were serious "level differences," even between the Companions of the noble Prophet, the most influential guide, who consisted of, and emanated, blessed light in every way. It is not possible for ordinary people like us to categorize those radiant figures.[196] Despite this, it is definite that few Companions shared the same level with people like Abu Bakr and Umar. We can say that every one of the Companions of the noble Prophet benefited from God's Beloved one, who was the focal point of Divine manifestations, in-as-much as their personal aptitudes and capacities allowed.

Such a difference of level is also true for the devoted souls in our time. For example, some of them can live of barely enough food for sustenance—sometimes they even starve; but they still do not ask anything from others, and keep their dignity.

However, some of them cannot forebear such sacrifice; they might adopt attitudes and expectations to violate the principle of dignified contentment. Similarly, as some people lead their lives by keeping up a serious consciousness of death, the dominant feeling in others might be a longing for worldly goals and delusion of permanence. I heard a few days ago that an old person—who has one foot in the grave as they say—visited a doctor and asked: "I heard some rumors, is there anything real as the potion of immortality?" In my opinion, delusion of immortality for a person of that age is nothing but seeking disgrace. It is a reality that a wish for an everlasting life, together with the feeling of cherishing worldly goals and endless desires, is inherent in human nature. However, it should not be forgotten that this feeling in human nature is supposed to be directed to the eternal afterlife.

As is the case with devotedness and other qualities, despite spending time with the devoted ones, a person may not quite share the same spirit. Some people always have their eye on higher worldly benefits. For this reason, they do not feel content with the payment, title, and status they have; they expect to have these increased at certain intervals. When they get what they desire, they set about seeking even more. Their lack of thankful contentment causes them to complain all

---

[196] Aliyyulqari, *Al-Asraru'l-Marfua*, 388; Al-Humaydi, *Al-Musnad*, 250; Al-Hakim at-Tirmidhi, *Nawadiru'l-Usul*, 3/62

the time. For this reason, it needs to be accepted as a reality that such people can be found even within the sphere of the devoted ones.

Responsibilities Must Be Entrusted to Eligible Ones

When needs to be done about dealing with this reality? First of all, people in certain positions should discern well the personality and natures of the people they are responsible for; they should consult with as many people as possible. This shared information should serve as a criterion that can assess the levels of individuals who act with commonsense and ascend to higher steps in life. If this can be done, people with worldly ambitions will not be able ascend to certain positions and breach the principle of dignified contentment. In fact, sometimes you need to employ someone in an important position, and cannot find anybody that suits your criteria. The only candidates for the job might possess some weaknesses, such as greed and envy. Then, even though they do not meet your standards of virtue, you may choose the lesser of two evils,[197] and will temporarily entrust that important responsibility to such a person, rather than leaving things undone. But when you find the eligible one to carry out the job, you shift the former to a more suitable position and let the deserving one assume control. Entrusting a duty to someone else while there is an eligible one will be a betrayal to that duty, or a breach of trust.

When somebody asked the noble Prophet about the Last Day, he told him that breach of trust would herald the coming of the Last Day. When the man asked about this breach of trust, the beloved Prophet told him to expect the time of Last Day when responsibility is given to the ineligible.[198] Accordingly, if you entrust some responsibilities to one who is not eligible for them, then it is a kind of "Last Day" for that particular responsibility. If this state becomes general and permanent, then the Last Day can come. It appears that when the appointed hour for the world comes, betraying the trust will have become a grave, worldwide issue.

---

[197] *Majallah al-Ahkam-i Adliya*, article 29
[198] *Sahih al-Bukhari*, Ilm, 2; Riqaq, 35; Ahmad ibn Hanbal, *Al-Musnad*, 2/361

Having More Abundant Means and Real Economy

Another thing that needs to be done about people who never feel satisfied but always have their eye on more worldly benefits is to remind them that self-sacrifice and sufficing with the available means is not a principle only to be followed during hard times; it is necessary to help them attain a character of living with economy and dignified contentment in all conditions.

Gaining access to more abundant means should not change our general discipline. As the noble Prophet stated, even a person making ablutions near a river should avoid wasting water.[199] Accordingly, as it is a waste for such a person to dip one arm in water and wait for two or three minutes; washing the limbs four or five times instead of three is wastefulness as well. A religious teaching that places so much emphasis on frugality also requires the same sensitivity in other matters. That is, if a person near a sea needs to act frugally, then a person in charge of a wealth like the sea should also live frugally, avoid wastefulness, and never change his or her lifestyle. For example, they should keep their habit of eating within the limits brought by Islam and never waste anything. As it is known, Bediüzzaman pointed out the fact that unnecessary eating triggers a false appetite.[200] Then instead of sufficing with a single kind of food, having a diverse spread and tasting various dishes will trigger such a false appetite, which is harmful to health. Therefore, no matter how much wealth God Almighty grants, individuals should eat the necessary amount and avoid excess.

Some of the Companions led very austere lives in spite of being very wealthy. For example, Uthman ibn Affan had abundant means to donate three hundred camels and also to provide ten thousand soldiers with equipment.[201] In spite of that, he never changed his life standards. He mostly spent his life on the sands of the Prophet's Mosque. He would make a little heap of sand and use it as his pillow. He ate the same meal

[199] *Sunan ibn Majah*, Taharah, 45; Ahmad ibn Hanbal, *Al-Musnad*, 2/221

[200] Nursi, *The Gleams*, p. 197

[201] *Sunan at-Tirmidhi*, Manaqib, 18; Ahmad ibn Hanbal, *Al-Musnad*, 4/75

with others.[202] Ali ibn Abi Talib, who also lead his life in the same simplicity, had only one dress to wear.[203] He wore it both in summer and
winter. As a matter of fact, he was a caliph who ruled an affluent state
in a very extensive region. He and other great personalities followed
the way of the blessed Prophet and continued to lead a simple life.
These are very important examples for us. If we are to change our
lives after gaining access to better means, then—may God forbid—it
means that we have stepped into a vicious circle of unending negative change.

A Bohemian Life Has No Limit

You need to be so steadfast on this issue, so that even if God Almighty
makes money shower down from the sky and form a heap before you,
you should still say, "No matter how abundantly you come, you cannot find any way into my heart. I know where to use you." Some saintly figures spent all of the goods God bestowed them without leaving
anything for the morrow. A report included in the collection of Imam
Bukhari teaches us the attitude to be adopted in the face of worldly
means. Accordingly, while the Messenger of God, peace and blessings
be upon him, was about to lead a Prayer at his mosque, he suddenly
stopped and rushed to his room. After that, he returned and led the
Prayer. When the Prayer was over, he turned to the puzzled congregation and explained that at the moment he was about to start the
Prayer, it occurred to him that somebody had given him a present. Since
this worldly property could occupy his mind during the Prayer, he
told his wife Aisha to give it to someone else so that he could free his
heart and stand in God's presence thus.[204] This perfect lifestyle of God's
Messenger, together with his blessed light and atmosphere, made such
an impact on those around him that their attitudes and behaviors were
never changed by their opportunities. Bediüzzaman's treatise "On

---

[202] Abu Nuaym, *Hilyatu'l-Awliya*, 1/60; Al-Bayhaqi, *As-Sunanu'l-Kubra*, 2/446
[203] *Sunan ibn Majah*, Muqaddima, 11; Ahmad ibn Hanbal, *Al-Musnad*, 1/99
[204] *Sahih al-Bukhari*, Amal fi's-Salah, 18; *Sunan an-Nasa'i*, Sahw, 104; Ahmad ibn Hanbal, *Al-Musnad*, 4/7, 384

Frugality"[205] is a very important guideline on this issue. Reading it from time to time will be very helpful in terms of getting used to living contently with frugality. Otherwise, there is no limit to leading a bohemian life. If people indulge themselves in such a life—may God forbid—they spend an entire life controlled by their carnal desires. For this reason, frugality and contentment is an important value for everyone, poor or rich.

Particularly for the believers dedicated to serving faith, thankful contentment has a special significance. It is the duty of those who employ them to provide them with a sufficient payment for a decent living; on the other hand what falls on the devoted souls is to live with frugality and contentment, and to not compare their own lives with their counterparts outside their spiritual sphere. Home and abroad, wherever they are, the volunteers had better become accustomed to living with a modest income, like the scholarship of a student. Other people's working for very high salaries cannot be an example for those who soar through the horizons of self-sacrifice. They do not care about owning worldly property; they rent an apartment to reside and support their family with what God Almighty grants them. This is the basic discipline of devotion. The desire to be like those who chase money and status is a violation of this discipline. Others may lead a heedless life by eating and lying lazily. This cannot be a criterion for the devoted soul. God Almighty grants some worldly means to some of those who run lawfully on His path, such as the private business they run; that is a different issue. However, those who are paid through the financial means of serving the truth need to be very careful on this issue. Nobody must take anything more than they deserve. When Abu Bakr was given a little more than the sufficient amount to support his family, he put the remaining amount to a pot and willed it to be given to the next caliph after he passed away. When it was brought to Umar ibn al-Khattab, in accordance with the will, he could not hold back his tears and said, "You presented an inimitable example of righteous-

---

[205] Included in *The Gleams* as "The Nineteenth Gleam."

ness and responsibility for those to come after you."[206] Thus he voiced the greatness of the first caliph. Actually, this is how the devoted souls in our time have to be. If they look at the means and payment others enjoy and hold the mistaken idea, "It seems that these are the real rewards of the job I am doing," they should know that even if they run breathlessly on that path, this very thought will cause them to consume the blessings meant for the afterlife.

Constant Self-Criticism

Another point that needs concern on this issue is having in mind the question, "I wonder whether I really deserve this salary I get?" We need to maintain this self-criticism by praying somewhere open to the public, or by eating at an establishment and asking ourselves: "I am consuming the water, using the carpet, and eating the food here, so I wonder whether..." Even if we are in the places that belong to the circle we are devoted to, we need to be suffering with such concerns in our inner world.

Even things gained while fighting for a righteous cause are lawful to take only in certain conditions. According to a *hadith* related in *Sahih al-Bukhari*, making personal claim on any possession left from a particular enemy depends on having eliminated him personally.[207] But when a nameless hero was offered a share from the gains of a battle he joined, he rejected the offer since was fighting not to gain benefits but to sacrifice himself.[208] As our way is "serving" for the sake of God, we are supposed to adopt the philosophy of selflessness and lead our lives in dignified contentment. God loves those who sincerely act this way. Attitude and behaviors of such people have an effect on others, and seeing them reminds others of God.[209] There is no need for them to tell so much with words. Their attitudes become an eloquent tongue and an articulate speech. Otherwise, those who can-

---

[206] Ibn Sa'd, *At-Tabaqatu'l-Kubra*, 3/186; At-Tabari, *Tarikhu'l-Umam wa'l-Muluk*, 2/354

[207] *Sahih al-Bukhari*, Khums, 18; Maghazi, 54; *Sahih Muslim*, Jihad, 41

[208] *Sunan an-Nasa'i*, Janaiz, 61; Abdurrazzaq, *Al-Musannaf*, 7/271; At-Tabarani, *Al-Mu'jamu'l-Kabir*, 2/271

[209] *Sunan ibn Majah*, Zuhd, 4

not maintain this fine state cannot convey any good message even if they start shouting. Even if such people hold others' attention temporarily, they can never help others make spiritual progress. Maybe some of us find it very difficult to lead such a life. But we mean to attain the difficult. The Qur'anic address to the noble Prophet "...*the Hereafter (what comes after) will be better for you than this world (what has gone before)...*" (ad-Duha 93:4) is also true for ordinary people like us. God Almighty makes the following warning to those who think otherwise, "...*but you (people) love and prefer what is before you (the present, worldly life), and abandon that which is to come later (the Hereafter)*" (al-Qiyamah 75:20–21). In one of the letters he wrote to his students, Nursi refers to the same fact by stating that this age made (most) followers of Islam prefer this life over the afterlife, willfully and gladly.[210] That is, he pointed out that the greatest disaster in the contemporary age was that love for this material world gained priority over love for the Hereafter; he commented that this verse refers to our time. From a perspective of Qur'anic exegesis, the original Arabic word in the verse is inflected in simple present tense (*mudari*); we can infer that this situation is one that continues for a long time. Therefore, it is possible to say that this understanding of preferring this worldly life over the next is likely to continue in the years to come. Probably in criticism of such facts, Muhammad Qutb chose the title *Are We Muslims?* for one of his books. According to the commentary of the great Imam Abu Hanifa in his *Al-Fiqh Al-Akbar*, making such a statement in the sense of not really being sure whether one really accepts faith or not is an expression of unbelief.[211] But there is nothing wrong in this one, for it is used in a sense of making self-criticism. The poet Mehmed Akif referred to the same problem thus:

> *Let alone being Muslim, we can hardly be called human;*
> *Let us make no pretense, we cannot fool anyone.*
> *All the true Muslims I knew are already in their graves.*
> *The real Islam is I guess, nowhere else but in heavens.*

---

[210] Nursi, *Kastamonu Lâhikası*, p. 82
[211] Aliyyulqari, *Sharhu'l-Fiqhi'l-Akbar*, 241–242

It is a reality that this is a diabolical age. We are living in an era of people whose sole concern is to indulge in consumption, to satisfy their appetites, and to lead an indolent life; their notion of Hereafter was destroyed, buried under the ground and huge boulders were heaped on it so that it could not be resurrected. Then, it should never be forgotten that the influence we are to make on others is closely related to the shadow we cast on the ground. If we are really upright, so will be our shadow, and our state will have a relevant effect in the hearts of others.

Perfection and Modesty

Question: *It is stated that the devoted souls who will realize a new revival are supposed be no different than ordinary people. On the other hand, they are continuously encouraged to be the cultured people who represent the best way by personal example. How can we strike the balance between these seemingly conflicting aspects?*

Answer: If we evaluate the issue from the perspective of guiding others and conveying the Divine message to them, it is essential to believe that the following two qualities constitute the "must" of this path: targeting perfect standards along with adopting an understanding of nullifying oneself. For being able to convey relevant points to others and making an impact on consciences by God's grace, it is essential to make an effort to be well-equipped with the knowledge and practices of faith, as well as possessing humility and modesty, and viewing oneself as an ordinary person among other people. Any attempt to guide that is not based on knowledge and actual spiritual depth will not evoke any trust in those being addressed. Word polluted with arrogance and pride will never diffuse into hearts; and even if they do, their effect will never be permanent. Consider the works of Bediüzzaman: He highlighted how serious a problem ignorance was.[212] On the other

---
[212] Nursi, *Tarihçe-i Hayat*, p. 61

hand, he also emphasized that arrogance has become a widespread disease in our time.[213]

Two-Winged Spirit of Guidance, with Knowledge and Humility

Let us expound on these two aspects a bit. In order to achieve a thorough representation, a Muslim, first, needs to "read" very well the contemporary age, social structure, contemporary events, and Divine principles operating in the universe, and then interpret them correctly. On the other hand, a Muslim also needs to know religious commandments and what they mean in our age, and thus become a "child of the time." Otherwise, so many truths will be victimized by their poor representation, and their values will be condemned to seem worthless in the eyes of others. As "everything is, by its nature, essentially dependent on knowledge,"[214] it is very important for Muslims to express their own values well. What we mean by knowledge (*ilm*) here is not having information about a particular subject as it is commonly used in our day; it is the knowledge based on an evaluation of realities with their internal and external dimensions, which can help us draw a conclusion and deepen in knowledge of God. In fact, it is not possible for a believer to make any individual progress without such knowledge, let alone guide others. Until the moment people are equipped with knowledge, including knowledge of God, they will not be able to refuse their carnal self, and not be able to rid themselves of confusion and instability. Individuals who do not solve the problems of their own heart and mind will have real difficulty conveying the truths of faith to others; unaware, they will probably resort to demagogy and dialectics. Until the moment they overcome the doubts and suspicions in their own mind, they will not be able to avoid faltering at their statements. For this reason, we firstly need to have insight into our own matters, knowing them deeply, with their spirit, essence, background, and basis. After that, we need to feel and sense in our conscience that, with the

---

[213] Nursi, *The Words*, p. 206
[214] Ibid., p. 332

initial theoretical knowledge we have, we can attain knowledge of God (*marifah*), then love of God through that knowledge, and then zeal and yearning for God through their totality. If we can truly make these ingrained in ourselves, and behold in our heart and mind a picture of what comes out of our mouth, then we can be saved from having inner conflicts and falling into contradictions. For this reason, those who wish to guide others and share the beauties of their teaching with others must definitely do everything they can to have a profound and multi-dimensional knowledge that will be pleasing to God Almighty. However, mere knowledge does not suffice for conveying the message to others. At the same time one needs to be conscious of the fact that these very important inspirations and gifts are pure blessings and bestowals of God Almighty. As Bediüzzaman points out in *The Letters*, all of these blessings can be compared to a fur coat presented by a king.[215] Their value should not be overlooked. On the other hand, we should never give up the consideration that they do not essentially belong to us. That is, what we need to do is to direct the appreciation to the One who truly deserves it. If we can attain this perspective, we will have started opening the doors of modesty, humbleness, and humility. Thus we will have realized the truth expressed by Imam Ali ibn Abi Talib: "Live among people as one of them." And this means combining absolute humility and perfection. Ingraining this feeling and thought in ourselves depends on acknowledging the True Owner of everything we possess, and making our conscience accept the fact that we are nothing. I would like to reiterate one point I previously made. If we were to be asked to put aside what essentially belongs to God and stand before Him with what remains, nothing would be left, I think. For this reason, what befalls on us is constantly being oriented to him in humbleness, modesty, and humility. As a matter of fact, it can be said that these points are related to the wisdoms behind the command to pray five times a day. Standing in awe of God five times a day at Prayer is an expression of submission to Him. As bowing before God is a form of modesty, prostrating oneself before Him is an expression of humbleness; it is a person's

---

[215] Nursi, *Mektubat*, pp. 416–417

closest state to God Almighty, as related in a hadith.[216] Actually, the time of prostration is the moment when a person is freed from one's own self and dyed with the hue of manifestations from Him. That is, you reach such a state of "I" during prostration that, this "I" is nothing but a work of His manifestations. Then, closeness to God depends on a person's nullifying oneself.

The Most Modest Person

As it is stated in the Qur'an: *"Assuredly you have in God's Messenger an excellent example to follow..."* (al-Ahzab 33:21), the Messenger of God presented the best example in every respect in all of his attitudes and behaviors. The Prince of both worlds was honored with the Divine address "Had it not been for you, I would not have created the worlds."[217] In the words of the poet Necip Fazıl: "He, for whose sake we exist." As his blessed light was the first light that appeared in the realm of existence,[218] he is the most perfect fruit of the tree of existence. In other words, the light of Muhammad is the seed of the tree of universe and the ink of the pen of Divine Power that writes this "book of universe." And he is the curator in this great exhibition of the universe. In the words of insightful scholars, the blessed Prophet is a person who was gifted with the beginning and end of wisdom, with respect to the knowledge of the Divine. By God's grace, every kind of problem was solved in the hands of that blessed settler of problems. He is the teacher for everybody to learn how to evaluate the world and its contents with the eye of wisdom. In addition to being such a distinguished person, God's Messenger, peace and blessings be upon him, is at the same time a monument of modesty and humility. When somebody addressed him as "our master," he expressed his protest for such address—even though it was true.[219] At another case when the following Divine command was revealed, *"So wait*

---

[216] *Sahih Muslim*, Salah, 215; *Sunan Abu Dawud*, Salah, 148; *Sunan an-Nasa'i*, Tatbik, 78

[217] Aliyyulqari, *Al-Masnu*, 150; *Al-Asraru'l-Marfua*, 295; Al-Ajluni, *Kashfu'l-Khafa*, 2/214

[218] As-Suyuti, *Al-Hawi*, 1/325; Al-Halabi, *As-Siratu'l-Halabiyya*, 1/240

[219] *Sunan Abu Dawud*, Adab, 9; An-Nasa'i, *As-Sunanu'l-Kubra*, 6/70

patiently for your Lord's judgment, and do not be like the companion of the fish, when he called out choking inwardly (with distress)..." (al-Qalam 68:48), he stated, not assuming superiority, "Do not prefer me over Yunus ibn Matta."[220] At another time, he told someone who felt overawed before him "Do not be afraid, I am the child of a woman who ate dried meat."[221] During the construction of the Prophet's Mosque in Medina, he carried two bricks on his back while others carried a single brick.[222] While they needed to cook during travel, as all of his Companions contributed to it, he undertook the task of collecting firewood;[223] he always made an effort to not avoid at any kind of responsibility. So the Perfect Guide, under whose blessed feet the stars were like a stairway, combined such opposite virtues in his person, and thus he reached into souls with his most perfect and trustworthy example. Then what befalls believers should be faithfully following the footsteps of that Perfect Guide.

[220] *Sahih al-Bukhari*, Anbiya, 35; *Sahih Muslim*, Fazail, 166–167

[221] *Sunan ibn Majah*, At'ima, 30; Tabarani, *Al-Mu'jamu'l-Awsat*, 2/64

[222] Ahmad ibn Hanbal, *Al-Musnad*, 2/381; Ibn Sa'd, *At-Tabaqatu'l-Kubra*, 2/66

[223] At-Tabari, *Khulasatu Siyari Sayyidi'l-Bashar*, 87; As-Safadi, *Al-Wafi bi'l-Wafayat*, 1/7

The Devoted Souls with Enthusiasm and Commonsense

Question: *What are the indications of being devoted to serving humanity for the sake of God? What are your suggestions for evoking enthusiasm in new generations and making it last?*

Answer: First of all, developing a spirit of devotedness depends on people's having a sound belief in the religion they represent. A spirit of devotedness cannot be evoked without a sound faith, and the formation period for such faith can differ according to individuals. Very short rehabilitations might suffice for some people; they get what they should within forty hours. On the other hand, some others may need forty days, months, or even forty years to make the same progress. Even Junayd al-Baghdadi, a person with a good potential for spiritual progress, expressed that he began to sense and feel certain things after the age of sixty. Surely, this should not be misunderstood as he did not have any spiritual experiences until the age of sixty, which would be obviously disrespectful to that noble soul. But how are we supposed to take that statement? Junayd al-Baghdadi always targeted the horizon of being *al-insan al-kamil* (the universal man). Sensing certain breezes of that horizon can take time. Or maybe, he wished to draw attention to the difference in potential between people. In short, whatever he intended, we need to be cautious and avoid making off-handed remarks and having negative thoughts about those great guides. Regarding the possibility of speaking ill of them, and invoking Divine wrath, we need to seek refuge in God.

The Greatest Favor That Can Be Done to Today's Generations

Returning back to our essential subject, illuminating the feeling and thought of devotedness in hearts has become more difficult in our time. This is an era where the home does not offer much in terms of metaphysical immensities. Educational institutions do not offer that feeling and thought either. Our streets have become enemies of spirituality. Mosques do not inspire hearts with love and enthusiasm, and establishments to guide people to the horizons of the heart and spirit do not exist... In such a period, making hearts feel the spirit of devotedness depends on certain specific efforts. We must help people resist their body's influence, and save them from being held captive by their carnal desires. We must orient them toward the level of the heart and spirit, and make the attainment of God's good pleasure their ultimate purpose in life. Lastly, we must teach them to pray all the time as, "My God, I ask for forgiveness, well-being, and Your good pleasure." Maintaining this requires very serious effort.

A desire for the world and its temptations is inherent in human nature. Particularly in our time, as worldly goals and ambitions have gained priority, people have been consumed by these worldly issues. For this reason, I think that the best kind of goodness for today's generation is evoking in their hearts a desire and enthusiasm to live for others. Such love and enthusiasm is a very important principle that belongs to the very essence of Islam. When this feeling is reflected in Prayer, it reveals itself as consciousness of God, and awe; when it comes to glorifying the Name of God, it reveals itself as an urge to be constantly on the move with a spirit of devotedness. No matter what you teach someone whose heart is devoid of such essential love and enthusiasm, you will not see much effort in terms of selflessness and sacrifice.

Being Devoid of Enthusiasm Means Death for the Heart

First of all, believers need to have a boundless enthusiasm; this makes them restless with suffering to reach this noble ideal. They must feel a throbbing in their temples from the intensity of this suffering, and be exhausted by the strain on their hearts and minds. If a person possesses such an intense enthusiasm, you can temper their feelings with reason and the sensibility of Islam. In other words, you can channel this overflowing enthusiasm toward goodness. For example, you can help them use their love and enthusiasm for maintaining steadfastness and continuity on the righteous path. This enthusiasm is essential; it is not possible to make any permanent and long-term achievement in the spirit solely with reasoning and logic. It is only with this love and enthusiasm that people will have the resolve to spend a lifetime upholding this noble ideal.

As is the case with every laudable virtue, the noble Prophet presents the best example for us, as confirmed by the Qur'an: "*Yet, it may be that you (O Muhammad) will torment yourself to death with grief, following after them, if they do not believe in this Message,*" (al-Kahf 18:6) and "*It may be that you (O Messenger) will torment yourself to death because they refuse to believe*" (ash-Shuara 26:3). The meaning of these verses show the level of enthusiasm the Messenger of God possessed. God Almighty tempered his enthusiasm with the commandment "*You cannot guide to truth whomever you like, but God guides whomever He wills*" (al-Qasas 28:56). Therefore, if anybody overflows with such an Islamic enthusiasm, it can be tempered with the commandments of the Qur'an. We can tell that person to appraise the possible costs of acting impulsively, and to reckon the requirements of time, conjuncture, the feelings of people they address, and how they will probably respond. But if there is no initial enthusiasm, what is there to be tempered? A fully enthusiastic mood like this is necessary in order to maintain continuity and determination. However, reason and commonsense should never be sacrificed to emotion and over-enthusiasm. These can give way to imbalance and extremism. For this reason, while hearts need enthusiasm, reason and commonsense must always supersede emotion, and passion must be channeled constructively.

Sensibility and Enthusiasm Should Support One Another

In addition, if there is a noble ideal we pursue, some obstacles on the way should not deter us from our path. As faithful servants, when we come up against an obstacle, we find an alternative way and keep walking from there. If the same thing happens with that path, then we find a new one again. If all the roads become impossible to walk, we continue striving for a lifetime without losing hope and say, "If we cannot, then the next generation will; if they cannot either, then, with the permission and help of God, the generation after them will realize this noble ideal." If necessary, we will bring down the stars in the sky as if they were playthings. We always try to keep our standards high, with the consideration that making no efforts for progress kills a person spiritually.

On the other hand, we abide by the requirements of reason and commonsense and thus pay attention to making realizable plans. There should never be contradiction between the reason and enthusiasm of a believer. On the contrary, these two must support and feed one another. Many people, despite acting in the name of righteousness, have harmed Muslims because they were guided only by emotion. Others used straightaway logic and thought that they could give good messages through pompous talks, demagogy, and dialectics. Yet they failed to make a lasting influence on others; they just lost energy and failed to carry on.

To find proper balance, we need enthusiasm at full gallop, but also sound principles tested through the essentials of the Qur'an. In fact, all of our attitudes and behaviors must be constantly tested to see whether they are right or wrong from the perspective of the Qur'an and Sunnah. The beloved Messenger of God, peace and blessings be upon him, stated that what Muslims need is to follow his Tradition and that of the Rightly Guided Caliphs. He told his followers to keep a firm hold on these, as if with clenched teeth.[224] Accordingly, another important criterion by which to test our behaviors on a certain issue is the approach of Rightly Guided Caliphs.

As we believe in the righteousness of the cause and ideal we are totally committed to, the path we use to reach that ideal must inspire trust in others' hearts. This can only be achieved by following the way of the Companions, particularly that of the Rightly Guided Caliphs, and the way of the Qur'an and the Sunnah.

One of the most important means of evoking such an enthusiasm is stimulating a person's *tafakkur* (reflection) and deepening their system of thought. The Arabic definition of *tafakkur* means a person does more than just think; they make serious mental efforts. Therefore, the perspective of *tafakkur* is acquired when one makes reflecting deeply their habit. *Tafakkur* does not mean sitting there and brooding over matters, or making superficial and simple connections about things one sees or hears. On the contrary, *tafakkur* means taking the beginning and end into consideration together; moving one's reason between the cause and effect like a shuttle and developing wisdom through that thinking; absorbing the consequent inspirations into one's soul and making these inspirations into a part of their feelings; and even seeking to make more of these inspirations by examining them further. For people to learn fervor and enthusiasm, they must become habituated to serious thinking and reasoning, and they must be able to see right and wrong correctly.

One Should Always Be Spelling the Name of God, Living with This Truth, Each and Every Night

Continuity of the mind is very significant. It is so important that even if we think those around us are journeying down the paths pointed out by the verse, "*It is in the remembrance of, and whole-hearted devotion to God, that hearts find rest and contentment,*" (ar-Ra'd 13:28) one should never see his or her own spiritual level, or rather another's

---

[224] *Sunan at-Tirmidhi*, Ilm, 16; *Sunan Abu Dawud*, Sunnah, 5; *Sunan ibn Majah*, Muqaddima, 6

level, as sufficient. Believers need to support one another in this pursuit. As the great thinker Bediüzzaman put it, like stones that make up a dome, we need to support one another in order to not fall.[225] Taking this example solely as advice about avoiding disagreements and upholding social unity is a deficient understanding. We need to tackle it from a wider perspective: We should adopt serving religion as the highest ideal of our lives and always support one another at maintaining our spirituality on the path to realizing this noble ideal. Accordingly, when we gather to worship, we should never be unserious. We should make the assembly meaningful by reading and discussing subjects to make us more conscious of God. After such gatherings, we need to question whether we experienced any of the truths expressed in the supplication:

"O God, increase us in knowledge (*ilm*), faith (*iman*), certainty (*yaqin*), reliance on You (*tawakkul*), surrender to You (*taslim*), commitment to You (*tafwiz*), knowledge of You (*marifah*), love of You (*mahabbah*), intense love of You (*ashq*), yearning for reunion with You (*ishtiyaq ila liqaik*), chastity (*iffah*), innocence (*ismah*), perspicacity (*fatanah*), and wisdom (*hikmah*)." Even at our gatherings for worldly matters, when we find a chance, we should shift the subject to such topics and try to whisper the beauties of faith into our hearts.

Knowing what happens in our present culture, it is understandable that people are influenced by popular norms. Knowing what happens in our day and following certain matters of actuality is surely acceptable. However, given that there are so many people immersed in these matters, those who devoted themselves to serving the truths of the Qur'an should try to fulfill their spiritual potential, and deepen their faith. For this reason, they should always be spelling the Name of God, and living with this truth each and every night.

In short, we are supposed to do whatever must be done to help people passionately love God Almighty, and to cherish their love for the blessed Messenger, peace and blessings be upon him. This love should be so intense that upon hearing his blessed name, the listener

---

[225] Nursi, *The Gleams*, p. 255

should feel a shiver down his spine. Sustaining our enthusiasm for this cause, and keeping our devotional spirit fresh, requires continuous maintenance.

The same principle is true in our physical life. For example, when a certain limb is not used for a long time, the muscles atrophy until they finally become completely useless. The same is true of our heart and spirituality. We cannot overlook the wisdom in the commandments to pray five times a day and to fast during the month of Ramadan. Believers who release their buckets into the fresh fountain of Islam five times a day are washed and purified with what they receive from it. That is, they try to feel Him, sense Him, and know Him five times a day. We are supposed to grasp this essential point in the act of worship, and orient our behavior and our time toward sustaining the Islamic love and enthusiasm.

The Seas before Us Cannot Be Passed with a Ramshackle Ship

In order to emphasize the importance of continuous spiritual maintenance, the beloved Prophet's advice to his Companion Abu Dharr is very important: "Restore your ship, for the sea is deep. Take your provisions perfectly, for the journey is long. Lighten your load, for the ascent is steep. Be sincere in your acts, for the Watchful One sees everything."[226]

As the distance to be covered is very long, and the sea to pass is very deep, there is no tolerance on the journey for the slightest heedlessness. May God forbid, but in the face of temptation, one can sink like the Titanic to the bottom of the sea. If the ship represents our spiritual life, and our heart's relation with God Almighty, then we need to restore it with every new dawn. It is not possible to undertake a long journey with a ramshackle ship, a neglected heart, and a faulty mentality.

The wise pieces of advice continue. The noble Prophet, peace and blessings be upon him, advised his Companion to take his provisions

---

[226] Ad-Daylami, Al-Musnad, 5/339

perfectly, for the journey would be very long. That long journey begins in this world and ends in the next. The provisions are neither food or drink, nor weapons; they represent a person's servitude and obedience to God. For example, our Prayers will accompany us in the intermediary realm of the grave,[227] and our fasting will help us pass through the Rayyan gate of Paradise.[228] If these are not taken here, on Earth, as provisions for the afterlife, then a person will face misery there.

There is also the warning about the steep ascent, and the recommendation to lighten one's load. Accordingly, believers are supposed to avoid immersing themselves in worldliness—to keep the load on their backs light so they can surmount that steep ascent. Finally, we are reminded to be sincere in our actions, for the Watchful One sees us every moment.

Although such preparations are important to our worldly life because they uphold the truth, establish justice, and continue efforts to dignify believers, they are even more important to our eternal life.

God Almighty reveals the following truth in the Qur'an: "*If He so wills (for the fulfillment of His purpose in creation), He can put you away and bring a new generation (of humankind in your place)*" (Ibrahim 14:19; Fatir 35:16). Here, rather than meaning a new people appearing on the stage of history, we can take the phrase "a new generation" to mean enthusiastic souls devoted to God—ones who did not give in to weariness, who did not take their religion for granted but felt its profundity freshly. In the next verse, it is stated, "*That is surely no great matter for God*" (Fatir 35:17). "*When He decrees a thing, He does but say to it, 'Be!' and it is*" (al-Baqarah 2:117). Unless they welcome a spiritual revival, those who become weary, who resemble worn-out goods, and who lose their spirit of religious enthusiasm are replaced by a new generation, through the noble lives of the Great Prophets or the activities of the respected expounders of Islamic laws, or the renovations of the great revivers of faith.

---

[227] *Sahih al-Bukhari*, Tahajjud, 2, 21; Fazailu Ashabi'n-Nabi, 19; Tabir, 35, 36; *Sahih Muslim, Fazailu's-Sahaba*, 139, 140

[228] *Sahih al-Bukhari*, Sawm, 4; *Sahih Muslim*, Zakah, 85

If those who experience a revival by showering God with favors become proud of their status as the "new generation," they risk losing the Divine blessings and support. This support depends on humility and modesty. When we are given a responsibility, we should carry it out in the best way, while still remaining humble by remembering our servitude to our Creator.[229] Only through an active understanding and faith can we survive long journeys, even those that take centuries. With a renewed enthusiasm and devotional spirit, we can walk toward the future.

---

[229] Nursi, Şuâlar, p. 424

Are We Faithful to the Trust?

Question: *There is a prayer at the end of "The Sixth Word": "O Lord, forgive our sins and accept us as your servants. Enable us to remain faithful to Your trust until the time of restitution (returning the trust) arrives."*[230] *Could you explain what is meant by "the trust?" Is it only the blessing of "life?" Could you also elucidate the term "trust," with respect to our duties and responsibilities?*

Answer: Since trusts are the first blessings God Almighty grants human beings, each thing a person gains—through giving freewill its due and making good use of the first blessings—is a trust as well. Actually the real catalyst in what a person gains is God, too. However, there is a general principle of law: "If the real catalyst is not apparent, then an action is ascribed to the closest cause."[231] Based on this principle, when a man gains something by using his freewill, we accept him as the cause of the act, even though he is not the actual catalyst.[232] There-

---

[230] Nursi, *The Words*, p. 39

[231] *Majallah al-Ahkam-i Adliya*, article 90

[232] As it is revealed in the Qur'an, "...*it is God Who has created you and all that you do*" (as-Saffat 37:96). This means that it is God Almighty Who creates us and enables us to do things. He has given us will and power so that we are able to will something and do it. However, it is He Who creates and gives external existence to what we do. Our performing an action does not mean that that action must come about. Were it not for His creation, we could do nothing. We are doers or agents, while

fore, as the attributes God Almighty grants people are blessings, what people gain through using their freewill should also be considered among the Divine blessings granted to them. If people can acquire this perspective, they will be able to discern that what actually operates behind those blessings, with all of their internal and external dimensions, is the hand of the Almighty Power. Those who possess this perspective will be full of praise and gratitude for the One who grants them those blessings. They will sing praise for God from the bottom of their heart, and feel that blessed phrase resonate through their entire body.

Faith: The Greatest Trust

As viewed from this perspective, the issue is extensive. For example, just as our life is a Divine trust to us, the seeds of eternal bliss such as faith, constant awareness of God's omnipresence (*ihsan*), knowledge of God (*marifah*), and love of God (*muhabbah*) are also important blessings. Without faith, people spend a temporary life in this world, like other creatures do; they condemn themselves to non-existence. Attaining eternal bliss depends on faith.

For this reason, exerting oneself to protect an important trust like faith by erecting barriers and using research to bring evidence in support of faith still does not give this important issue its proper due. What befalls on individuals is regarding such a valuable trust is to ask for more all the time and keep on walking in the path of servanthood. Imagine that a box of valuable jewels is given to your custody and you risk losing your head if anything happens to it. That trust will surely be treated with the utmost seriousness. However, the worth of such a box is nothing next to faith. For this reason, believers should build fortifications around their faith, being certain not to leave any gaps that the devil and the carnal soul can sneak through; such behavior stems from remaining faithful to such a great trust. In addition to

---

God is the Creator. If we had no ability to do something and God did not create our actions, then our having freewill would be meaningless and we would have no responsibility for our deeds.

being steadfast in faith, diligence in observing worship is also a very important part of preserving the trust of faith. A person needs to continuously pray to God for this sake, seeking refuge in His protection and help. As such, the Messenger of God never gave up praying as, "O Turner of hearts! Bind my heart to Your religion!"[233] or "O Turner of hearts, turn our hearts to Your obedience."[234]

Who Is Islam Entrusted To?

The Holy Qur'an is also a trust given to believers. It is necessary to preserve it not only in the minds, through memory, but also by being loyal to its meaning and content. If the Qur'an is not understood in meaning and content, its value is not appreciated. It should not be forgotten that we cannot pretend to be faithful to the Qur'an by entrusting its message to vocal performers, and by finding consolation while listening to them. To be truly faithful to this trust, we must keep Qur'anic values alive in society by exerting ourselves to make it the most cherished teaching in the world, and by blowing its spirit to other souls.

If we cannot be faithful to the Qur'an in this way, then we are actually betraying it, even though we might show shallow respect by hanging it in velvet covers on our bedroom walls. The Islamic teaching, with all of its essentials and principles that must be practiced in real life, is a trust to all Muslims from God Almighty and His Messenger.[235] The Pride of Humanity has presented the framework for this teaching and showed the truth of everything explicitly, he showed believers the ways to true happiness in this world and the next. Therefore, the noble Prophet entrusted Islam to his Companions first, and then to generations to follow. With the hopes of making it more practicable in their age, every one of the saintly figures (mujaddid, mujtahid, awliya, asfiya, and abrar) of later centuries brought clarity to certain vague religious points; with their judgments and elucidations, they

---

[233] *Sunan at-Tirmidhi*, Qadar, 7; Da'awat, 89, 124; *Sunan ibn Majah*, Dua, 2

[234] *Sahih Muslim*, Qadar, 17; Abd ibn Humayd, *Al-Musnad*, 137

[235] *Sunan at-Tirmidhi*, Manaqib, 77; *Muwatta*, Qadar, 3

revealed the fact that Islam can be lived afresh in every era. Thus they fulfilled their duty and entrusted it to the following generations.

The trust that was placed on the shoulders of earlier generations is on our shoulders now; it will be transferred to the next generation tomorrow. It would be terribly irresponsible to transfer that trust to later generations in a deformed condition. If we are not faithful to the trust, protect it as we should, and hand it to our successors in sound condition, we will have betrayed this trust and done a grave disservice to the next generations. Particularly in our time, serving faith and the Qur'an has gained more importance owing to neglect. In the past, people risked their lives for this noble ideal. Under difficult circumstances, they responded in the best way possible; they upheld this trust so it could reach our hands. Now it is our duty to uphold the service of faith as it was entrusted to us, ensuring its message does not lessen during our lives by conveying this message, untainted, to those who need it. If we fail and the trust is tainted, we have betrayed God Almighty, and He will bring us to account in the Hereafter.

Let me state an example: If a volunteer of faith, without working for sixteen hours, says that things are not running smoothly and asks for an assistant, then this person can be seen as giving in to laziness. If a devoted soul works for sixteen hours and still feels that certain things are left undone, then he can ask for a helper. If we really care about not bearing the stigma of betrayal in the sight of God Almighty, we must approach the trust with this mindset, and then seek refuge in Divine Power and Mercy through considerations and prayers such as, "My God! Please send trustworthy people eligible to bear the trust as soon as possible, so that we can transfer these trusts to them untainted."

Betraying the Trust is a Characteristic of Hypocrites

The noble Prophet stated that anyone who has the following four characteristics is a pure hypocrite; if he has one of them, he possesses some hypocrisy until he gives it up: When he is trusted, he betrays this trust; when he speaks, he lies; when he makes an agreement, he breaks it;

and when he becomes hostile he has no limits.[236] Accordingly, neglecting the trust—taking all of the points we mentioned into consideration—can be taken as a sign of hypocrisy. This also means losing one's trustworthiness, which is among the characteristics of the Prophets. People gain value in so much as much as they adopt characteristics of the Prophets, and vice versa.

Let me make a final point that those who act in such a carefree manner regarding issues concerning all Muslims' rights commit a serious wrong by betraying the trust without even being aware of it. Therefore, all of us must shake with anxiety at the thought of ruining this trust, which has been placed on our shoulders by the Divine Grace.[237] Taking fellow believers into consideration as well, we should constantly pray: "O Lord, protect us from a wrongdoing like betraying the trust and make us trustworthy hearers until the day You take it from us."

---

[236] *Sahih al-Bukhari*, Iman, 24; Mazalim, 17; *Sahih Muslim*, Iman, 106
[237] Nursi, *The Gleams*, p. 225

Seeking Recognition

Question: *People have an innate inclination towards self-appreciation and seeking recognition. What is the suitable attitude for a believer to have to counter such urges?*

Answer: One can sometimes realize good things with the help and support of God Almighty. However, we cannot always be sure that we did everything in the best way possible. Perhaps it was possible to do something better with the means available. For this reason, even in the face of seemingly great accomplishments, believers must reflect on their actions by questioning themselves and their deeds thinking, "I wonder whether I was efficient in using the means granted to me. Have I given a satisfactory performance and did I really do my best?"

If this self-examination is done, I think even in the face of one's greatest accomplishments, one will realize that they were not able to carry out their actions properly and failed to act in a way that complied with the intent of God Almighty; one will not be satisfied with her or his efforts. Thus, let alone taking pride in their actions, they will even begin to blame themselves and find avenues for improvement through this process of self-evaluation.

Carry out or Establish?

The Turkish people use the verb *kılmak* (to carry out) when referring to the observance of Prayers. However, the Holy Qur'an[238] and the

---

[238] Al-Baqarah 2:43; an-Nisa 4:77; al-Maeda 5:55

Authenticated Sunnah[239] refer to the same issue using the word *iqamah* for establishing the Prayers. This means separating one's self from anything other than God and perfectly fulfilling the Prayer's inward and outward dimensions. In other words, one gives that Divine trust its due with perfect sensitivity and performs that pillar in a flawless fashion with its special hues, patterns, and lines. For this reason, if someone says, "I have established the Prayer" then others may ask that person "Have you really fulfilled the Prayer thoroughly with all of its outward and inward requirements?"

As for the use of the term *kılmak* it rather gives a sense of finishing a task one has to complete. Therefore, I find it safer to refer to the Prayers with the phrase *kılmak*; it sounds humbler. It calls to mind a consideration that if the Prayer has not been perfectly fulfilled with its inward and outward dimensions, then one cannot say they have established it. Instead, I performed the Prayer to the best of my ability. However, I have hope in the infinite mercy of God that He will forgive a person like me who carries out the Prayers imperfectly. I truly love this way of thinking, because I believe it is a reflection of a humble and modest personality.

When this is not the case, then there is a danger in one's becoming confident in their good acts. Instead, one must think, "I could not do it properly," and seek to do better and to hold the firm belief that God Almighty may forgive His servants even with deeds performed imperfectly and accept them. Hopefully, God Almighty will fill the gaps in the deeds of a person who possesses this type of attitude with regard to their intention and treats that person accordingly. It is wrong to think about the good things one accomplished, to seek recognition for them, and to wish for their good deeds to be talked about; similarly, it is wrong to claim the appreciation and compliments of others. Other people can say, 'this person made such and such achievements', but we are supposed to take it as an exaggeration that stems from their positive view and take such remarks as mistaken judgment.

---

[239] *Sahih al-Bukhari*, Adab, 98; *Sahih Muslim*, Iman, 26

In fact, mistaken judgments based upon thinking positively of others cannot be evaluated as a sin. In Islamic ethics, it is better to prove wrong a good opinion of a person than prove right a negative opinion. Muslims are supposed to hold a good opinion of one another with the condition of not losing the balance of making exaggerations in singing someone's praises. Otherwise, this resembles dealing a fatal blow to them by evoking arrogance.

Do Not Reduce the Reward for Good Acts into the Expectation of Appreciation from People

It is very important for a believer to aspire to make others love God and His Messenger with an insatiable ambition. However, even if a man succeeds in becoming a means for making all hearts feel and appreciate the true spirit of the noble Prophet, he should see what he did as insufficient; he should not reduce the value of those good acts by seeking recognition in return for them. Even others' appreciative remarks should not change his feelings and opinion with regards to this issue. Those who seek an opportunity to talk about their achievements and live with this feeling will not find the opportunity or time to detail what they really should. However, our care and concern should be only for God and His Messenger. We should see this as the greatest ideal and act upon it all the time. It is the right of God Almighty to be loved by people, whereas its realization is a duty and responsibility for the believers. One of the most dangerous factors for those who try to serve for this sake is trying to express and prove oneself by mentioning certain things one achieved. In fact, if others heedlessly praise a person's ideas, suggestions, projects, and organizational or communicative skills, then the situation is more dangerous. When we cherish a worldly goal such as recognition by others, although it is possible to realize in this world, it reduces the reward and will bring a disappointment beyond description in the next one. For this reason, a true believer should see the issue from the perspective of the immensity of Divine Mercy, always seek God's good pleasure, and never render their actions worthless by attaching them to simple expectations.

It is not a virtue for a person to memorize personal achievements and acts of goodness. There is a proverb that reflects this meaning: "Do a good deed and let it into sea; even if the fish do not appreciate it, the Creator will."

When someone performs an act of goodness, it is possible to praise God and offer thanks to Him for making it possible for one to perform that good deed. That is a different issue. However, if someone mentions his or her achievements and good deeds in a boastful manner, it will cause them to lose the otherworldly rewards that would have accompanied their good deeds. Believers must act so sensitively with regards to this issue that when someone comes and mentions their good act, they should be able to say that they do not even remember that and not spare any place in their memory for it. If needed, they should make serious efforts to erase it from their memory.

The Greatest Shortcoming: Not Seeing One's Own Shortcomings

Someone with sound belief should have a guilty conscience even about a single bad deed and feel remorse as if it was done yesterday, even if they committed it seventy years ago and asked forgiveness for it seventy thousand times. They must kneel in shame and keep asking for forgiveness from God. Perhaps the mistakes that existed in the mind and imagination will never be recorded in a person's record of deeds; however, if a person commits a mistake even at such a level, he or she must feel ashamed, saying, "My God! How could I even think such unbecoming things before You... How could I allow such things to enter my imagination? What a disrespectful person I am!" In other words, a person should feel ashamed for the wrongs they commit. A person who acts in this manner will not lose anything. On the contrary, one who leads a life in this way will attain the reward of so much repentance by seeking forgiveness. The Messenger of God gave glad tidings to those whose record of deeds is rich in seeking forgiveness (*istighfar*).[240]

---

[240] *Sunan ibn Majah*, Adab, 57; *Sunan an-Nasa'i*, As-Sunanu'l-Kubra, 6/118; Al-Bazzar, *Al-Musnad*, 8/433

In one instance, he stated that he asked forgiveness from God at least seventy times a day,[241] and another time, he said it was a hundred times a day.[242] However, we already know that God Almighty did not let him commit the slightest wrong in his entire lifetime. The beloved Prophet, peace and blessing be upon him, was born innocent and always lived innocently. He led his life under the protective shade of Divine revelation. Despite this fact, he still asked for forgiveness seventy or a hundred times a day.

In conclusion, it is a great gain for a person to rise from bed at night with a guilty conscience about a single sin, shed tears about it, and say, "O God, I ask forgiveness a million times from You." As for those who are dizzy from their achievements, which see themselves as free from guilt and live in the magical atmosphere of their own virtues, it is very difficult for them to turn toward God in humility and humbleness. It is only those who see themselves as criminals even for making the slightest wrong that turn toward God with complete sincerity, open up to Him and start imploring Him to forgive them. Therefore, a person that seeks appreciation from others is contemptible, whereas questioning oneself is a virtuous deed. May God include us among His fortunate servants who criticize themselves in the true sense!

---

[241] *Sahih al-Bukhari*, Da'awat, 3; *Sunan at-Tirmidhi*, Tafsir as-Surah (47), 1; *Sunan Abu Dawud*, Witr, 26; *Sunan ibn Majah*, Adab, 57; Ahmad ibn Hanbal, *Al-Musnad*, 2/282
[242] *Sahih Muslim*, Dhikr, 41; *Sunan at-Tirmidhi*, Tafsir as-Surah (47), 1; *Sunan ibn Majah*, Adab, 57; Ahmad ibn Hanbal, *Al-Musnad*, 4/211, 26

How Muslims Benefit from Their Own Sources to the Maximum Degree

Question: *It is stated that a true disciple of the Qur'an should benefit from Islamic sources directly and from other sources by filtering them. What are the points of consideration for benefiting from Islamic sources in the most efficient manner?*

Answer: Before directing people to the essential sources, evoking a feeling of curiosity and an ardor for learning is necessary. In other words, love for the truth must be evoked in the conscience of society and then a thirst for knowledge and exploration in order to reach that truth must be present to such a degree that people become ardent seekers of knowledge who study phenomena tirelessly. If such ardor can be evoked, then a wish for studying the sources that constitute the identity of Muslims will begin to form in the hearts of the people. When hearts are seized by a passionate desire for learning, people will turn to their own sources and wish to drink abundantly from that fountain of knowledge.

You Cannot Direct Stagnant Water Anywhere

I would like to give an example from another issue. The volunteers who wish to revive their own thought or realize a revival within their own line of thinking must possess enthusiasm to the degree of madness; this excited state makes them unable to contain themselves to stay where they are. It is very difficult to save people from inertia, languor, and weariness without such an excitement. As for a person full of enthusiasm, although they might go to excesses in some respects, it is easier to moderate them within the disciplines of the religion they respect. For example, you can tell them, "You are so enthusiastic, but going to extremes will bring more destruction than progress, and this contradicts the values you cherish and the essentials of your religion. Instead, let us use your enthusiasm in a constructive way. Perhaps, your enthusiasm will be a seed of active patience for a few centuries and an example of remaining steadfast on this path. Even if it takes centuries, let us exert our brains to come up with beautiful projects."

This may help channel their enthusiasm to constructive projects. The same fact is true for deepening one's knowledge and reading more. In other words, it is very difficult to direct people toward reading certain sources without evoking in them a passion for knowledge, truth and exploration. No matter how much you try to encourage people who are devoid of such enthusiasm to read certain sources, they will remain sufficed with a single reference book. A passion for knowledge must be stimulated first, and then it must be channeled to a productive course; it is not possible to channel stagnant water anywhere.

The Essentials Should Be Known First

The second point of consideration here is to determine our priorities with respect to our own world of thinking. In other words, what should our priorities be with regards to learning and establishing a base and criteria to follow? What are the essentials that serve as our standard to test the new things we learn and where are they found? The answers to these questions lie in the essential sources of religion which consists of the major evidences of Islamic Law[243]—the Qur'an, Sunnah, *ijma* (consensus of Muslim jurisprudents), and *qiyas* (logical deduction by analogy in Islamic jurisprudence)—and the minor evidences of Islam-

---

[243] Al-Pazdawi, *Al-Usul*, 1/221; As-Sarahsi, *Al-Usul*, 1/279

ic Law[244] (i.e. taking decent customs and the public interest into consideration, choosing the better option, etc.).

Reading different sources without understanding the primary sources and learning the established principles set forth in them confuses minds most of the time. An example of such confusion happened with the Ottomans, with the process that began with the Tanzimat Period and continued later on. Their failure to show fidelity to a methodology is evidenced by their accepting everything they found to be true without testing whether they were right or wrong. Thus, they ran after different fantasies leading to a period of confusion. For example, it is a reality that much discussion has been made concerning issues of self-improvement nowadays. However, if we do not refer to the invaluable statements of the noble Prophet regarding this important matter and only read self-improvement theories devoid of metaphysics, so many aspects of the issue will remain deficient. If we cannot guide people toward becoming heroes of spirit that glorify God in a universally comprehensive sense within the essentials taught by the Perfect Guide, the Messenger of God, then it resembles—God forbid—seeing the system he brought as a deficient one, as if the Qur'an left many things incomplete, or as if the great scholars of the classic period did not understand Islam at all. All of these are examples of obvious deviation. Then why should Muslims follow other ways? What others wrote or said may have a point within their own discourse, terminology, and system, but Muslims are supposed to evaluate matters from the perspective of their own values and essential sources so that they do not conflict or contradict the essentials of faith while making a statement about pedagogy, psychology or other sciences.

If we begin to travel without determining the *qiblah* first, then we wander here and there in a perplexed fashion but cannot find the right way or direction. If establishing this *qiblah* can be assured well, namely, after Muslims first learn their own sources and internalize the essentials in them as their criteria, they can read any book they wish. I do not even object to reading Sartre and Marcus, whose thoughts might

---

[244] Mehmed Seyyid, *Madhal*, 323

misguide particularly young believers. There can be some good things to be taken from their philosophies, but if you are to take what you wish in the correct way, you definitely first need a criterion in hand. Before making embroidery, you first need a canvas to work on. If you do not have an established structure of values, then you may drift away in pursuit of different currents and will not obtain anything in the end. Unfortunately, this has been the miserable condition of some intellectuals from Muslim lands for a few centuries.

The Tripod

The knowledge obtained from other sources by one who understands the essential sources well can elevate one to a different kind of richness. Until the fifth century of the Islamic Calendar, and even until the 11th and 12th centuries in way, Muslims took what they could from other sources, benefited from them, and experienced no serious problems with regards to this issue. They filtered things they took, revised them, and determined very well what to take and what to leave out. If we can realize this same methodology today, then we can attain a serious wealth of knowledge.

On the other hand, in order to benefit from our invaluable essential sources efficiently, we need to have a magnanimity of conscience that allows us to journey through the horizons of the heart and spirit and enables us to identify what we need to know; in addition, we should also possess a perspective that draws the correct meanings while reading the universe like a book in order to benefit from those sources of knowledge and interpret them correctly. I doubt many people with such horizons and understanding can be found in our time. For a long time, we have been deprived of the establishments that raise individuals with a holistic approach and appeal to all of their material and spiritual aspects—their heart, spirit, reason, and thinking altogether. Unfortunately, the *madrasas* (traditional Islamic schools), that were once the centers of knowledge and wisdom and where so many great personalities were raised, lost their progressive qualities. They just began to repeat what had previously been said. Since they could not keep pace with their time, eventually they were far behind and, as a result, unable to meet the needs of their society. Sufi lodges, which had flourished within the Islamic tradition, similarly lost their progressive quality. Since they did not take the principles of Islamic theology and the methodology of jurisprudence into consideration, they interpreted religion according to certain personal feelings and experiences. As the understanding of religion was built upon certain subjective considerations, it was pushed into the frame of mysticism. When this became the case, the reactionary movements against them totally ended up in naturalism and materialism. Therefore, the schools and Sufi lodges, which were supposed to support another, fell into serious conflict. Imitating the West, some even took it to the extreme of completely separating the fields of science and religion.

In the end, Muslims were the ones to pay the price. As the madrasas and Sufi lodges were closed to the world, the spiritual and scholarly life of Islam became separated from one another. As these two were devoid of the support of "time," an important interpreter, they condemned themselves to narrowness of ideas. Consequently, the religion was shattered into pieces and it lost its true identity. In this respect, without striking a balance between the madrasa and the Sufi lodge—or between reason and spirit—and then completing this into a tripod of discipline, it is impossible for Muslims to become themselves again or to think like themselves and analyze matters related to their true identity.

I would like to mention one final point here. If we have a serious love for truth and knowledge, and if this becomes reflected in our character, then I think we give the message we wish to convey by our representation of it. The most influential, permanent, and consistent lesson is the one that individuals give through their attitude and behaviors. The most important dynamic for making hearts feel a reality is presenting a practical example of the truths one believes and seeks. The real duty of books and speeches must be shedding light on the points that are not clear through practical examples. However, we suffice with solely transferring information as if it could possibly convey everything. Unfortunately, the Holy Qur'an has been waiting desolately in a special corner of Muslims' homes, unable to guide them even though it is shown ceremonial respect by being placed in velvet covers. If the meaning and contents of the Qur'an, the Book of Wisdom, begin to be practiced and becomes the spirit of our lives, then the Divine Word will be given its due. Only then will you be able to hear the voices from beyond the physical realm and feel the breathing of the angels in it. If you concentrate on it in an even more resolved fashion, then you can listen to it as if it were coming out of the blessed mouth of the Messenger of God, peace and blessings be upon him. A scripture that is not practiced and whose language is not understood will not tell you much, no matter how exalted it is. For this reason, all of our spoken or written statements must be under close inspection and command of the heart.

A Balanced Figure of Love and Enthusiasm: Jalaluddin Rumi

Question: *Mawlana Jalaluddin Rumi is misunderstood in our time by some and is subjected to unfair criticism concerning his Sufi path. Could you evaluate the Sufi path of Rumi with respect to his compliance with the essentials of Islam?*

Answer: There have been so many great personalities throughout the history of Islam whose knowledge, spiritual depth, love, and enthusiasm made their voices reach beyond the centuries. Particularly, there are some exceptional figures with immense personalities such as Imam al-Ghazali, Imam Rabbani, and Mawlana Khalid al-Baghdadi; they are in a rather distinguished position. Jalaluddin Rumi is one such monumental personality. Those great people that enlightened the spiritual darkness of different eras had excellent insight into their time, analyzed it well, and concentrated on the issues of the highest priority in order to answer the needs of the people. Jalaluddin Rumi must be seen from this aspect. The matters he emphasized served as an antidote against the poisons and negative influences prevalent in his time and an elixir to cure even the worst diseases.

Rumi and the Emergence of the Ottomans

The era in which Rumi lived was a difficult time period. On the one hand, there were the damages inflicted by the Crusader attacks. On the other hand, there was the Mongolian invasion that shattered Muslim lands into different fragments, causing discord and sedition throughout the Muslim world. As a result, the Seljuk state was greatly weakened, the royalty lost authority of their people and all of these negative effects extended throughout Anatolia. During this troubled era, Jalaluddin Rumi opened his arms wide with an immense understanding of tolerance and magnanimity to embrace everyone. Thus, he virtually offered a cure for that environment of chaos, discord, and fragmentation. This immense understanding represented by Rumi and other spiritual masters prepared new ground to cultivate people with Islamic values.

At the same time, the princedom of the Ottomans found an opportunity to stand on their feet in a small corner of Anatolia. Such an understanding of agreement and unity was needed more than anything else in that era. Rumi saw this urgent need at a time when Anatolia was shattered into fragments, different princedoms emerged, people became disoriented, and everyone was going about their own ways. By uniting people around a certain understanding, he paved the way for the birth of the Ottomans. I think this understanding, which we can refer to as the spirit of Rumi, played an important role in their successful flourishing in just a short time period. Had the Ottomans displayed brutality instead of leniency and magnanimity, they would have become stuck and would have been unable to further their progress. In this respect, along with the distinguished qualities of the people who governed the state, the contributions and efforts of Rumi and other dervishes must not be overlooked when examining the continuity of the same dynasty for six centuries, something unparalleled in the history of humanity.

An immense figure of spirituality who took flight with love and enthusiasm to the horizons of knowing God, Rumi formed such a warm atmosphere during his time that most people came under its influence and stepped into his circle. At a certain period, even the famous Yunus Emre[245] joined his circle. The great master poured the inspira-

---

[245] Yunus Emre (d. 1321), Turkish Sufi poet.

tions of his soul into the hearts of the people who gathered around him and raised exemplary guides to light up the ages after him.

Attracted toward the Divine (*Jadhb* and *Injidhab*) within the Axis of Faith and Knowledge of God

Rumi possessed an understanding of extending a hand of immense tolerance and compassion to everyone. On the other hand, overlooking his depth of worship and devotion as well as his loyalty to the Qur'an and Sunnah might lead one to some misconceptions about him. Indeed, if he had not been so sincerely devoted to the essentials of religion, as is claimed by some, neither would the people of Konya allow him live among them nor would the devout Muslim rulers let him convey his radiant teachings. In addition, none of the scholars among his contemporaries criticized him. For example, his contemporary Sadreddin Konevi was a great scholar who wrote explanatory commentaries about Ibn Arabi's *Shajarat al-Numaniyya* and Qadi Baydawi's Qur'anic exegesis. When we study the life and works of this great scholar, we do not find a single word of criticism for Rumi. Rumi displayed immense compassion and magnanimity by embracing others, and he adhered to the essentials of Islam and did not possess any attitudes or behaviors that contradicted the religious commandments. Unfortunately, some people today view him as a person who jumped to his feet in momentary excitement, put on a costume and started whirling ecstatically, and who contributed to others taking up his whirling. Actually, there is no issue with whirling itself. Rumi was a person of great spiritual depth who weaved a pattern of knowledge of God by constantly moving his shuttle of reflection between human, universe, and God; he became saturated with the knowledge of the Divine and thus made others overflow with love and zeal.

Bediüzzaman follows a system of thought regarding this issue: faith in God, knowledge of God, love of God, and spiritual pleasure, respectively.[246] Accordingly, one must have perfect faith first, then practice Islam without any flaws, and then try to feel sincerity (*ikhlas*) in

---

[246] Nursi, *The Letters*, pp. 239–240

their conscience with its complete profundity and try to awaken the consciousness of *ihsan*, a state of constant awareness of the omnipresence of God. They must be on the way to know God thoroughly by means of the conscience and make their good deeds become a depth of their character so that they can attain the level of spiritual pleasure and zeal for God. In other words, attaining true love and zeal is not possible without sound faith, sound practice of Islam, sound awareness of God, and a deep knowledge and love of God. Rumi's attraction toward the Divine and becoming enraptured with love and zeal needs to be seen from this perspective.

An Immense Inclusiveness within the Framework of Essential Disciplines

On the other hand, certain words Rumi uttered while in a trance or while he whirled to a particular level are related to the spiritual states he personally experienced. These stem from the entranced states of *hayrah, dahshah, hayman, and qalaq*. Although acting in vigilance is essential for a person in a wakeful state and of a sound mind, consideration of the words and behaviors of a person while in an entranced state of spiritual intoxication should be considered accordingly.

For this reason, what is incumbent upon people like us is to take the special cases of the great figures like Jalaluddin Rumi into consideration and find a plausible explanation for their words and behaviors that are likely to be misinterpreted. For example, one of the most criticized statements of Rumi is his famous call: "Come, come, whoever you are; even if you are an unbeliever, a fire-worshipper, or idolater... come. Our lodge is not a place of hopelessness, even if you have backed from your vow of repentance for a hundred times, still come."

We are not sure whether these are the exact words that were originally uttered by Rumi or not. However, even if this statement is not his, Rumi has many other statements reflecting this spirit. I believe those who criticize these words are not fully aware of the point being made. In my opinion, there is nothing wrong in making such a statement. When Rumi's life and works are viewed as a whole, it is clear that they reflect the meaning of "Come, whoever you are, discover the beauties in our world, and find your true essence." On the other hand, as Rumi himself expressed, one of his feet walks through the nations of the world, and the other stays fixed in the center of Islamic principles. As a person who never wavered in his fidelity to religious ways and essentials, it is unthinkable to say that he abandoned any religious practices that were obligatory (*fard*), necessary (*wajib*), or commendable (*sunnah*) to do. It is not correct to solely approach him in terms of his relations with others without seeing the excellent depth of his religious life.

Jalaluddin Rumi has two sides. On the one hand, he lives in strict adherence to the essentials of Islam; on the other hand, he lives among people and teaches the religion to them in a form that they can love and sincerely embrace. Those that criticize him see the second side only and fail or refuse to see the depth of his spiritual life. As a matter of fact, today as well, certain volunteers with love for God and humanity try to show sensitivity in observing acts of worship and complying with the essential disciplines of the religion on the one hand, and they try to come into contact with the entire world on the other. Similarly, those who criticize the volunteers do not pay attention to their religious devotion but only see their efforts for dialogue with others from a narrow-minded perspective. However, in our time when the world is full of antagonism and weapons of mass destruction, dialogue activities centered around love, respect, compassion, and tolerance are very important. If you really wish to eliminate the menacing, negative tension in humanity, you need to use the mysterious key of love. Actually, there is no door this magical key cannot open, no heart it cannot enter, and no face it cannot make smile. Still, it should not be forgotten that one could convey positive thoughts and feelings to others not through a frown but with a warm smile. When others step into your heart, they must find a magnanimous conscience so that nobody worries about failing to find a seat reserved for them. It is commendable to follow the ways and methods presented by heroes of guidance such as Jalaluddin Rumi, Imam Rabbani, Mawlana Khalid al-Baghdadi, and Bediüzzaman Said Nursi, whose guide was the Qur'an and Sunnah. Although they possessed certain differences of secondary importance, all of those great figures of immense conscience beamed with love, overflowed with mercy and showed compassion to all; they opened their bosom to everyone and they neither returned any negative behavior with a physical or verbal response, nor did they respond by breaking others' hearts as they did to them. What is incumbent upon us in our time is to take the lesson we learn from these historic figures and use this mysterious and magical power of love for the good of humanity.

Reflections on the Day of Hunayn

Question: *What are the messages that can be drawn from the verse (translated as): "God has already helped you on many fields, and on the day of Hunayn, when your multitude was pleasing to you, but it availed you nothing, and the earth, for all its vastness, was too narrow for you, and you turned back, retreating" (at-Tawbah 9:25).*

Answer: After the conquest of Mecca, the tribes of Thaqif and Hawazin were allied with other tribes and prepared to attack the Muslims. In addition to being an excellent head of state, the Messenger of God, peace and blessings be upon him, was a unique commander. Upon receiving the news, he immediately took action to launch a preemptive strike. Thus, he aimed to win without much bloodshed and not to give way to much rancor. As a matter of fact, so many people from those tribes became Muslim later on. As a matter of fact, the noble Prophet utilized the same practice and strategy during the process that started with the Treaty of Hudaybiya and resulted in the conquest of Mecca. Imagine that the Messenger of God, a person who is held in high esteem beyond the heavens, accepted the articles of the treaty although they asserted demands seemingly disadvantageous to the Muslims for the sake of gaining the hearts of those people.[247] Later on, the Meccans themselves breached the treaty. Upon this, the Pride of Humanity gath-

---

[247] *Sahih al-Bukhari*, Shurut, 15; *Sahih Muslim*, Jihad, 90–92

ered an army and camped outside Mecca. During that time, he could easily have said "Might is right," and charged at them. However, that noble soul never did and would not do such a thing, because, had he entered Mecca through bloodshed, it would have hurt the people's pride and possibly given way to long-standing bitter feelings.

Hunayn: A Hard Test

Getting back to our main subject, 2,000 new Muslims from Mecca were added to the 10,000 Companions who conquered Mecca and an army of 12,000 marched toward Hunayn. Therefore, those the army was compiled of mostly young soldiers who were dizzy from the conquest of Mecca and people who had newly embraced Islam. In this state, such a thought may have occurred: "Nobody can stand before this army. Just as we have conquered Mecca by God's grace, we are going to defeat Thaqif and Hawazin as well."

At this point, let me note that I always have a spirit of showing respect toward the Companions, seeing them as pure souls, and choosing carefully selected words when talking about them so much so that I take heed not to use the slightest expression of questioning where the Companions are concerned. However, in this incident, some of the blessed Companions may not have adhered to the refined state God Almighty expected of them that was becoming of their distinguished position. Consequently, they may have received a Divine warning, so that they gave the due of their elevated status. However, this is a matter between God Almighty and them. Our making off-handed remarks regarding this issue will be impertinence and a transgression.

Now, keeping this point of view and criterion in consideration, let us look closer at the mood of the Companions on their way to Hunayn. First of all, they had formed the greatest army until that day. In addition, they had won so many battles against greater forces than theirs, by God's grace and permission. Despite the adverse conditions they faced, they had always emerged victorious. Now they were marching upon the enemy with the Pride of Humanity riding his camel in front of them and they were very hopeful; may our souls be sacrificed for them and may God make us steadfast upon their righteous path. Describing their state, the Qur'an first reminds us how they received Divine help, *"God has already helped you on many fields..."* alluding to the instances such as the battles of Badr and Uhud and the conquest of Mecca. God Almighty makes the first reference to Hunayn by stating that they received Divine support on that day as well. Later, He describes their mood at the time, but it needs to be reminded once more that the mistakes of theirs must be approached with the consideration "The good, righteous deeds of the virtuous would be regarded as vices for those who are nearest to God Almighty."[248] For example, just as you can be held responsible for something negative you thought about, they might even be responsible for such a thing merely passing their imagination. God Almighty states, *"and the earth, for all its vastness, was too narrow for you."* The same expression is used in another verse for Ka'b ibn Malik and his friends.[249] In fact, there is an idiom meaning, "to feel suffocated" that happens when some place is not as roomy as you expected. So, the temporary troubled state experienced by the Companions at Hunayn is described as the earth's being too narrow for them, and this is underlined by the fact that they came to the point of retreating. Despite all of this, God Almighty sent down His gift of *sakina* (inner peace and reassurance) upon them, as is expressed in the next verse: *"Then God sent down His gift of inner peace and reassurance on His Messenger and the believers..."* (at-Tawbah 9:26). Hearing this, they experienced heartfelt repentance, pulled themselves together, and became victorious by God's permission and grace.

Dizziness That Comes along with Glory

Let us consider the lesson to be drawn from this historical event, as expressed in the initial question. Just as the blessed Companions of the noble Prophet had Divine providence and support behind them, today's Muslims can be granted different Divine favors and blessings as well. What really matters is to keep one's inner purity at such

---

[248] Al-Khatib al-Baghdadi, *Tarikh Baghdad*, 4/276; Ibn Asakir, *Tarikh Dimashq*, 5/137
[249] At-Tawbah 9:118

times by acknowledging Him as the only one who really makes things happen. Even in the face of the greatest achievements that seemingly depend on our free will and efforts, we need to shatter the veil of causality and see the Causer of causes beyond and say, "Everything is from You."

From a worldly perspective, success and achievements can be seen as good things to sing praises about, but such things must never make a believer feel dizzy or forget their position of servitude for God. No matter how great the accomplishments we make, we always need to see ourselves as loyal slaves at His door. In fact, if we can achieve to see ourselves as His slaves, we will be freed from being slaves to everything else. This, at the same time, means freedom from different systems of manipulation and abuse. Those who do not become slaves to God Almighty become slaves to different things—some to lust, bohemianism, worldly benefits, and fame, while others become slaves to power and commit different forms of oppression thinking that might set everything right. You can view all of these people as captives. I can even say that if you swear they are being captives, you will not have made a false statement, because, some of those people bear two, five, or even ten shackles of captivity around their necks. Ones devoid of wisdom might ascribe good things being achieved to certain individuals and groups on stage and extol them. Those with character flaws and a weakness for fame and praise might grow arrogant and insolent in the face of such applause. They might have claims on what does not belong to them. In truth, it is a downfall to make such claims by forgetting that their achievements are blessings granted by God Almighty. For example, if a preacher sees that the audience is deeply moved and are listening to him in tears, he will corrupt what he did if he takes any personal pride and sees it as a consequence of his powerful oratory; in reality, people's hearts are in God's hand of power. Being granted oratory skills is both a blessing and a test. Making a claim of such things is a form of usurpation. Let us not forget that a love and desire for fame is such a trouble that one with such a character flaw can make claims on what belongs to God, the noble Prophet, and the Qur'an when they keep being extolled. May God protect us from such a disaster!

In conclusion, if you wish to build up the statue of your soul one more time, you need to know that this can neither be achieved through worldly opportunities nor through different means of power. As the poet Mehmed Akif put it, "One must always rely upon God, work diligently, and comply with what wisdom requires." With this understanding, if you try to always speak up for the truth by taking Qur'anic reasoning as the basis and without engaging in polemics, God lets you see and speak correctly; eventually, He makes the impossible become real for you and grants you success on the path you walk.

Suicide

Q **uestion:** *What is the Islamic perspective on suicide, which has become a social disaster in our time? What are the underlying reasons that lead a person to suicide?*

Answer: Even though no explicit statement is found in the Qur'an, we can say that the prohibition against taking life is also true for a person's taking his or her own life. Killing oneself is murder in the same way killing another person is murder. God Almighty considers taking one life equal to killing all of humanity: *"He who kills a soul unless it be (in legal punishment) for murder or for causing disorder and corruption on the earth will be as if he had killed all mankind"* (al-Maedah 5:32). Indeed, human life is among the five essentials people are responsible for protecting.[250] It can even be said—as Shatibi systematically expounds on in his *Muwafaqat*—all of Islamic law is based upon these five essentials of protecting a person's life, religion, property, mental health, and offspring. Protection of life is the foremost among these essentials. It is so important to protect one's life that somebody under assault is allowed to harm the assailant in self-defense.

Breaching the Trust

Human life is an important trust from God. In other words, just as faith is a God-granted trust in the name of serving the religion, the blessing

---

[250] Ash-Shatibi, *Al-Muwafakat*, 1/38, 2/10

of life, which makes all of these possible, is such a trust as well. For this reason, a person's taking his or her own life willfully means ruining this Divine bestowal through which people are commissioned to fulfill certain responsibilities.

People come to this world like recruits to an army, to undertake a responsibility. What is required of people is waiting patiently until the appointed time when they will be summoned to the Divine presence. Just as a soldier that leaves his regiment without a leave signed by his commander is considered a fugitive, a person who leaves the duty of life without a Divine command is similarly considered a fugitive deserving punishment. All of the good actions a person did in their lifetime will be wasted. In fact, even wishing that God would end one's life due to certain sufferings is a sin; making such a wish means rebelling against the fate ordained by God Almighty. For this reason, somebody who utters such words of rebellion by mistake needs to seek Divine forgiveness in prostration as if they committed a grave sin. Given that such wishes—much less severe in comparison to taking one's life—is so wrong, then it is a much worse disrespect toward God Almighty to commit suicide, because it is an attempt to interfere with the time of dismissal from duty without waiting for the command of God, the rightful authority. Just as He is the one who sends people into the world, He must also be the one to send them to the next world. No human is given the right for self-decided intervention.

A person can even die in the lawful defense of their life, religion, or property. Even though there may seem to be an outward human intervention, this is actually a form of passing to the next world within the command of God Almighty. The Messenger of God stated that one who is killed in defense of their property, religion, life, or family is a martyr.[251] Therefore, dying in such situations is a form of taking leave from service with Divine permission. Some scholars of Islamic jurisprudence made the judgment that a person who commits suicide is like a person who renounced faith and therefore is not eligible for an Islamic Funeral Prayer. However, there is also the consideration

---

[251] *Sunan at-Tirmidhi*, Diyat, 22; *Sunan an-Nasa'i*, Tahrimu'd-Dam, 23

that a person might commit suicide during a temporary state of insanity. Since people in such a state are not responsible for their actions, it is possible to carry out a Funeral Prayer with this consideration.

Sometimes, intolerable sufferings might lead one to suicide. Indeed, such an incident took place during the time of the blessed Prophet. A person named Quzman was wounded during the Battle of Uhud. To end his suffering, he committed suicide by leaning his body weight on the tip of his sword. Seeing this, the Messenger of God stated that the man is a dweller of Hellfire.[252] Imagine that he fought near the beloved Prophet for the defense of Medina and received a fatal wound that would make him a martyr, but this unfortunate man became a loser in a zone of winning for not being patient with the suffering. Without waiting for the Divine decree, he made the judgment for himself and thus became deserving to be a dweller of Hellfire. What befalls a believer, however, is showing patience during such times of trouble. A person is supposed to remain patient against all odds, until they are summoned by the Divine will. In other words, one must seek what God wills even while dying.

The commandment *"O you who believe! Keep from disobedience to God in reverent piety, with all the reverence that is due to Him, and see that you do not die save as Muslims (submitted to Him exclusively)"* (Al Imran 3:102) also implies that people should not end their own life. However, suicide is a consequence of not submitting to God and is contrary to this commandment. In addition, just as killing oneself means ruining an entire past, suicide means ending one's life in a very ominous way.

A Multiple Murder: Suicide Attacks

There is another form of suicide called a "suicide attack" that started in the West first and then, unfortunately, became present in some Muslim countries as well. Those who commit this act try to justify it by asserting that it is a meaningful suicide. In other words, with these attacks they undergo for the sake of their ideologies, they are pre-

---

[252] At-Tabari, *Tarikhu'l-Umam wa'l-Muluk*, 2/73

tending to ascribe a positive meaning and value to suicide as if it were possible to protect their religion with it. However, when we look into the truth of the matter, we see that such suicide bombings are no different than the suicide we previously mentioned.

Suicide attacks can even be seen as a form of murder, because just as those heedless murderers who have nothing to do with humanity and who have no idea about the true spirit of Islam go to Hell head-first by killing themselves, they kill so many innocent people as well. Therefore, just as they will be called to account on the Day of Judgment for taking their own lives, they will have the same trouble for the people they killed—for every child, woman, man, Muslim, and non-Muslim victim one by one.

In Islam, laws and disciplines explicitly define the acts that are permissible during peace and wartime. Nobody can declare a war or decide to kill another person by himself, and nobody has the right to kill children, women, or the elderly on the opposite side during battle. This being the case, suicide attacks or other similar acts of terrorism can never be compatible with Islam. To shed light on the issue, we take the statement of the noble Prophet that a person does not commit adultery as a believer, does not drink wine as a believer, does not steal as a believer, and does not commit murder as a believer.[253] We understand from this *hadith* that a murderer is not a believer while committing murder. In other words, a person committing these sins cannot be called a Muslim in terms of their state, intents and plans while committing them. When you study their character during these moments, what appears before you is not the portrait of a Muslim; indeed, such character cannot fit within the Islamic frame. For this reason, let us emphasize once more that a person who acts as a suicide bomber and kills innocent people, no matter what country or religious group they are from, the murder they commit has absolutely nothing to do with being a Muslim. A person taking so many lives cannot be saved in the next world. Of course, it is always possible for

---

[253] *Sunan an-Nasa'i*, Qasama, 48–49; Qat'u's-Sarik, 1; Abdurrazzak, *Al-Musannaf*, 7/415; Ibn Abi Shayba, *Al-Musannaf*, 6/169

a person who commits those grave sins[254] to repent and ask forgiveness from God, and the Almighty One can forgive their sins.[255] In this case, God knows how they will be treated in the Hereafter.

On the other hand, it is a reality that such murders smear the beautiful face of Islam. The crimes, which are committed by those appearing to be Muslim and pretending to commit murder for the sake of religion, are attributed to Islam in the sight of people who do not know the original teachings of Islam. Therefore, it becomes exceedingly difficult for believers to change this mistaken image. Clearing people's minds of this negative image will take intensive effort for many years. For this reason, no matter who commits those suicide attacks, they can be defined as twice as bad, or rather a manifold worse form of murder. A few people who were not very knowledgeable about the genuine teachings of Islam asked me once, "Is it the love of going to Paradise that leads Muslims to become suicide bombers?" I answered them saying, "If those people are acting on such a motive, then they hold a mistaken consideration, for a person who makes such an attempt does not go to Paradise but goes headfirst into Hellfire."

In conclusion, those horrible murders committed under the name of suicide attacks are hidden under the guise of religion, which takes the issue to much more dangerous dimensions. In this respect, let us state once more that no matter what motive and method such brutality is committed, it is a condemnable act God Almighty dislikes and is not pleased with and is never compatible with Islam whatsoever.

---

[254] An-Nisa 4:93; al-Maeda 5:32; *Sahih al-Bukhari*, Tafsir as-Surah (24), 5; *Sahih Muslim*, Tafsir, 16
[255] Al-Furqan 25:68–70

Loving One's Nation

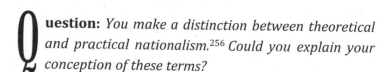

Question: *You make a distinction between theoretical and practical nationalism.*[256] *Could you explain your conception of these terms?*

Answer: From the past to the present, there have been very different conceptions of nationalism. What I mean by nationalism is the consciousness of being the children of the same heritage, which may date back as far as a few thousand years, who shared the same destiny, joys, and troubles throughout history, who held a composition of common values and were fed from the same spiritual teachings, and whose world of thought was made up of the essences distilled from these values. As for the people of Anatolia, they found what they sought in Islam. Islam enabled them to hear the voice of their spirit and heart; they discovered the concept of eternity, struck a balance between this world and the next, and found a means of opening into different dimensions.

In other words, as descendants of a people who established different states throughout history, they found what they sought in Islam, completed their quest, and transformed into their natural state with it. Indeed, the Qur'an states that true perfection was revealed with Islam: "*This day I have perfected for you your Religion (with all its rules,*

---

[256] The original word Gülen uses is not exactly nationalism, but "*milliyetperverlik,*" a term that rather means "loving one's nation," which is an allusion to Bediüzzaman's criticism of the negative sense of nationalism in "The Twenty-Sixth Letter."

commandments and universality), completed My favor upon you, and have been pleased to assign for you Islam as Religion" (al-Maedah 5:3).

In other words, religion was truly perfected with the example and the message of the noble Prophet and the Qur'an, and the people of Anatolia found their ideal state when they were honored with Islam.

A Composition of Values Filtered by Religion

The customs and traditions dating back to the distant past reached our time after being filtered and distilled by religious commandments and Divine criteria, and they have become the character of our people. Since these customs and traditions were already filtered through religious criteria, they should be seen as values allowed by our religion. Indeed, Islamic jurisprudence is based upon the Qur'an, the *Sunnah, ijma (consensus of Muslim jurisprudents on a ruling for a new issue)*, and *qiyas (logical deduction by analogy in Islamic jurisprudence)*.[257] In addition, there are other criteria of a complementary nature[258] and some scholars counted custom (*urf*) of a given culture as one of them.[259] According to the Qur'an, following custom is counted as a good act that God Almighty commands us to carry out.[260] In this respect, custom denotes a composition of values that do not conflict with the essential teachings of Islam. The main components that form the make-up of the people of Anatolia are the entirety of the essences that were distilled from their spiritual heritage.

Racism and Hypocrisy

The people of Anatolia lived together for centuries and shared the same culture, belief, joys, troubles, and sorrows. It is such a bitter reality that in the unfortunate regions where Muslims live, some hypocriti-

---

[257] Al-Pazdawi, *Al-Usul*, 1/221; As-Sarahsi, *Al-Usul*, 1/279

[258] There are secondary criteria in Islamic jurisprudence such as *istishab, istihsan, maslahah,* and *sadd al-dharai*. For example, if something has benefits but no harm, it is accepted as lawful in Islam.

[259] Mehmed Seyyid, *Madhal*, 323

[260] Al-A'raf 7:199; at-Tawbah 9:71

cal thoughts and behaviors have dominated the fate of the region for a few centuries. Some people whose words and behaviors are in total conflict with one another tried to divide societies by causing dissent and thus did the greatest evil to them. In a way, this was a greater threat to Muslims than disbelief because those who absolutely denied God and reduced everything to materialism were soon to fade away in the sight of people. However, the hypocrisy that continued under different masks is much more difficult to fade away. For this reason, what really paralyzed Muslims for the last few centuries is the virus of hypocrisy that has cut through the veins of society and is sucking its blood. The notion of nationalism was a means of abuse for these circles of hypocrisy. Nationalism was a tool for dividing society through chauvinistic heroism. Even though some appeared to work for the future of their society, the practical result was bloody clashes.

To give a concrete example, we were put into prison together with people who fought against one another for different ideologies during the 70s and 80s. On both sides, there were sincere young people who possessed the chivalrous spirit of their Anatolian heritage. Those young people were misguided, provided with arms, and provoked to fight on streets on opposite sides. Unfortunately, they were obsessed with the thought of bloodshed. However, when one gained insight into their inner worlds, as if conducting psychoanalysis, one would see that their hearts beat for their people. Unfortunately, the circles of hypocrisy hiding behind different ideologies and currents turned those sincere people into enemies against one another.

As a matter of fact, Persian culture had a negative effect on Muslims. This issue dates all the way back in Islamic history to the first emergence of hostility toward the caliphs, Abu Bakr and Umar. Hypocritical thoughts continued ever since then under different names and titles. The idea of racism is also a product of such a hypocritical understanding. During the final days of the Ottomans, the national cause was corrupted with racist considerations, the religion was disregarded, and some people tried to present the spirit of the Turks to be rebellious against their Prophet and God Almighty. When the reality of the situation became apparent later on, a certain philosopher-poet expressed which facts were distorted and how and wrote an apologetic poem confessing and expressing his regret for misunderstanding the great ruler, Sultan Abdulhamid II. For this reason, it is not possible for us to exclude the considerations of God Almighty, the noble Prophet, and the Qur'an from our understanding of loving one's nation; even the attitudes that imply taking them lightly cannot have a place in this understanding. We cannot use such holy concepts in our arguments as if they are ordinary objects. We can only show respect and pay tribute to them. This is the foundation of our nationality.

The Embodiment of Love for One's Nation

We believe that the Muslim nations' continuity depends on cherishing these values, and their gaining a place in the balance of powers and taking the lead in representing human virtues also depends upon keeping this composition of values.

Indeed, we believe that the right and lawful will find their true meanings, blood and tears will come to an end, justice—absolute or relative—will take place, and humanity will regain peace in safe hands. Why should a person who believes this ideal not try to proclaim this composition of values to the entire world?

At this point, there comes a distinction between theoretical and practical nationalism. Let me remind you of our approach to religious life: establishing belief as an ingrained part of our character through practical actions. In *The Critique of Pure Reason*, the German philosopher Immanuel Kant says that God can be known not through theoretical reason but only through practical reason. This idea is in compliance with Bergson's "intuition." Bediüzzaman also referred to sensing the conscience; he emphasized that people must feel how helpless and poor they really are and turn to God with this consciousness and realize their actions and give thanks to Him.[261] In the same way, theoretical nationalism without practical goodness means paying lip service to the issue and comforting oneself with stories of chauvinistic heroism.

---

[261] Nursi, *The Letters*, p. 443

However, what really matters is working ceaselessly for noble ideals without expecting any benefit and doing what needs to be done. Why should I not teach my language to anybody else? As English has become a world language, why should mine not become a worldwide means of attachment between people? Referring to the Arabic, Turkish, and Persian in use today, Ali Shariati said that it is not possible to develop knowledge with such shallow languages. In fact, we can enrich Turkish by referring to the Central Asian languages of Turkic origin, bringing different locally used words into common use, benefiting from stories and novels, and by reviving the words forgotten between pages of dictionaries. If we are to practically prove that we love our people, then we should try to develop the language and also seek to introduce the positive feelings of our people and the values of our historical heritage to the entire world.

Introducing Turkey to others is an ideal for so many people. But how are they supposed to do it? So much investment was made, but to what extent did it work? I saw a TV program, in the middle of New York, the speaker extended a microphone to passersby and asked whether they had ever heard of a country called Turkey. Most of them had not heard of it, and some even said, "I think it is a country in Africa." This is a clear indication that the efforts to introduce Turkey to others have been insufficient.

Nowadays however, some volunteers made up their minds to realize this ideal in different parts of the world by God's grace and permission. I wish the country had better economic means so that the schools opened by the faithful people of Anatolia would number two thousand, instead of one. Then, the number of people learning Turkish would amount to a million; they would love our country and people. If the slightest amount of harm came to Turkey, people in different parts of the world would voice their sorrow about it. Let me also add that in spite of everything, the people of Anatolia showed a great example of faithfulness and realized good works both at home and abroad by making use of their means to the utmost degree. Taking no notice of those praiseworthy activities is akin to being unfaithful. We see that there is serious public support and concern for these benevolent activities that have become a source of joy for many people. If God Almighty does not send an adverse wind, we hope that the establishments supported by those altruistic people will increase manifold and the regions where they exist will turn into a land of dreams envied by all. What we call practical nationalism means to strive for a sublime ideal and present an excellent performance for this sake.

In short, if you really believe that your values are of Divine origin and you see them as having the utmost importance and vitality with respect to their extending to eternity toward the past and future, then you cannot contain yourself from sharing them with all of humanity. The people you address may not accept all of them, but at least they appreciate you and your true identity and inner beauty. In this way, you will have formed friendly circles around you and will be saved from confining yourself to isolation in a shrinking World.

Properties of Perfect Intention

Q uestion: *What does "perfect intention" mean? What are the properties of an intention, which is stated as being better than one's deeds?*

Answer: Scholars of both Islamic Jurisprudence and discipline of *Hadith* defined intention as "what the heart truly wills."[262] As for what is meant by perfect intention, as the true will of the heart, it can be defined as a person solely turning toward God, who is the Absolute One to be worshipped and the True Desired One, and seeking His approval in all their deeds. As it is known, the most famous saying of the noble Prophet about intention is the first one Imam Bukhari included in his classic work:

"Actions are judged by intentions, and a person will get a reward according to the intention. So, whoever emigrated for God and His Messenger, his emigration will be for God and His Messenger; and whoever emigrated for worldly benefits or for a woman to marry, his emigration would be for what he emigrated for."[263]

According to this *hadith*, if somebody observes the Prayers to deceive people by attempting to appear pious, they find no reward in the Afterlife for such deeds; since their heart was not oriented to God

---

[262] Al-Gazali, *Al-Wasit*, 2/519

[263] *Sahih al-Bukhari*, Bad'ul-Wahy, 1; Iman, 41; Itq, 6; Manaqibu'l-Ansar, 45; Ayman, 23; Hiyal, 1; *Sahih Muslim*, Imara, 155

but to appreciation by people. Actually, such an attitude is the character of hypocrites. They do not believe in making ablution, observing Prayers, guiding others, and serving their people and humanity with altruistic attitude. By stating that actions are judged by intentions, the *hadith* lets us know that actions which do not seek God's good pleasure bear no value.

Varying Degrees of Intention

On the other hand, we need to admit that not everybody is on the same level. A person's purity of intention is directly proportional with their horizons of knowledge of God. Their intention will vary in accordance with how sound their faith is, how immersed they are in knowledge of God, and how the consciousness of omnipresence of God flourishes in their hearts. For this reason, those with broad horizons in regards to knowledge of God need to aim higher with their intentions, which can be seen as the starting point of worship. One who makes a sound intention, which we can call the *basmala* of worship, can offer acts of worship—such as the Prayers, fasting, and *Zakah* (prescribed purifying alms)—with due awareness and consciousness.

In the Hanafi school of thought, pronouncing one's intention was seen as preferable.[264] On the other hand, even though he is not renowned as a jurist, the great guide Imam Rabbani objected pronouncing the intention.[265] Accordingly, since intention is what the heart truly wills, the heart must become oblivious to all other things than God and totally become fixed on Him in full concentration. Pronouncing the intention with the mouth must not busy the mind and having such additional concern might make it difficult to become fully concentrated. Therefore, that great imam held such a profound and immense consideration about intention for Prayer. Personally, even though I say the intention with my tongue, I favor this view of Imam Rabbani, since making the intention with the tongue might sometimes be misleading. Believers might feel content with having said the words but fail to ori-

---

[264] Al-Marghinani, *Al-Hidaya*, 1/45; Ibn Abidin, *Hashiya*, 1/108
[265] Imam Rabbani, *Al-Maktubat*, 1/160 (Letter 186)

ent themselves to God Almighty with all of their outward and inward faculties. They may not achieve a full concentration of the heart. The voice of their heart may not have accompanied the voice coming out from the mouth. However, words being uttered are not the basis for intention; they only bear a meaning as far as they are the voice of the heart. On the other hand, holding everybody responsible for such a level of intention means expecting everybody to be at the same horizons of the heart and spirit, which will not be a realistic expectation. For this reason, it is best to believe that the acts of worship will be accepted from those who turn to God with a sincere intention at their giving alms as *Zakah*, fasting, and going to Hajj. At the same time, such an approach is an expression of taking into consideration that Divine Providence will help the worshipper, the principle of easiness in religion, and having a positive opinion of people. It should not be forgotten that holding a positive opinion about others is one of the branches of worship.[266]

The Connection between Pure Intention and Deeds

We need to expound on what we mean by "what the heart truly wills," the phrase we used while defining intention. "What the heart truly wills" does not denote something passing a person's mind or heart. On the contrary, it denotes being resolved at one's intention and making a serious effort to put that intention to practice. In other words, as orienting oneself to God is the theoretical side of intention, attempting to do this is the practical side. In this respect, one needs to be resolved at putting the intention into practice by achieving such concentration. In other words, although intention is an issue to be considered within religious commandments, its realization depends on an individual's religious practices. Seriousness of intention reveals itself in having the theory and practice together. This is not only limited to essential acts of worship such as fasting and Prayers, but applicable for all acts of goodness. The practical value of intention can be understood from the following statement of Bediüzzaman: "The intention

---

[266] *Sahih Muslim*, Jannah, 82; *Sunan Abu Dawud*, Janaiz, 12; *Sunan ibn Majah*, Zuhd, 14

to be humble spoils humility, the intention to be great provokes con-tempt...".[267] Lowering one's wings of humility down to the ground is an important virtue in Islamic morality, but the thought "Let me appear a tad humble," eliminates it; because it is an indication of running after one's desires and fancies. It may turn out that the speaker's intent is not being humble, but being appreciated, applauded, and becoming a person recognized by others. Similarly, attempting to appear great provokes contempt in others, the exact opposite of the intended pur-pose. Or, for instance, assuming a proud attitude toward a proud per-son is not an indication of being proud, since there is a different intent. In sum, an intention finds its value in practice, the real motive is revealed through its practical dimension.

The Reward that Corresponds to the Intention

As the Messenger of God, peace and blessings be upon him, once stat-ed in the name of stressing the importance of intention, a man's inten-tion is better than his deed.[268] At another instance, he stated that a person who intends to do something bad but then desists from it, and a person who intends to do something good but does not find the chance to do it will also gain rewards.[269] Accordingly, if someone who intends to do an evil act and is determined to do it desists from that act for the sake of God, this will be recorded as one good deed. In the same way, someone who cannot find the chance to do and intended an act of goodness will be rewarded for this intention.

To give an example, the volunteers disperse to the four corners of the world for the sake of humanity to share their values and spiri-tual heritage, and they act sincerely. Their devotion reaches such a degree that when they think about it, their eyes fill with tears and they cry their hearts out. At the same time, they make use of every oppor-tunity for the sake of their sublime ideals. However, they cannot real-ize their intent owing to adverse conditions. So the glad tidings of the

---

[267] Nursi, *Al-Mathnawi Al-Nuri*, p. 279

[268] At-Tabarani, *Al-Mu'jamu'l-Kabir*, 6/185–186; Al-Bayhaqi, *As-Sunanu's-Sughra*, 2

[269] *Sahih al-Bukhari*, Riqaa, 31; Tawhid, 35; *Sahih Muslim*, Iman, 203, 206, 207, 259

noble Prophet are true for believers in this situation; their intention is more valuable than their deed, and they will be rewarded as if they realized that deed, according to their intention.

Intention is of a crucial importance with respect to a person's eternal bliss. However, the intention that helps a person to be saved is one that serves as a motive for good deeds. In other words, perfect intention is a complementary component for good deeds and this makes it resemble a mysterious key unlocking doors to infinity in this finite worldly life. To clarify that with an example, if people observe the Divine commandments for worship such as the Prayers and fasting as much as they can, these acts will not amount to even a tenth of the due of the blessings to be granted by God Almighty in Paradise; not even when these deeds are multiplied by twenty, or a hundred, because Paradise is a place adorned with blessings surpassing human imagination.[270] Bediüzzaman also stated that thousands of years of happy life in this world cannot be compared to an hour of life in Paradise.[271] The blessings of Paradise narrated in the Qur'an and authenticated sayings of the noble Prophet, peace and blessings be upon him, provide us with some food for thought; they give us an idea about the issue.[272] Otherwise, the blessings in Paradise are far beyond human conception and imagination. Therefore, it is not possible for us to become eligible for and deserve such a Paradise with our acts of worship. But let's say that you try to avoid sins and carry out Divine commandments—observe the Prayers, speak the truth, follow right guidance, give the *Zakah*, go to Hajj, and strive to uphold the Divine teaching—all along this finite worldly life. All of these will be too little with respect to the worth of Paradise. However, through your attitude and intention, you virtually say, "O God, to the Ruler belongs the Royal manner that befits Him, just as servitude befits a slave. As a poor servant, this is what I can do." Thus in return for such an immense intention, God Almighty will say, "This servant of mine lived for sixty years and spent his (or her) life

---

[270] *Sahih al-Bukhari*, Badu'l-Khalq, 8; Tafsir as-Surah (32), 1; Tawhid, 35; *Sahih Muslim*, Iman, 312; Jannah, 2–5

[271] Nursi, *The Letters*, p. 245

[272] Al-Baqarah 2:25; Al Imran 3:198; al-Kahf 18:31

in obedience to Me. If he were to live for a million years, he would spend his life in the same way. So I consider him as if he worshipped Me that much." That is, God Almighty will replace a person's intention with their practical deeds, and count their intention as better than their deeds.

Keeping up the Initial Sincere Intention

There is another reason for an intention being better than the deed: a person can be sincere with respect to their initial intention. However, when the deed is being put to practice, other considerations such as showing off to others and taking sanctimonious pride can spoil sincerity. As for intention, it does not face such a degree of risk as the deed does. Since it is a will in the heart, it is not possible for others to see it. For example, one man can say, "I gladly accept it even if God takes my life a thousand times, if only the blessed name of the Messenger of God was honored in these lands." Even his closest friends cannot exactly know the feeling and the excitement in his heart. Seeing the entire world dark without him, believing that everywhere will gain light with him, feeling agony with this concern, suffering with shame for failing to be true to him, and living with a troubled conscience with this concern—such feelings and considerations enveloped by sincerity in one's heart have great value in the sight of God, for they cannot be spoiled by sanctimonious concerns of showing off to others. In this respect, it can be said that as these feelings and thoughts inside are not exposed to the destructive effect of negative considerations, God Almighty accepts them as if they were actions carried out, counts them as compensation for the gaps one's deeds fail to fill, and grants that person eternal bliss in return for them.

People can erase their wrongs and sins through repentance and penitence. However, even if sins are removed, there will be certain gaps in one's record of deeds. The mysterious capital to fill up those gaps is a person's sincere intentions, orienting oneself heavenwards, and their intents and wills bound to put into practice. We hope that God Almighty accepts them as if they were actual deeds and fill the gaps in the record of deeds with them, and thus will not let His servant in shame on the day of reckoning. In this respect, great guides gave much importance to intention.

One of the Most Eloquent Invitations for Divine Providence

As intention is an invitation for Divine help in order to realize the intent, then one should never refrain from making it. In the face of loads of work to do, one should make an intention and begin working, do as much as she can do, which is an invitation of great significance in the name of asking from God Almighty to make it possible to complete the task, instead of waiting idly in hopelessness. Then it is not right for a person to neglect this petty task they are responsible for in terms of apparent causes. People should target great ideals and keep their standards high, at least in terms of their intention. Besides that, when they cannot realize all that they desired to, they should not give in to disappointment, be respectful to how Divine Justice operates, and after having done what they were supposed to, they should wait for the right time to do what remains undone.

Intentions That Surpass the Available Means

Those who fail to do what they planned to do owing to valid excuses beyond their power will be treated in accordance with their intentions. For example, the Qur'an praises the ones who felt sad since they could not find the means for making a contribution to the Tabuk Campaign: "...*they returned, their eyes overflowing with tears in sorrow that they could not find anything to spend*" (at-Tawbah 9:92). As those who donated for the campaign were praised for their deed, the ones who could not were appreciated for the purity of their intention, depth of their heart, and immensity of their feelings. Referring to those who could not join the army for a valid excuse, who could not find a mount or who had relatives they had to look after, the noble Messenger of God stated, "There are some men in Medina who are with you (on account of their intention) wherever you march and whichever valley you cross..."[273] and gave the glad tidings that they would also have their share of the Divine reward like others. In other words, the noble Prophet meant to say that if they had the same means and conditions as others, they would also join them, practically make the same efforts, and therefore receive the same reward. In one case, the Pride of Humanity even spared a share from war-gains for Uthman ibn Affan, who was unable to join the Battle of Badr for a certain reason, and that distinguished Companion was also counted among the blessed souls who attended the Battle of Badr.[274]

As it is seen, those who cannot realize what they wish to do for a valid reason are excused according to the Qur'an and Sunnah, and they are counted as if they realized their intent. Even during our times, there are various people who serve in different areas of life enthusiastically. They are full of enthusiasm for carrying out the duty that falls on their part. So those people, by God's grace, will be rewarded as people who strived for a sacred cause. Their intention, determination, efforts, and resolution will meet them in the other world as such a pleasant surprise that most others will not be able to help but envy them for the blessings God Almighty will grant them. For this reason, it is always commendable to cherish high intentions and ideals. It should never be forgotten that a person who aims at and endeavors for the good of their whole nation, is a nation; further than that, a person who aims at and endeavors for the good of the entire humanity, is like a huge humanity.[275]

---

[273] *Sahih al-Bukhari*, Maghazi, 81; *Sahih Muslim*, Imara, 159

[274] Ibn Abi Shayba, *Al-Musannaf*, 6/361; Ibn Sa'd, *At-Tabaqatu'l-Kubra*, 3/56; Al-Bayhaqi, *As-Sunanu'l-Kubra*, 9/174

[275] Nursi, *Tarihçe-i Hayat*, p. 95

Jealousy

Question: *What should an appropriate attitude be towards those who envy us and cannot stomach our achievements?*

Answer: First of all, it needs to be known that not being able to stomach others' merits is a serious spiritual illness. The example of Satan's attitude towards Adam and his later going completely astray is the most striking example of just that. Considering the words of Satan in different verses of the Qur'an, it is seen that he is a creature that knows God. But in spite of that, he refused to prostrate himself before Adam for the sole reason of his jealousy and not being able to stomach God's honoring Adam. While mentioning Satan's disobedience to the Divine command, the Qur'an uses the word "*aba*" (refused), which denotes insistent refusal. That is, he was insistent at his haughty refusal to prostrate himself before Adam. Since he was full of grudge and hatred, this prevented him from seeing goodness and thinking positively. Had it been easy to overcome jealousy and inability to stomach others' merits, Satan's end would probably not be so pitiful. Perhaps, realizing Adam's relation with the Almighty Creator and the angels' respect for him would bring Satan to his senses. However, that poor victim of jealousy fell headlong and is still falling. It is narrated in a parable that Satan once asked God Almighty, "You forgive so many people, should my punishment and suffering not be over?" God Almighty reminded him of the first test that he failed, "Go and

prostrate yourself before the grave of Adam. Then I will forgive you."
However, Satan was totally seized by his jealousy and inability to
stomach Adam's merits once again that he continued his refusal and
denial. Jealousy has such a compact potential for evil that Satan threw
himself headfirst into disbelief.

From Jealousy to Fratricide

On the other hand, God Almighty relates the parable of Adam's two sons
in the chapter Al-Maedah (5:27–31), in order to show where jealous-
ly and inability to stomach others' merits can destroy a person. Although
the names of the two sons are not specified in the Qur'an and the
Tradition of the noble Prophet, earlier scriptures refer to them as Cain
and Abel.[276] They were born into a family blessed with Divine revelations, which was also a nucleus for the final Prophet. One of these
two sons, whose father was mentioned as "the Pure Servant of God,"[277]
was an unfortunate one who could not stomach the merits of his
brother and turned so furious as to kill him in the end.

When we review history, we come across many examples of this
kind. The lesson to extract from these is that jealousy caused many
people to fall. Grudge and jealousy even caused some people to be
antagonistic toward the Pride of Humanity, who would not hurt anybody in the slightest degree. At one instant, Abu Jahl confessed this
truth with the following words, "All that he conveys is true. He does
not lie; we have never witnessed that. However, his tribesmen (Banu
Abdul Muttalib) already said, 'We have the honorable duties of giving
Zamzam water to pilgrims, keeping custody of the keys of the Ka'ba,
and offering food to pilgrims.' If they say now, 'The Prophet has
appeared from among us,' I cannot stand that!"[278] Until the day he met
his end at the Battle of Badr,[279] that unfortunate one spent all of his
days in enmity towards the Messenger of God, and then drifted to

---

[276] *The Old Testament*, Genesis, 4

[277] Abu'sh-Shayhk, *Al-Azama*, 5/1596; As-Sa'labi, *Al-Kashf wa'l-Bayan*, 6/51

[278] Ibn Ishaq, *As-Sirah*, 4/191; Ibn Abi Shayba, *Al-Musannaf*, 7/255–256

[279] Ibn Hisham, *As-Siratu'n-Nabawiyya*, 3/183; Ibn Kathir, *Al-Bidaya wa'n-Nihaya*, 3/287–289

eternal perdition in the vice of his jealous grudge. He could perhaps be granted Divine forgiveness if he had said even as late as a few minutes before his death, "Until this moment, I have always been trying to destroy what you built up. But now, I am asking for forgiveness," and then accept faith. However, he was absorbed in a jealous grudge, arrogance and envy even during his death throes. Let us give it a thought; his inability to stomach others' value was like an inauspicious iceberg not melting even in the significant atmosphere of the Messenger of God.

Not even a Ladder to Paradise

Some people might entirely object acts of benevolence for the sole reason that they did not personally take part in initiating, planning, and realizing these initiatives, no matter how significant, beneficial, and beautiful they could be. For example, in recent years, Language Olympiads have been held in Turkey with students from four corners of the world. The organization is realized by devoted teachers, selfless tutors, and philanthropic people of Anatolia; it is a fruit of the concerted efforts of so many self-sacrificing souls. This organization does not only stand for teaching language, but also for sharing significant values. The values of a deep-rooted spiritual heritage are presented for others to see, without missionary like intentions or imposing things on any of the contestants or audience members. Every language carries with it the culture and world of thought it is based on. People of Turkey did not achieve an organization of such success, even in their most prosperous periods. Now, at a time of economic crises, philanthropic souls of Anatolia face variations of possible difficulties, send help to different areas, and carry out a very important service by the grace of God. However, still you see that some people of the same land express their uneasiness by remarking that the concept is exaggerated. At another instance, a columnist makes an accusation and defines all those altruistic services as mere show. Although the educational activities are realized through so much suffering and troubles, some cannot find acceptance towards these and attempt to discredit them in many different ways. Some even take jealousy to the degree of wishing to destroy all these acts of goodness. Sometimes, this feeling causes them to make groundless accusations and complaints to the authorities in different countries, with an intention to eliminate the services. Even "jealousy" is too innocent a term for such a degree of loath and grudge. I think the word "envy" could petition to be excluded from a relevant glossary; such a destructive spirit can only stem from animosity toward faith. Those people do not show their true face and it would be too unmannerly for us to label them hypocrites. But their souls are seized by such malignant feelings that even if you offer them a ladder to Paradise, they will do everything to destroy that blessed ladder.

Stomaching the Inability to Stomach

In sum, we need to take into consideration that such negative attitudes are always present. Not only those hostile to faith, but even those who supposedly share the same feelings, thoughts and teachings with the volunteers, will present their jealousy and inability to stomach the achievements from time to time. The becoming response for us is to stomach these as an outcome of human nature and embrace everyone despite this factor. Ideal believers are described in the Qur'an (Al Imran 3:134) as ones who are ever-restraining their rage (even when provoked and able to retaliate), and pardoning people their offenses. Accordingly, you should swallow your anger, forgive people, and even if you meet some evil, you should leave this evil one sided by not responding in the same way. If a vehicle crashes into a stationary one, the damage will be halved. However, when two vehicles crash into one another with speed, both will be compressed into a heap of metal. In the same way, you can halve the damage by leaving vice on its own; you must condemn the jealousy and intolerance of the adversaries to melt the vices away.

On the other hand, for the sake of overcoming such problems, you must help others around you by showing them the ways to deepen their faith, emphasize the importance of sincerity (*ikhlas*) and brotherhood, and constantly rehabilitate them with circles of contemplative dialogue. Thus, you must struggle to help them realize annihilation (in the Sufi sense) of their carnal soul and arrogance, and then take wing in their spiritual life to the horizons of *Baqa Billah* (Subsistence with God).[280] Our contemplative dialogues must be revising our relations with God, whether we stand where we should or not, and whether we are in line with the Qur'anic teachings in terms of our world of thoughts. We must be rekindled with "contemplative dialogue on the Beloved," to become revitalized and reinvigorated. Issues such as founding schools or universities in various countries are too simple in comparison to this notion. When matters are seen from this perspective, it is more possible to spot our shortcomings. Since we do not constantly burn to engage in the contemplative dialogue on the Beloved, we do not bring up the subject of God and His Messenger, peace and blessings be upon him, all the time, and we do not keep trying to orient others toward sound faith, we fail to seal up the mouth of the green-eyed monster that is unable to stomach others' merits. Since we fail to do that, this monster is making Muslims talk in an unbecoming fashion and is pushing them to inappropriate behaviors.

---

[280] *Baqa billah* is covered as an entire chapter in the second volume of Gülen's *The Emerald Hills of the Heart: Key Concepts in the Practice of Sufism*, New Jersey: Tughra Books, 2010.

References

Abd ibn Humayd (d. 249 AH), *Al-Musnad*, (Ed. Subhi al-Badri as-Samarrai, Mahmud Muhammad Halil as-Saidi), Maktabatu's-Sunnah, Cairo, 1988.

Abdurrazzaq, Abu Bakr Abdurrazzaq ibn Hammam (d. 211 AH), *Al-Musannaf*, I-XI, (Ed. Habiburrahman al-A'dhami), Al-Maktabu'l-Islami, Beirut, 1983.

Ahmad ibn Hanbal, Abu Abdillah Ahmad ibn Muhammad ash-Shaybani (b. 164–d. 241 AH), *Al-Musnad*, I-VI, Muassasatu Cordoba, Egypt, nd

Ahmed Cevdet Paşa, (d. 1895), *Tarih-i Cevdet*, I-XII, Üçdal Neşriyat, İstanbul, 1976.

Al-Ajluni, Ismail ibn Muhammad (b. 1087– d. 1162 AH), *Kashfu'l-Khafa wa Muzilu'lilbas*, I-II, Muassasatu'r-Risala, Beirut, 1985.

Aliyyulqari, Abu'l-Hasan Nuraddin Ali ibn Sultan Muhammad (d. 1014 AH/1606 CE), *Al-Asraru'l-Marfua fi'l-Akhbari'l-Mawdua*, (Ed. Muhammad ibn Lutfi Sabbagh), Al-Maktabu'l-Islami, Beirut, 1986.

_____, *Mirqatu'l-Mafatih Sharh Mishkati'l-Masabih*, I-XI, Daru'l-Kutubi'l-Ilmiyya, Beirut, 2001.

_____, *Al-Masnu fi Marifati Hadithi'l-Mawdu*, (Ed. Abd al-Fattah Abu Ghudda), Maktabu'l-Matbuati'l-Islami, Cairo, 1984.

_____, *Sharhu Kitabi'l-Fiqhi'l-Akbar*, (Ed. Ali Muhammad Dandal), Daru'l-Kutubi'l-Ilmiyya, Beirut, 1995.

Al-Alusi, Abu's-Sana, Shihabuddin Mahmud ibn Abdillah (d. 1854), *Ruhu'l-Ma'ani fi Tafsiri'l-Qur'ani'l-Adhim wa's-Sab'u'l-Masani*, I-XXX, Daru Ihyai't-Turasi'l-Arabi, Beirut, nd.

Al-Amidi, Abu'l-Hasan Sayfuddin Ali ibn Muhammad ibn Salim, *Al-Ihkam fi Usuli'l-Ahkam*, IV, Daru'l-Kitabil-Arabi, Beirut, 1984.

Al-Baghawi, Abu Muhammad Muhyissunna Husayn ibn Mas'ud, (d. 516 AH/1122 CE), *Ma'alimu't-Tanzil*, I-IIX, Daru'l-Ma'rifa, Beirut,1987.

Al-Bayhaqi, Abu Bakr Ahmad ibnu'l-Husayn (b. 384–d. 458 AH), *Shuabu'l-Iman*, I-IX, (Ed. Muhammad as-Said Basyuni az-Zaghlul), Daru'l-Kutubi'l-Ilmiyya, Beirut, 1990.

Al-Bazzar, Abu Bakr Ahmad ibn Amr ibn Abdilkhaliq (b. 215–d. 292 AH), *Al-Musnad*, I-IX, (Ed. Mahfuzurrahman Zaynullah), Muassasatu Ulumi'l-Qur'an/Muassasatu'l-Ulumi wa'l-Hikam, Beirut-Medina, 1989.

Al-Buhari, Abu Abdillah, Muhammad ibn İsmail (d. 256 AH), *Al-Adabu'l Mufrad*, I-VIII, (Ed. Muhammad Fuad Abdulbaqi), Daru'l-Bashairi'l-Islamiyya, Beirut, 1989.

_____, *Sahih al-Bukhari*, I-VIII, Al-Maktabatu'l-Islamiyya, İstanbul, 1979.

Ad-Darimi, Abdullah ibn Abdirrahman (181–255 AH), *As-Sunan*, I-II, Daru'l-Kitabi'l-Arabi, Beirut, 1987.

Ad-Daylami, Abu Shuja' Shirawayh ibn Shahradar (b. 445–d. 509 AH), *Al-Musnadu'l-Firdaws bi Ma'suri'l-Khitab*, I-V, (Ed. Muhammad as-Said Basyuni az-Zaghlul), Daru'l-Kutubi'l-Ilmiyya, Beirut, 1986.

Abu Dawud, Suleyman ibn Ash'as as-Sijistani (b. 202–d. 275 AH), *As-Sunan*, I-V, Çağrı Yayınları, 2nd ed., İstanbul, 1992.

Abu Nuaym, Ahmad ibn Abdillah al-Isbahani (d. 430 AH), *Hilyatu'l-Awliya wa Tabaqatu'l-Asfiya*, I-X, Daru'l-Kitabi'l-Arabi, Beirut, 1985.

Abu'sh-Shayh, Abdullah ibn Muhammad ibn Jafar ibn Hayyan Al-Asbahani (274–369 AH), *Al-Azama*, (Ed. Rizaullah ibn Muhammad Idris al-Mubarak Furi), I-V, Daru'l-Asima, Riyad, 1988.

Abu Ubayd Qasim ibn Sallam, Al-Harawi al-Azdi (d. 838), *Al-Amwal*, Daru'l-Fikr, Beirut, 1998.

Abu Ya'la, Ahmad ibn Ali ibn Musanna al-Mawsili at-Tamimi (d. 307 AH), *Al-Musnad*, I-XIII, (Ed. Husayn Salim Asad), Daru'l-Ma'mun li't-Turas, Dimashq, 1984.

Al-Ghazali, Abu Hamid Muhammad ibn Muhammad (b. 450–d. 505 AH), *Ihya Ulumi'd-Din*, I-IV, Daru'l-Ma'rifa, Beirut, nd.

_____, *Al-Wasit fi'l-Madhab*, I-VII, (Ed. Ahmad Mahmud Ibrahim, Muhammad Muhammad Tamir), Daru's-Salam, Cairo, 1997.

Gülen, M. Fethullah; *Kırık Mızrap*, Nil Yayınları, İstanbul, 2011.

Al-Hakim at-Tirmidhi, Abu Abdillah Muhammad ibn Ali ibn Hasan (d. 360 AH), *Nawadiru'l-Usul fi Ahadisi'r-Rasul*, I-IV, Daru'l-Jil, 1st ed., (Ed. D. Abdurrahman Umayra), Beirut, 1992.

Al-Halabi, Ali ibn Burhanaddin (d.1044 AH), *Insanu'l-Uyun fi Sirati'l-Amini'l-Ma'mun* (Sirat-i Halabiyya), I-III, Daru'l-Ma'rifa, Beirut, 1980.

Al-Humaydi, Abu Bakr Abdullah ibnu'z-Zubayr (d. 219 AH), *Al-Musnad*, I-II, (Ed. Habiburrahman al-A'zami), Daru'l-Kutubi'l-Ilmiyya-Maktabatu'l-Mutanabbi, Beirut-Cairo, nd.

Ibn Arabi, Muhammad ibn Ali Muhyiddin (d. 1240), *Al-Futuhatu'l-Makkiyya*, I-VIII, Al-Majlisu'l-A'la li'th- Thaqafa, Cairo, 1983.

_____, *Ash-Shajaratu'n-Nu'maniyya bi Sharhi Sadriddin al-Konawi*, Daru'l-Kutubi'l-Ilmiyya, Beirut, 2004.

Ibnu'l-Jawzi, Abu'l-Faraj Abdurrahman ibn Ali ibn Muhammad (508–597 AH), *Al-Muntazam fi Tarikhi'l-Muluki wa'l-Umam*, Daru Sadir, Beirut, 1939.

Ibn Abi'd-Dunya (d. 894), *Husnu'z-Zanni billahi*, (Ed. Muhammad Muhlis), Daru Tayba, Riyad, 1988.

Ibn Abi Shayba, Abu Bakr Abdullah ibn Muhammad (d. 235 AH), *Al-Musannaf fi'l-Ahadis wa'l-Athar*, I-VII, (Ed. Kamal Yusuf al-Hut), Maktabatu'r-Rushd, Riyad, 1989.

Ibn Hajar, Abu'l-Fazl Shahabaddin Ahmad ibn Ali al-Askalani (773–852 AH), *Talkhisu'l-Khabir*, (Ed. Abdullah Hashim al-Yamani), Medina, 1964.

Ibn Hallikan, Abu'l-Abbas Shamsuddin Ahmad ibn Muhammad ibn Abi Bakr ibn Hallikan (d. 681 AH), *Wafayatu'l-A'yan wa Anbai Abnai'z-Zaman*, I-VIII, (Ed. Ihsan Abbas), Darul Saqafa, Beirut, nd.

Ibn Hibban, Abu Hatim Muhammad ibn Hibban ibn Ahmad at-Tamimi al-Busti (d. 354 AH), *Sahih Ibn Hibban*, I-XVI, (Ed. Shuayb al-Arnawut), Muassasatu'r-Risala, Beirut, 1993.

Ibn Hisham, Abdulmalik ibn Hisham ibn Ayyub al-Himyari (d. 213 AH/828 CE), *As-Siratu'n-Nabawiyya*, I-VI, (Ed. Taha Abdurrauf Sa'd), Daru'l-Jil, Beirut, 1991.

Ibn Khuzayma, Abu Bakr Muhammad ibn Ishaq as-Sulami an-Naysaburi (223–311 AH), *As-Sahih*, I-IV, (Ed. Muhammad Mustafa al-A'zami), Al-Maktabu'l-Islami, Beirut, 1970.

Ibnu'l-Imad, Abu'l-Falah Abdulhay ibn Ahmad ibn Muhammad (1032–1089 AH), *Shadaratu'z-Dhahab fi Ahbari man Dhahab*, I-VIII, (Ed. Abdulqadir al-Arnawut, Mahmud al-Arnawut), Daru Ibn Kathir, Dimashq, 1985.

Ibn Ishaq, Muhammad ibn Ishaq ibn Yasar, *Siratu Ibn Ishaq*, I-III, (Ed. Muhammad Hamidullah), Ma'hadu Dirasat wa'l-Abhas li't-Ta'rif, Beirut, nd.

Ibn Kathir, Abu'l-Fida Ismail ibn Umar ibn Kathir ad-Dimashqi (d. 774 AH), *Al-Bidaya wa'n-Nihaya*, I-XIV, Maktabatu'l-Ma'arif, Beirut, nd.

_____, *Tuhfatu't-Talib*, Daru Hira, Mecca, 1985.

Ibn Majah, Muhammad ibn Yazid al-Kazwini (b. 207–d. 275 AH), *As-Sunan*, I-II, Çağrı Yayınları, 2nd ed., İstanbul, 1992.

Ibnu'l-Mubarak, Abdullah ibnu'l-Mubarak al-Marwazi (b. 118–d. 181 AH), *Kitabu'z-Zuhd wa'r-Raqaiq*, (Ed. Habib al-A'zami), Daru'l-Kutubi'l-Ilmiyya, Beirut, nd.

Ibn Nujaym, Zaynuddin Zayn ibn Ibrahim ibn Muhammad al-Misri al-Hanafi (d. 1563), *Al-Bahru'r-Raik Sharhu Kanzi'd-Dakaik*, I-VIII, Daru'l-Ma'rifa, Beirut, nd.

Imam Rabbani, Ahmad ibn Abdilahad ibn Zaynilabidin Sarhandi (d. 1624), *El-Mektubat*, I-II, Fazilet Neşriyat, İstanbul, nd.

Ibn Sa'd, Abu Abdillah Muhammad ibn Sa'd az-Zuhri (d. 230 AH), *At-Tabakatu'l-Kubra*, I-VIII, Daru Sadir, Beirut, nd.

Al-Kalabazi, Abu Bakr Muhammad ibn Ibrahim (d. 990), *At-Taarruf li Madhabi Ahli't-Tasawwuf*, Daru'l-Kutubi'l-Ilmiyya, Beirut, 1980.

Al-Kurtubi, Muhammad ibn Ahmad ibn Abi Bakr ibn Farah (d. 670 AH), *Al-Jami' li Ahkami'l-Qur'an*, I-XX, Daru'sh-Sha'b, Cairo, 1372 AH.

Malik ibn Anas, Abu Abdillah al-Asbahi (93–179 AH), *Al-Muwatta*, I-II, Daru'l-Hadith, Cairo, 1993.

Al-Marghinani, Abu'l-Husayn Ali ibn Abi Bakr ibn Abdiljalil (d. 593 AH), *Al-Hidaya Sharhu'l-Bidaya*, I-IV, Al-Maktabatu'l-Islamiyya, Beirut, nd.

Muslim, Abu'l-Husayn al-Hajjaj an-Naysaburi (b. 206–d. 261 AH), *Sahih Muslim*, I-V, (Ed. Muhammad Fuad Abdulbaqi), Dar'ul-Ihya Turasi'l-Arabi, Beirut, nd.

Al-Hakim, Abu Abdillah Muhammad ibn Abdillah an-Naysaburi (d. 405 AH), *Al-Mustadrak ala's-Sahihayn*, I-IV, (Ed. Mustafa Abdulqadir Ata), Daru'l-Kutubi'l-Ilmiyya, Beirut, 1990.

Al-Munawi, Zaynuddin Muhammad Abdurrauf ibn Tajilarifin ibn Ali (d. 1622), *Fayzu'l-Qadir Sharhu Jamii's-Saghir*, I-VI, Al-Maktabatu't-Ticariyyatu'l-Kubra, Egypt, 1356 h.

An-Nasa'i, Abu Abdirrahman Ahmad ibn Shuayb (b. 215–d. 303 AH), *As-Sunan*, I-VIII, Çağrı Yayınları, 2nd ed., İstanbul, 1992.

_____, *As-Sunanu'l-Kubra*, I-VI, (Ed. Abdulghaffar Sulayman al-Bundari), Daru'l-Kutubi'l-Ilmiyya, Beirut, 1991.

Nursi, Bediüzzaman Said (b. 1877–d. 1960 CE), *Barla Lahikası*, Şahdamar Yayınları, İstanbul, 2010.

_____, *Kastamonu Lahikası*, Şahdamar Yayınları, İstanbul, 2010.

_____, *Emirdağ Lahikası*, Şahdamar, İstanbul, 2010.

_____, *İşaratü'l-İ'caz*, Şahdamar, İstanbul, 2010.

_____, *Mektubat*, Şahdamar, İstanbul, 2010.

_____, *Tarihçe-i Hayat*, Şahdamar, İstanbul, 2010.

_____, *Şualar*, Şahdamar, İstanbul, 2010.

_____, Münazarat, (Ed. Abdullah Aymaz), Şahdamar, İstanbul, 2006.

_____, *The Gleams*, New Jersey: Tughra Books, 2008.

_____, *The Reasonings*, New Jersey: Tughra Books, 2008.

_____, *The Letters*, New Jersey: The Light, 2007.

_____, *Al-Mathnawi al-Nuri*, New Jersey: Tughra Books, 2007.

_____, *The Rays*, New Jersey: Tughra Books, 2010.

_____, *The Words*, New Jersey: The Light, 2010.

Ar-Razi, Abu Abdillah Fahruddin Muhammad ibn Umar ibn Husayn (d. 1210), Ar-Razi, Muhammad ibn Umar ibn al-Husayn (544–606 AH), *Al-Mahsul*, I-V, Jamiatu'l-Imam Muhammad ibn Suud al-Islamiyya, Riyad, 1980.

_____, *Mafatihu'l-Ghayb*, I-XXXII, Daru'l-Kutubi'l-Ilmiyya, Beirut, 2000.

As-Safadi, Abu's-Safa Salahuddin Halil ibn Aybak ibn Abdillah (d. 1363), *Al-Wafi bi'l-Wafayat*, XXIX, (Ed. Ahmad al-Arnawut), Dar'ul-Ihya Turasi'l-Arabi, Beirut, 2000.

As-Sa'labi, Abu Ishaq Ahmad ibn Muhammad ibn Ibrahim an-Naysaburi (d. 1035), *Al-Kashf wa'l-Bayan fi Tafsiri'l-Qur'an*; I-X, (Ed. Muhammad ibn Ashur), Dar'ul-Ihya Turasi'l-Arabi, Beirut, 2002.

As-Sahawi, Abu'l-Khayr Shamsaddin Muhammad ibn Abdurrahman (d. 902 AH/1497 CE), *Al-Maqasidu'l-Hasana*, (Ed. Muhammad Uthman) Daru'l-Kitabi'l-Arabi, Beirut, 1985.

As-Samarqandi, Abu'l-Layth Imamu'l-Huda Nasr ibn Muhammad ibn Ahmad (d. 983), *Tanbihu'l-Ghafilin fi'l-Maw'izati bi Ahadisi Sayyidi'l-Anbiya*, Muassasatu'l-Kutubi's-Thaqafiyya, Beirut, 1988.

As-Sarakhsi, Abu Bakr Muhammad ibn Sahl (d. 483 AH/1090 CE), *Al-Mabsut*, I-XXX, Daru'l-Ma'rifa, Beirut, 1986.

As-Suyuti, Abdurrahman ibn al-Kamal Jalaladdin (849–911 AH), *Al-Hawi li'l-Fatawa fi'l-Fiqh wa Ulumi't-Tafsir*, I-II, (Ed. Abdullatif Hasan Abdurrahman), Daru'l-Kutubi'l-Ilmiyya, Beirut, 2000.

_____, (Abdulghani and Fakhru'l-Husn ad-Dihlawi), *Sharhu Sunani Ibn Majah*, Kadim-i Kutuphana, Karachi, nd.

At-Tabarani, Abu'l-Qasim Sulayman ibn Ahmad (b. 260–d. 360 AH), *Al-Mu'jamu'l-Awsat*, I-IX, (Ed. Tariq ibn Iwazillah ibn Muhammad, Abdulmuhsin ibn Ibrahim al-Husayni), Daru'l-Haramayn, Cairo, 1994.

_____, *Al-Mu'jamu'l-Kabir*, I-XXV, (Ed. Hamdi ibn Abdulmajid as-Salafi), Maktabatu'z-Zahra, Musul, 1983.

At-Tabari, Abu Jafar Muhammad ibn Jarir (d. 310 AH), *Jamiu'l-Bayan fi Tafsiri'l-Qur'an*, I-XXX, Daru'l-Fikr, Beirut, 1985.

_____, *Khulasatu Siyari Sayyidi'l-Bashar*, Maktabatu Nizar Mustafa al-Baz, Mecca, 1997.

_____, *Tarikhu'l-Umam wa'l-Muluk (Tarikhu't-Tabari)*, I-V, Daru'l-Kutubi'l-Ilmiyya, Beirut, 1987.

At-Tayalisi, Abu Dawud Suleyman ibn Dawud (d. 204 AH), *Al-Musnad*, Daru'l-Ma'rifa, Beirut, nd.

At-Taftazani, Sa'duddin Mas'ud ibn Umar ibn Abdillah, (d. 1390), *Sharhu'l-Maqasid*, Daru'l-Ma'arifi'n-Nu'maniyya, Pakistan, 1981.

At-Tirmidhi, Abu Isa Muhammad ibn Isa ibn Sawra (b. 209–d. 279 AH), *Al-Jamiu's-Sahih*, I-V, Çağrı Yayınları, 2nd ed., İstanbul, 1992.

Al-Waqidi, Abu Abdillah Muhammad ibn Umar ibn Waqid al-Aslami (d. 823), *Kitabu'l-Maghazi*, I-III, (Ed. Marsden Jones), Alamu'l-Kutub, Beirut, 1966.

Az-Zahabi, Shamsuddin Muhammad Ahmad (d. 1347), *Tarikhu'l-Islam*, (Ed. Umar Abdussalam), Daru'l-Kitabi'l-Arabi, Beirut, 1987.

Az-Zamahshari, Abu'l-Qasim Jarullah Mahmud ibn Umar ibn Muhammad (d. 1144), *Al-Kashshaf'an Haqaiqi Ghawamizi't-Tanzil wa Uyuni'l-Aqawil fi Wujuhi't-Ta'wil*, I-IV, (Ed. Abdurrazzak al-Mahdi), Daru'l-Ihya Turasi'l-Arabi, Beirut, nd.

Index